CHEVELLE & SS
MUSCLE PORTFOLIO
— 1964-1972 —

Compiled By R.M. Clarke

ISBN 1 85520 1887

Brooklands Books Ltd.
PO Box 146, Cobham, KT11 1LG
Surrey, England.

Printed in Hong Kong

BROOKLANDS BOOKS

BROOKLANDS ROAD TEST SERIES
AC Ace & Aceca 1953-1983
Alfa Romeo Alfasud 1972-1984
Alfa Romeo Alfetta Coupes GT. GTV. GTV6 1974-1987
Alfa Romeo Giulia Berlinas 1962-1976
Alfa Romeo Giulia Coupes Gold Portfolio 1963-1976
Alfa Romeo Giulia Coupes 1963-1976
Alfa Pomeo Giulietta Gold Portfolio 1954-1965
Alfa Romeo Spider Gold Portfolio 1966-1991
Alfa Romeo Spider 1966-1990
Allard Gold Portfolio 1937-1959
Alvis Gold Portfolio 1919-1967
American Motors Muscle Cars 1966-1970
Armstrong Siddeley Gold Portfolio 1945-1960
Aston Martin Gold Portfolio 1972-1985
Austin Seven 1922-1982
Austin A30 & A35 1951-1962
Austin Healey 100 & 100/6 Gold Portfolio 1952-1959
Austin Healey 3000 Gold Portfolio 1959-1967
Austin Healey Sprite 1958-1971
Avanti 1962-1990
BMW Six Cylinder Coupes 1969-1975
BMW 1600 Col. 1 1966-1981
BMW 2002 1968-1976
BMW 316, 318, 320 Gold Portfolio 1975-1990
BMW 320, 323, 325 Gold Portfolio 1977-1990
Buick Automobiles 1947-1960
Buick Muscle Cars 1965-1970
Buick Riviera 1963-1978
Cadillac Automobiles 1949-1959
Cadillac Automobiles 1960-1969
Cadillac Eldorado 1967-1978
Chevrolet Camaro SS & Z28 1966-1973
Chevrolet Camaro & Z-28 1973-1981
High Performance Camaros 1982-1988
Camaro Muscle Portfolio 1967-1973
Chevrolet 1955-1957
Chevrolet Corvair 1959-1969
Chevrolet Impala & SS 1958-1971
Chevrolet Muscle Cars 1966-1971
Chevelle and SS Muscle Portfolio 1964-1972
Chevy Blazer 1969-1981
Chevy EL Camino & SS 1959-1987
Chevy II Nova & SS 1962-1973
Chrysler 300 Gold Portfolio 1955-1970
Citroen Traction Avant Gold Portfolio 1934-1957
Citroen DS & ID 1955-1975
Chevrolet Corvettee Gold Portfolio 1968-1977
High Performance Corvettes 1983-1989
Daimler SP250 Sport & V-8250 Saloon Gold Portfolio 1959-1969
Datsun 240Z 1970-1973
Datsun 280Z & ZX 1975-1983
De Tomaso Collection No.1 1962-1981
Dodge Charger 1966-1974
Dodge Muscle Cars 1967-1970
Excalibur Collection No.1 1952-1981
Facel Vega 1954-1964
Ferrari Cars 1946-1956
Ferrari Dino 1965-1974
Ferrari Dino 308 1974-1979
Ferrari 308 & Mondial 1980-1984
Ferrari Collection No.1 1960-1970
Fiat-Bertone X1/9 1973-1988
Fiat Pininfarina 124 + 2000 Spider 1968-1985
Ford Automobiles 1949-1959
Ford Aanchero 1957-1959
Ford Bronco 1966-1977
Ford Bronco 1978-1988
Ford Consul. Zephyr Zodiac MkI & II 1950-1962
Ford Cortina 1600E & GT 1967-1970
Ford Fairlane 1955-1970
Ford Falcon 1960-1970
Ford GT40 Gold Portfolio 1964-1987
Ford Zephyr Zodiac Executive MkIII & MkIV 1962-1971
High Performance Capris Gold Portfolio 1969-1987
High Performance Escorts MkI 1968-1974
High Performance Escorts MkII 1975-1980
High Performance Escorts 1980-1985
High Performance Escorts 1985-1990
High Performance Fiestas 1979-1991
High Performance Mustangs 1982-1988
Holden 1948-1962
Honda CRX 1983-1987
Hudson & Railton 1936-1940
Jaguar and SS Gold Portfolio 1931-1951
Jaguar XK120 XK140 XK150 Gold Portfolio 1948-1960
Jaguar MKVII VIII IX X 420 Gold Portfolio 1950-1970
Jaguar Cars 1961-1964
Jaguar Mk2 1959-1969
Jaguar E-Type Gold Portfolio 1961-1971
Jaguar E-Type 1966-1971
Jaguar E-Type V-12 1971-1975
Jaguar XJ12 XJ5.3 V12 Gold Portfolio 1972-1990
Jaguar XJ6 Series II 1973-1979
Jaguar XJ6 Series III 1979-1986
Jaguar XJS Gold Portfolio 1975-1990
Jeep CJ5 & CJ6 1960-1976
Jeep CJ5 & CJ7 1976-1986
Jensen Cars 1946-1967
Jensen Cars 1967-1979
Jensen Interceptor Gold Portfolio 1966-1986
Jensen Healey 1972-1976
Lagonsa Gold Portfolio 1919-1964
Lamborghini Cars 1964-1970
Lamborghini Countach & Urraco 1974-1980
Lamborghini Countach & Jalpa 1980-1985
Lancia Fulvia Gold Portfolio 1963-1976
Lancia Stratos 1972-1985
Land Rover Series I 1948-1958
Land Rover Series II & IIa 1958-1971
Land Rover Series III 1971-1985
Land Rover 90 & 110 1983-1989
Lincoln Gold Portfolio 1949-1960
Lincoln Continental 1961-1969
Lincoln Continental 1969-1976
Lotus and Caterham Seven Gold Portfolio 1957-1989
Lotus Cortina Gold Portfolio 1963-1970
Lotus Elan Gold Portfolio 1962-1974
Lotus Elan Collection No.2 1963-1972
Lotus Elite 1957-1964
Lotus Elite & Eclat 1974-1982
Lotus Turbo Esprit 1980-1986
Lotus Europa Gold Portfolio 1966-1975
Marcos Cars 1960-1988
Maserati 1965-1970
Maserati 1970-1975
Mazda RX-7 Collection No.1 1978-1981
Mercedes 190 & 300SL 1954-1963
Mercedes 230/250/280SL 1963-1971
Mercedes Benz SLs & SLCs Gold Portfolio 1971-1989
Mercedes Benz Cars 1949-1954
Mercedes Benz Cars 1954-1957
Mercedes Benz Cars 1957-1961
Mercedes Benz Competion Cars 1950-1957
Mercedes 'S' Cars 1965-1972
Mercedes 'S' Class 1972-1979
Mercury Muscle Cars 1966-1971
Metropolitan 1954-1962
MG TC 1945-1949
MG TD 1949-1953
MG TF 1953-1955
MG Cars 1959-1962
MGA & Twin Cam Gold Portfolio 1955-1962
MGB MGC & V8 Gold Portfolio 1962-1980
MGB Roadsters 1962-1980
MGB GT 1965-1980
MG Midget 1961-1980
Mini Cooper Gold Portfolio 1961-1971
Mini Moke 1964-1989
Mini Muscle Cars 1961-1979
Mopar Muscle Cars 1964-1967
Morgan Three-Wheeler Gold Portfolio 1910-1952
Morgan Cars 1960-1970
Morgan Cars Gold Portfolio 1968-1989
Morris Minor Collection No.1
Mustang Muscle Cars 1967-1971
Oldsmobile Automobiles 1955-1963
Old's Cutlass & 4-4.2 1964-1972
Oldsmobile Muscle Cars 1964-1971
Oldsmobile Toronado 1966-1978
Opel GT 1968-1973
Packard Gold Portfolio 1946-1958
Pantera Gold Portfolio 1970-1989
Panther Gold Portfolio 1972-1990
Plymouth Barracuda 1964-1974
Plymouth Muscle Cars 1966-1971
Pontiac Tempest & GTO 1961-1965
Pontiac Firebird and Trans-Am 1973-1981
High Performance Firebirds 1982-1988
Pontiac Fiero 1984-1988
Pontiac Muscle Cars 1966-1972
Porsche 356 1952-1965
Porsche Cars in the 60's
Porsche Cars 1960-1964
Porsche Cars 1964-1968
Porsche Cars 1968-1972
Porsche Cars 1972-1975
Porsche 911 1965-1969
Porsche 911 1970-1972
Porsche 911 1973-1977
Porsche 911 Carrera 1973-1977
Porsche 911 Turbo 1975-1984
Porsche 911 SC 1978-1983
Porsche 914 Gold Portfolio 1969-1976
Porsche 924 Gold Portfolio 1975-1988
Porsche 928 1977-1989
Porsche 944 1981-1985
Range Rover Gold Porfolio 1970-1992
Reliant Scimitar 1964-1986
Riley 11/2 & 21/2 Litre Gold Portfolio 1945-1955
Rolls Royce Silver Cloud Gold Portfolio 1955-1965
Rolls Royce Silver Shadow 1965-1981
Rover P4 1949-1959
Rover P4 1955-1964
Rover 3 & 3.5 Litre Gold Portfolio 1958-1973
Rover 2000 + 2200 1963-1977
Rover 3500 1968-1977
Rover 3500 & Vitesse 1976-1986
Saab Sonett Collection No.1 1966-1974
Saab Turbo 1976-1983
Shelby Mustang Muscle Portfolio 1965-1970
Stubebaker Gold Portfolio 1947-1966
Stubebaker Hawks & Larks 1956-1963
Sunbeam Tiger & Alpine Gold Portfolio 1959-1967
Thunderbird 1955-1957
Thunderbird 1958-1963
Thunderbird 1964-1976
Toyota Land Cruiser 1956-1984
Toyota MR2 1984-1988
Triumph 2000. 2.5. 2500 1963-1977
Triumph GT6 1966-1974
Triumph Spitfire Gold Portfolio 1962-1980
Triumph Stag 1970-1980
Triumph Stag Collection No.1 1970-1984
Triumph TR2 & TR3 1952-60
Triumph TR4-TR5-TR250 1961-1968
Triumph TR6 Gold Portfolio 1969-1976
Triumph TR7 & TR8 1975-1982
Triumph Herald 1959-1971
Triumph Vitesse 1962-1971
TVR Gold Portfolio 1959-1990
Valiant 1960-1962
VW Beetle Collection No.1 1970-1982
VW Golf GTi 1976-1986
VW Karmann Ghia 1955-1982
VW Kubelwagen 1940-1975
VW Scirocco 1974-1981
VW Bus. Camper. Van 1954-1967
VW Bus. Camper. Van 1968-1979
VW Bus. Camper. Van 1979-1989
Volvo Amazon & 120 Gold Portfolio 1956-1970
Volvo 1800 Gold Portfolio 1960-1973
Volvo P444 & P544 1945-1965

BROOKLANDS ROAD & TRACK SERIES
Road & Track on Alfa Romeo 1949-1963
Road & Track on Alfa Romeo 1964-1970
Road & Track on Alfa Romeo 1971-1976
Road & Track on Alfa Romeo 1977-1989
Road & Track on Aston Martin 1962-1990
Road & Track on Auburn Cord and Duesenburg 1952-1984
Road & Track on Audi & Auto Union 1952-1980
Road & Track on Audi 1980-1986
Road & Track on Austin Healey 1953-1970
Road & Track on BMW Cars 1966-1974
Road & Track on BMW Cars 1975-1978
Road & Track on BMW Cars 1979-1983
Road & Track on Cobra, Shelby & GT40 1962-1983
Road & Track on Corvette 1953-1967
Road & Track on Corvette 1968-1982
Road & Track on Corvette 1982-1986
Road & Track on Corvette 1986-1990
Road & Track on Datsun Z 1970-1983
Road & Track on Ferrari 1950-1968
Road & Track on Ferrari 1968-1974
Road & Track on Ferrari 1975-1981
Road & Track on Ferrari 1981-1984
Road & Track on Ferrari 1984-1988
Road & Track on Fiat Sports Cars 1968-1987
Road & Track on Jaguar 1950-1960
Road & Track on Jaguar 1961-1968
Road & Track on Jaguar 1968-1974
Road & Track on Jaguar 1974-1982
Road & Track on Jaguar 1983-1989
Road & Track on Lamborghini 1964-1985
Road & Track on Lotus 1972-1981
Road & Track on Maserati 1952-1974
Road & Track on Maserati 1975-1983
Road & Track on Mazda RX7 1978-1986
Road & Track on Mazda RX7 & MX5 Miata 1986-1991
Road & Track on Mercedes 1952-1962
Road & Track on Mercedes 1963-1970
Road & Track on Mercedes 1971-1979
Road & Track on Mercedes 1980-1987
Road & Track on MG Sports Cars 1949-1961
Road & Track on MG Sprots Cars 1962-1980
Road & Track on Mustang 1964-1977
Road & Track on Nissan 300-ZX & Turbo 1984-1989
Road & Track on Peugeot 1955-1986
Road & Track on Pontiac 1960-1983
Road & Track on Porsche 1951-1967
Road & Track on Porsche 1968-1971
Road & Track on Porsche 1972-1975
Road & Track on Porsche 1975-1978
Road & Track on Porsche 1979-1982
Road & Track on Porsche 1982-1985
Road & Track on Porsche 1985-1988
Road & Track on Rons Royce & B'ley 1950-1965
Road & Track on Rolls Royce & B'ley 1966-1984
Road & Track on Saab 1955-1985
Road & Track on Toyota Sports & GT Cars 1966-1984
Road & Track on Triumph Sports Cars 1953-1967
Road & Track on Triumph Sports Cars 1967-1974
Road & Track on Triumph Sports Cars 1974-1982
Road & Track on Volkswagen 1951-1968
Road & Track on Volkswagen 1968-1978
Road & Track on Volkswagen 1978-1985
Road & Track on Volvo 1957-1974
Road & Track on Volvo 1975-1985
Road & Track - Henry Manney at Large and Abroad

BROOKLANDS CAR AND DRIVER SERIES
Car and Driver on BMW 1955-1977
Car and Driver on BMW 1977-1985
Car and Driver on Cobra, Shelby & Ford GT 40 1963-1984
Car and Driver on Corvette 1956-1967
Car and Driver on Corvette 1968-1977
Car and Driver on Corvette 1978-1982
Car and Driver on Corvette 1983-1988
Car and Driver on Datsun Z 1600 & 2000 1966-1984
Car and Driver on Ferrari 1955-1962
Car and Driver on Ferrari 1963-1975
Car and Driver on Ferrari 1976-1983
Car and Driver on Mopar 1956-1967
Car and Driver on Mopar 1968-1975
Car and Driver on Mustang 1964-1972
Car and Driver on Pontiac 1961-1975
Car and Driver on Porsche 1955-1962
Car and Driver on Porsche 1963-1970
Car and Driver on Porsche 1970-1976
Car and Driver on Porsche 1977-1981
Car and Driver on Porsche 1982-1986
Car and Driver on Saab 1956-1985
Car and Driver on Volvo 1955-1986

BROOKLANDS PRACTICAL CLASSICS SERIES
PC on Austin A40 Restoration
PC on Land Rover Restoration
PC on Metalworking in Restoration
PC on Midget/Sprite Restoration
PC on Mini Cooper Restoration
PC on MGB Restoration
PC on Morris Minor Restoration
PC on Sunbeam Rapier Restoration
PC on Triumph Herald/Vitesse
PC on Triumph Spitfire Restoration
PC on VW Beetle Restoration
PC on 1930s Car Restoration

BROOKLANDS HOT ROD 'MUSCLECAR & HI-PO ENGINE SERIES
Chevy 265 & 283
Chevy 302 & 327
Chevy 348 & 409
Chevy 350 & 400
Chevy 396 & 427
Chevy 454 thru 512
Chrysler Hemi
Chrysler 273, 318, 340 & 360
Chrysler 361, 383, 400, 413, 426, 440
Ford 289, 302, Boss 302 & 351W
Ford 351C & Boss 351
Ford Big Block

BROOKLANDS MILITARY VEHICLES SERIES
Allied Mil. Vehicles No.1 1942-1945
Allied Mil. Vehicles No.2 1941-1946
Dodge Mil. Vehicles Col.1 1940-1945
Off Road Jeeps 1944-1971
Hail to the Jeep
Complete WW2 Military Jeep Manual
US Military Vehicles 1941-1945
US Army Military Vehicles WW2-TM9-2800

BROOKLANDS HOT ROD RESTORATION SERIES
Auto Restoration Tips & Techniques
Basic Bodywork Tips & Techniques
Basic Painting Tips & Techniques
Camaro Restoration Tips & Techniques
Chevrolet High Performance Tips & Techniques
Chevy Engine Swapping Tips & Techniques
Chevy-GMC Pickup Repair
Custom Painting Tips & Techniques
Engine Swapping Tips & Techniques
Ford Pickup Repair
How to Build a Street Rod
Mustang Restoration Tips & Techniques
Performance Tuning - Chevrolets of the '60s
Performance Tuning - Ford of the '60s
Performance Tuning - Mopars of the '60s
Performance Tuning - Pontiacs of the '60s

CONTENTS

ACKNOWLEDGEMENTS

It is some eight years now since we published our first book on the Chevelles: *Chevelle and SS, 1964-1972* in fact proved so popular that we had to reprint it no fewer than three times. When the time came for a fourth reprint, we decided to see if we could expand the book by including new material which had became availabe, and so that is what we have done with this Muscle Portfolio. Some 50% of the material in it did not apear in the earlier book.

Brooklands Books exist to provide an information service on the older cars which today's enthusiasts enjoy. Without the co-operation of the world's leading magazine publishers, however, we would be unable to fulfil our aims. It therefore gives me pleasure to express my thanks for the material used in this volume to the publishers of Autocar, Car and Driver, Car Craft, Car Life, Cars, Chevrolet High Performance, Hot Rod, Motor Trend, Musclecar Classics, Road & Track and Road Test.

R.M. Clarke

When the Chevelle appeared in 1964, its main aim was to tackle the intermediate sized sedan segment of the market in which Ford's Fairlane had been scoring heavily since 1962. Of course, the Chevelle came with a wide variety of body styles and engines and, of course, there was a performance package among the options. The performance models were known as the Malibu and SS.

During the 1960s, both sales and horsepower of the Chevelles embarked on a steep upward curve. In the best Chevy tradition, the performance models always ran V8 engines, ranging from a 220bhp 283 cubic incher in the '64 models to a massive 454 cubic inch motor with 450bhp in the 1970 SS-454. This latter machine could turn in six-second 0-60mph times and quarter-miles of under 14 seconds.

But somebody had to spoil all the fun, even if it was for a good reason. As unleaded gasoline became mandatory, so the Chevelle's horsepower came down. For 1971, the power losses were noticeable; for 1972, performance was down again; and after that, the high-performance Chevelle effectively ceased to exist.

This book celebrates the golden years of the Chevelles, when the range contained muscle cars which offered affordable high-performance motoring and fun by the ton. Today, the Malibu and SS models have a strong enthusiast following, and there can be no doubt that a read through these pages will make even more converts to the cause.

James Taylor

Chevelle Malibu

IT MAKES LITTLE difference whether the appearance of GM's new A-body structure preceded the decision by Chevrolet to shift its model alignment. The end result is the same and it is called Chevelle. This is the standard-sized Chevrolet line, with 11 models available in three series: the 300, the Malibu and the Malibu Super Sport—plus a sedan pickup El Camino in standard or de luxe trim.

The Super Sport comes as either a convertible or a coupe, both called 4-passenger by virtue of the individual bucket seats in front, separated by a central console extending along the transmission tunnel and bucket-like styling for the rear seats. The console has an automatic courtesy light styled into the aft end for back seat occupants. Leather grain vinyl is used to trim the seats in a choice of seven color-keyed all-vinyl interiors.

To power this, Chevrolet's 283-cu.

in. V-8, developing 220 bhp with a single 4-barrel carburetor, dual exhausts and different distributor advance, can be teamed with the new 4-speed all-synchromesh manual transmission. Gear ratios are 2.56 first, 1.91 second, 1.48 third and 1.00:1 high, and an axle ratio of 3.08:1 is standard (3.36:1 optional). While this engine is a special option for the Chevelle, the 283 with single 2-barrel is also available (195 bhp) as is the Chevrolet 7-main bearing 6-cyl. engine—120 bhp from 194 cu. in. and 155 bhp from 230. A 3-speed manual, with column mounted lever, is the standard transmission, although overdrive and Powerglide (with console-mounted selector) are also options.

In common with its B-O-P kissin' cousins, the Chevelle body is mounted on a perimeter-type frame of 115-in. wheelbase. Coil springs are used at each wheel and, while quite soft in

the modern manner, can be replaced by heavier duty components.

At 193.9 in. overall, the Chevelle is still some 16 in. shorter than the large-sized Chevrolet although its interior dimensions and entrance height are within an inch of the larger car. Wheels are 14 in. on all models; self-adjusting brakes operate on 9.5-in. drums. Gauges are used for oil pressure, coolant temperature and ammeter on the Super Sport, and are mounted along with an electric clock in a trio of large round dials.

Further setting off this SS model is a special yellow paint job which can be ordered rather than one of the 14 regular hues. A simulated wood grained steering wheel with spring steel spokes heads a list of optional equipment which includes power brakes, power steering, tilting steering wheel, built-in air conditioning, tinted glass and limited-slip differential. ∎

by Bob McVay, *Assistant Technical Editor*

ONE OF THE FEW all-new cars offered for 1964 is Chevrolet's Chevelle. We got our first chance to drive a production version at a press preview two weeks before the car was officially introduced. After that initial drive, we asked for a test car as soon as possible, and we got one of the first ones available in the Los Angeles area.

Our Chevelle Malibu Super Sport test car came with the biggest engine option (220-hp V-8), a four-speed all-synchro-mesh floormounted gearshift with a 3.08 rear axle, and loaded with accessories. After putting a few hundred easy break-in miles on the car, we picked up our test gear and our photographer and took off for Riverside International Raceway to see how it would perform. With our test equipment and two MOTOR TREND staff members aboard, the Chevelle tipped the scales at just under 3500 pounds.

We got lots of wheelspin on hard acceleration, but each run to 60 mph was under the 10-second mark — 9.7 was our best time. Zero to 30 and 45 mph took 3.6 and 6.2 seconds. The Malibu crossed the end of our measured quarter-mile test strip hitting an honest 80 mph and freezing our battery of stop watches at 17.4 seconds. Although the Chevelle's easy-to-read speedometer proved from two to three mph on the optimistic side, our Weston electric speedometer showed the car's top speed was 109 mph. (We

Dimensions and handling of all-new Chevelle Malibu reminded us of an old friend, the 1955 Chevy. Chevelle fills the gap between full-sized Chevrolets and Chevy II.

ROAD TEST

recalled that one of the preview Chevelles had the optional 3.36-to-1 "mountain" rear axle and felt quite a bit stronger off the line, since it allowed the 283-incher to reach its peak revs more quickly.)

Our test car's engine was the tried and proven 283-cubic-inch V-8, which hot rodders and racing mechanics have used to power practically anything on four wheels since its introduction. In its 220-hp Chevelle form, it was quiet, willing, and reliable during our test period. It's an engine that lends itself well to the owner who wants more than the 220 hp offered by Chevrolet.

We used 5500 rpm as our red line and for shift points for best acceleration. Third gear proved handy for any quick passing in normal cruising ranges of 45 to 75 and would wind right on up to 91 mph before a shift into fourth was necessary. Second-gear starts were easily possible.

For the performance-minded buyer, the combination of the top V-8 and a four-speed transmission is a good one (the gearbox goes as an option for $188.30). The shift lever is a man-sized unit, with a fist-filling chrome ball on top. A finger-operated lock-out gate prevents unwanted shifts into reverse, but it was quite easy to go from third into second unwittingly, unless we consciously applied side pressure on the shift lever.

Ride and handling were what we've come to expect from Chevrolet. Our Chevelle had a soft boulevard ride and showed considerable body lean in faster-than-usual corners. Fast cornering also caused the carburetor to flood and the car to lose power right in the middle of a bend, just when we needed it most to keep the car under control. Cornering power was about average, with the front end usually the first to lose adhesion. A wet track showed up the car's understeering characteristics even more strongly. It's handling struck us as being about average for an American passenger car — certainly not one that lends itself to overly fast driving.

We could feel small bumps and tar strips in the road transmitted to our hands through the steering gear. The suspension bottomed on moderate dips and bumps. When cruising at legal highway speeds of 65 mph, small bumps would cause the front suspension to oscillate up and down two or three times before settling down to level riding. A desirable option (at just $4.85) would be the heavier springs and shock absorbers offered as heavy- or special-duty equipment.

Our acceleration and top-speed runs gave the Chevelle's brakes a good workout. Six high-speed stops found them faded almost completely. They needed about 10 minutes to recover their stopping power. Our braking tests found the car giving reasonably good stops from 30 mph in 24 feet, but our maximum-effort stops from 60 mph required a longer-than-usual 162.5 feet. Wheel lock-up and swerving made straight-line stops difficult, and here's where we would've appreciated fewer turns of the power-steering unit.

Almost four turns (3.98) lock to lock are required by Chevelle's integral power steering. In our opinion, panic stops and winding roads, as well as tight parking spaces, needed too many wheel turns for reasonable safety. Any tight bend took at least one full turn, sometimes more.

It's hard to talk about steering without mentioning the steering wheel itself. Our test car was equipped with the optional sport wheel, a nice, two-spoke, plastic wheel that looks just like the wooden ones seen on some expensive sports cars. It adds a touch of glamor to the car for an extra $32.30.

Our test car had quite a long cruising range. With its 20-gallon gasoline tank and our top mileage figure of 18.4 mpg, we could drive well over 300 miles before looking for a service station. Extremely hard driving gave us a low figure of 9.6 mpg, but our overall average for 900 test miles was a high 16 mpg — quite good for the top performance car in the Chevelle line-up. Moderate driving would give even better mileage, especially on the six-cylinder models equipped with overdrive. It was refreshing to find a powerful hardtop that would still give such good gas mileage.

Somehow, we couldn't help feeling we'd driven the Chevelle before, about eight years ago. It's basically very similar to the popular 1955 Chevrolet — a shade shorter in overall length and height, but with the same basic engine-chassis combination. The Chevelle is a little faster, lighter, and costs more.

Chevelles come in three series; Chevelle 300, Malibu, and Malibu Super Sport, plus the regular and deluxe El Camino three-passenger pickup (probably the most interesting of the line). A full range of body styles is offered, in-

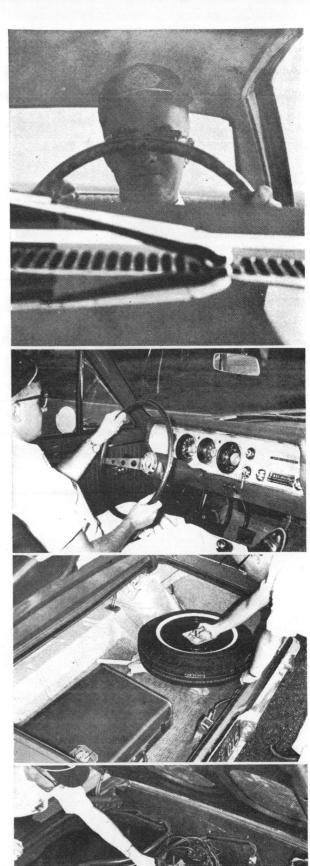

1) *Well known for power and reliability, Chevelle's 283-cubic-inch V-8 uses hydraulic lifters, five main bearings, and has a good torque supply. It lends itself well to power increases.*

2) *Instrument panel is simple and easy to read. Super Sport models have clock, use gauges. The others have warning lights.*

3) *Our test car's trunk had lots of room (16.9 feet) and a low lip for easy loading. The protruding bolt that holds the spare in place should be covered. It could damage expensive luggage.*

4) *High-mounted steering wheel cut right across our line of vision. Position is tiring after long stints behind the wheel.*

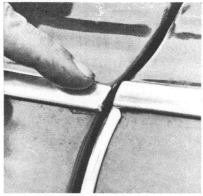
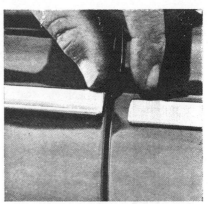

Fit and detail finish seemed below average for Chevy products. Straight-edge demonstrates front fender alignment and the gap between car's fender panel and door. Technical editor's finders point out the wide gaps and imperfect fit of Chevelle's chrome.

1

2

3

4

cluding two-door and four-door sedans and station wagons (two- and three-seat models), hardtops, and convertibles.

The standard engine is a 194-cubic-inch Six, rated at 120 hp. Next comes an optional 230-inch Six with 155 horses. Both Sixes use a single-barrel carburetor, have 8.5-to-1 compression, and use regular gas. Two V-8s are offered, both 283-inchers. The standard unit is rated at 195 hp and has a two-barrel carb, while the top engine (as on our test car) boasts 220 horses and has one four-barrel carb. Both have 9.5-to-1 compression ratios.

Transmissions include the standard three-speed column shift (3.08 axle), optional overdrive (3.70 axle), Powerglide automatic (3.08 axle), and the all-synchromesh four-speed box. A "special purpose" or "mountain" axle ratio of 3.36 to 1 is optional.

Chevelle joins other GM compacts in using separate body-chassis construction. It uses the 115-inch-wheelbase perimeter frame with coil springs at each corner. The ladder-type frame has three structural crossmembers and one nonstructural crossmember for the rear engine mount.

Chevrolet is offering enough options to please almost everyone. A look down the long list reveals such interesting performance items as metallic brake linings, air-suspension system, heavy-duty suspension options (mentioned earlier for $4.85), heavy-duty clutch, Positraction rear axle, and a host of optional tires ranging from 6.50 x 14 to 7.50 x 14-inchers of four-ply construction.

Starting from a base price of $2635, our test car had all the available options, with the exception of air conditioning and power seats. Its price tag came to $3462.35, plus tax and license. Air conditioning would increase this to $3830.90 — certainly not an economy price tag.

The Chevelle lines up between the full-sized Chevys and the diminishing Chevy II series. The top-line body styles of the Chevy II, the hardtop and convertible, have been dropped for '64, so it's only natural for people who would normally buy the SS model to look to the Chevelle.

Chevelle, along with other GM products, has a 24-month/24,000-mile warranty that applies to the original purchaser. A minimum 60-day or 6000-mile service period is required to keep the warranty in force.

Somehow, we couldn't get too excited over the Chevelle, even though it's a brand-new offering. The 1955 Chevy was a top seller, and this one's a lot like it. It does what it was designed to do, providing good reliable transportation for five with adequate power and luggage space. General overall quality and workmanship looked good inside the car, but body panels and outside chrome trim didn't match up very well. Ours was one of the first Chevelles in this area, but we've looked at more recent ones and they didn't look much better than our test car.

If public interest in our test car is any indication, there's a good market for the Chevelle. People were constantly asking about the car wherever we stopped. Only time will tell about the future of the Chevelle. It fills a gap in Chevrolet's extensive line-up — and that's an accomplishment. /MT

---

1) *Chevelle sports minimum of chrome trim, giving it a clean profile. The car has curved side glass and posts. A special adhesive cement is used to seal the windshield and rear window.*
2) *Brake fade occurred after a few high-speed stops, but brakes recovered their usefulness after they cooled for a few minutes.*
3) *Our SS hardtop had adequate leg- and head room for four, was a little tight for five. Doors open wide for easy entrance and exit. The long reach to third gear made us stretch a little.*
4) *Three-quarter-front view shows the pleasing Chevelle grille. Hood latch is outside, leaving the engine easy prey for vandals.*

CHEVELLE MALIBU SS
2-door, 5-passenger hardtop

OPTIONS ON CAR TESTED: 220-hp V-8, power steering-brakes-windows, special steering wheel, radio, heater, whitewalls, seat belts, misc. items.
BASIC PRICE: $2635
PRICE AS TESTED: $3462.35 (plus tax and license)
ODOMETER READING AT START OF TEST: 600 miles
RECOMMENDED ENGINE RED LINE: 5500 rpm

PERFORMANCE

ACCELERATION (2 aboard)
0-30 mph............................3.6 secs.
0-45 mph............................6.2
0-60 mph............................9.7
Standing start ¼-mile 17.4 secs. and 80 mph
Speeds in gears @ 5500 rpm
    1st ....51 mph   3rd ....91 mph
    2nd ....69 mph   4th ....110 mph
Speedometer Error on Test Car

Car's speedometer reading 32	46	52	62	72	83
Weston electric speedometer ...30	45	50	60	70	80

Observed miles per hour per 1000 rpm in top gear ....22 mph
Stopping Distances — from 30 mph, 24.0 ft.; from 60 mph, 162.5 ft.

SPECIFICATIONS FROM MANUFACTURER

Engine
Ohv V-8
Bore: 3.875 ins.
Stroke: 3.00 ins.
Displacement: 283.0 cu. ins.
Compression ratio: 9.25:1
Horsepower: 220 @ 4800 rpm
Torque: 295 lbs.-ft. @ 3200 rpm
Horsepower per cubic inch: 0.78
Carburetion: 1 4-bbl.
Ignition: 12-volt coil

Gearbox
4-speed manual, all synchro; floormounted lever

Driveshaft
1-piece, open tube

Differential
Hypoid, semi-floating
Standard ratio: 3.08:1

Suspension
Front: Single lower arm, with independent coil springs, direct, double-acting, hydraulic shock absorbers and stabilizer bar; spherically-jointed steering knuckle for each wheel
Rear: 4-link system; 2 upper and 2 lower control arms, coil springs, and direct, double-acting hydraulic shock absorbers

Steering
Recirculating ball nut, with integral power
Turns lock to lock: 3.98

Wheels and Tires
5-lug, steel disc wheels
7.00 x 14 Goodyear whitewalls

Brakes
Hydraulic, duo-servo, with vacuum power assist; self-adjusting; cast-iron drums
Front: 9.5-in. dia. x 2.5 ins. wide
Rear: 9.5-in. dia. x 2.0 ins. wide
Effective lining area: 172.7 sq. ins.

Body and Frame
Welded steel body on ladder-type welded perimeter frame, with torque box reinforced sections
Wheelbase: 115.0 ins.
Track: front and rear, 58.0 ins.
Overall length: 193.9 ins.
Curb weight: 3060 lbs.

Chevelle Chevelle Chi

1 Malibu, 1 El Camino, and 1 Super Sport Equal 1 Suburbia Set for Triple Trial . . .

O NE FORTE OF THE Chevrolet dealer organization is that it can sell just about any sort of rolling stock, provided the cars meet its conception of what an automobile should be. The Corvair did not and only a mushrooming public interest saved it from an apathetic fate at the dealers' hands. Then came the Chevy II, a car which the dealers could understand, and that reputation for salesmanship was maintained. It comes as no surprise, then, that Chevrolet's new line, the aggressively conventional Chevelle, has accounted for more than the 15% of production originally scheduled for it at introduction time.

What has been somewhat of a surprise, however, has been the continued demand for the Chevy II, which factory planners figured would have to face a dwindling market. The Chevelle was conceived as a bigger car, completely divorced from the austere economy image, which would allow Chevy

II customers to move into a larger car at a time when the pendulum of public taste was swinging back toward largeness and luxury. The top series in the Chevy II line had been dropped, only to be returned to production as 1963 drew to a close and the strong demand for the Chevy II line continued.

It was a late decision last spring to continue an emasculated Chevy II line as a hedge on the Chevelle bet and production continued with negligible appearance changes. Availability of the 283-cu. in. V-8 engine as an option, however, raised the Chevy II stakes in this popularity poker game.

With that in mind, the appearance of the Chevelle line then begins to seem a merchandising master stroke. Not only does it complete the "something for everybody" line which can snare a shopper into driving home from the Chevrolet dealership in a new car, it also retains for the Chevy dealer near-equal footing with the local Pontiac,

Buick and Oldsmobile stores. He had had a small advantage over the B-O-P smaller cars in a slightly better passenger package with the Chevy II before the A-series cars were introduced.

Chevrolet and its dealers are well aware that a vast segment of the motoring public couldn't care less about the things that, to the enthusiast, are the heart and soul of an automotive love affair. It is precisely for that great group, quite often seen choking the highways in dawdling drives on springtime Sunday afternoons, for whom the Chevelle was designed and built. Small wonder that its sales performance exceeds the forecast of the production planners.

Since it is a new line of standard-sized cars available in 13 models, *Car Life* editors decided to expand the usual test to include three varied examples with differing power trains. The result —a standard 6-cyl. 4-door sedan, a sporty V-8 El Camino pickup with Powerglide, and a sleek 2-door hardtop with the new Chevrolet-built "Muncie" 4-speed transmission—was a veritable suburbia kit: a car each for Mom, Dad and Junior.

As it worked out, Mom would have

been pleased to find the 2-speed Powerglide bolted behind the 230-cu. in., 7-main-bearing Six in her sedan, even though the testers would have preferred the 3-speed manual, with or without overdrive, to permit a more thorough evaluation of the available power trains. When announced, the Chevelle was to have four engine and four transmission options, for a total of 13 power trains. As *Car Life* testers began work, however, Chevrolet announced that the 327-cu. in. Corvette engine would be available in three bhp ratings, increasing the power options to 19. They are:

CHEVELLE POWER OPTIONS

Engines		Transmissions		
cu. in./bhp	3-speed	O/D	4-speed	PG
194/120	X	X		X
230/155	X	X		X
283/195	X	X	X	X
283/220	X		X	X
327/250	X		X	X
327/300			X	
327/365			X	

Father and son undoubtedly would have to Indian-wrestle for the keys to the El Camino, if both had surfing, motorcycling, hunting, or ranching as major interests. The reappearance of this stylish pickup truck, enhanced by the optional bucket-seated and carpeted interior, puts Chevrolet back into competition in that growing segment of the market—particularly in the Southwest and on the West Coast—that wants lushness with its load-carrying and has found that station wagons aren't the answer. For the past two years, Ford Rancheros have had this segment to themselves until Dodge edged in with its whimsically experimental (and subsequently adopted) "sports pickup."

Both the El Camino and the Malibu Super Sport hardtop (Dad, being a bit out of shape for physical exertion, settles for the latter) were powered by the 220 bhp V-8, the special Chevelle-only option that was the line's most potent powerplant before the addition of the 327s. Improved breathing from the four 1.44-in. barrels of the Carter carburetor (Rochester with Powerglide) instills new life into this 283-cu. in. engine. The breathless struggle in the higher rpm ranges to which our Chevy II test car was heir (Jan. CL) is not evident with the 4-barrel modification. The 4800 rpm power peak is readily attained, aided to some extent by the dual exhaust system which is standard with the 220 bhp version. A different distributor and incorporation of a rubber-mounted vibration damper to the crankshaft are the only other differences from the 195 bhp engine. Particularly with the automatic transmission, it appears that the more powerful of the two is the better choice for a car of this weight.

The data panel only partially illustrates the penalty extracted by the Powerglide transmission. Chevrolet could well use Buick's new variable vane torque converter automatic so long as it has no plans to build a true 3-speed automatic. Evidence abounds at most drag strips that the opposition knows the importance of a well-designed, modern 3-speed automatic. The transmission's lack of efficiency, demonstrated in sluggish starts from rest and in the gap in power transmission at medium speeds, is readily apparent in driving the Chevelles. However, past experience indicates that the more powerful 327 engines would overcome this deficiency by sheer brute force.

On the other hand, the Muncie 4-speed is an entirely different story. This robust gearbox does a most admirable job of transmitting power to the pavement. With ratios of 2.56 first, 1.91 second, 1.48 third and 1.00:1 high, the

IN LINE behind, our trio of test cars shows new silhouette for American car market.

Chevelle

unit is more evenly spaced than the formerly used Warner Gear T-10. It is fully synchronized in all four gears, which have wider faces to handle the torque loads from Chevrolet's largest engines and a different tooth design for noise reduction. Larger synchronizers and a new output shaft aid in measuring up to big inch engines, as do larger capacity bearings. The tubular shift lever, slightly bent for easier reach and topped by a chrome ball, has a spring loaded lock-out gate at the base to prevent accidental shifts into reverse. A sliding collar sprouting a pair of lifting pegs, which lives under the knob, unlocks the gate. Because of a more rigid bracket assembly, shifts have a some-

what tighter feel than the T-10 unit but are quick, positive and a wrist-flick apart.

This stout (0.68-in. diameter) stick reaches up from a console which hardly justifies the name. It is no more than a raised bright metal trim cover extending from firewall to rear seat footwell, with a light (which didn't work) at the aft end. When Powerglide is specified in the Super Sport, it also is controlled from a floor-mounted lever—in that case a T-shaped handle with a piano key-like button on top to control the Park-Reverse-Low lockout. The shift pattern, incidentally, is now in a straight line instead of requiring a stepped motion.

The single dry-disc centrifugal clutch betrayed no signs of either slipping or grabbing. It is 10.4-in. in diameter with the more powerful V-8s and is housed in a new ribbed aluminum casting. Positive clutch action even at high rpm was possible because of the "bent finger" design of the new pressure plate, and pedal effort seemed moderate despite the 2300 lb. plate pressure involved.

Only three axle ratios are listed for the Chevelle, effectively limiting any factory-installed improvement in performance for the line. Standard is 3.08:1 with 3.36:1—standard for the station wagons and El Camino—as the readily available option. Overdrive-equipped models have 3.70:1. The lighter El Camino, despite the higher gearing, still failed to match the hardtop because of its Powerglide handicap.

Chevrolet uses the 194-cu. in. Six of Chevy II heritage as the basic engine for the Chevelle line, teamed with a 3-speed synchromesh manual transmission as standard. Since this is the case, our data panel includes figures extrapolated from previous tests of this pow-

TILT-WHEEL option is available with power steering and was fitted to El Camino.

BUCKET seats in pickup tilt for access to spare tire, small stowage space.

FAMILIAR 283-cu. in. engine serves as optional power with up to 220 bhp.

er train weighted (literally) against Chevelle specifications.

The optional Six is, of course, the very familiar 7-main-bearing 155 bhp powerplant which has been doing yeoman service since it replaced the venerable "stovebolt six" in late 1962. It weighs 465 lb. and is readily identifiable in the Chevelle with its chromed air cleaner, rocker arm cover and oil filler cap. High performance is not this engine's plate of hashish, but economical, long-lived operation is; the sturdiness and smoothness resulting from the more expensive 7-main crankshaft help insure this. Breathing restrictions are built in with the single barrel (1.56-in. venturi) carburetor and manifold, to the point where 4000 rpm is barely within reach. The engine is easily capable (at 3000 rpm) of maintaining maximum legal cruising speeds, with some margin and minimum obtrusiveness, which should be acceptable, considering the market for which the Chevelle was designed. Except for the new 4-speed, then, there is nothing unfamiliar about Chevelle power trains.

An analysis of the body and chassis

is, of course, largely repetition of that for the Oldsmobile F-85 Cutlass (Jan. CL). The fact that about two-thirds of the 1965 American passenger cars will have almost identical design, however, makes it worthy of repeating.

The Chevelle shares General Motors' A-series body design, using a perimeter-type frame with torsional rigidity somewhat less than past practice. To this is attached a welded-up body structure which approaches unitized construction in structural rigidity. Suspension is by unequal length A-arms in the front and a 4-link live axle behind, all sprung via coils and damped with double-acting telescopic shock absorbers. All suspension attachment points and the 10 mounting points between chassis and body are heavily rubber-bushed, resulting in a progressive resistance to jolts and twists as they travel from roadbed to passenger compartment.

The frame consists of a pair of full-length side rails, joined laterally by three cross-members which form part of the structure. A large box-section cross-member loops down under the engine and forms the attachment point

for front suspension components. A deep C-section cross-member attached in front of the rear kick-up forms a similar base for rear suspension components. The third cross-member is a simple channel section joining the rear of the two side rails. A fourth, nonstructural cross-member is used to support the rear of the transmission housing and is fully rubber bushed at attachment points to eliminate vibration.

Side rails are of heavy gauge C-section construction, with welded-in torque boxes at the rear kick-up and between the passenger and engine compartments. On the convertibles and sedan pickups (El Camino), another C-section is welded over the usually-open inner side of the rails to provide greater beam strength. Side rails are located just inside the body rocker panels and no cross-member intrudes upon passenger compartment space.

The coil spring independent front suspension is little different from long-standing Chevrolet practice. Stamped short and long control arms swing from rubber bushed pivots and locate the ball jointed hub assembly. Coil

HIGH STYLE of utilitarian El Camino draws praise at every filling station, envy from every surfer.

TAILGATE of wagon provides a more fitting enclosure than usual pickup type.

Chevelle

springs and shock absorbers are concentric, seated in the lower arm and at the side-rail cross-member attachment point. A link-type stabilizer bar of 0.812-in. diameter connects the two lower arms and the short upper arm is inclined slightly at the front for anti-dive control. Lower wishbones are positioned with their pivots on a bias, angling the arm somewhat forward so that the curved leading edge forms a right angle to the car's centerline. In conjunction with rubber-bushed pivots

of different sizes and resiliencies, this arrangement provides controlled flexibility fore and aft at the same time high lateral stiffness is maintained. Coil springs are 10.51-in. high and have a rate of 90.5 lb./in. at the wheel, for the sedan.

Two sets of stamped control arms take up drive and brake forces in the rear suspension, which is designed to provide a quite high roll center for the desired understeer. The longer lower control arms attach to the side rails

through welded-on brackets, while the upper arms are attached to the kick-up cross-member. A large stamped plate, riveted to the cross-member and welded to the side rails, serves as upper spring seat and shock absorber mounting. The rigid Salisbury-type rear axle rides on brackets attached to the rear ends of the longer arms, with each end of the arm pivoting in compressed rubber bushings. Coil springs are 7.18-in. high and mount directly over the axle housing, while shock absorbers are attached to a bracket behind the axle. The shorter upper arms run diagonally from the differential and also are pivoted in compressed rubber bushings. The diagonal mounting is thought to restrict lateral movement of the axle sufficiently to eliminate the need for radius rods or track bars. Geometry of the rear suspension tends to lift the rear of the frame during acceleration.

SHIFT pattern is on console which really isn't a console.

BREATH of life is given to 283 by 4-barrel carburetor.

MORE THAN adequate baggage capacity is available in new line despite spare tire's location.

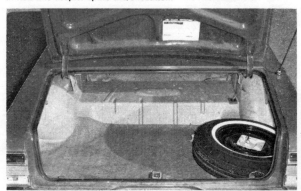

PARKED IN front of 3-car garage, a Chevelle suburbia set awaits Mom, Dad and Junior.

LOOKS REAL, but wood grained wheel is really plastic imitation.

Steering is by recirculating ball gear and has an overall ratio of 26.2:1 with 5.48 turns between locks in standard form. However, the test cars all were fitted with the integral power cylinder and control valve which reduced ratio to 19.1:1 and turns to 4.1.

Duo-servo hydraulic brakes are 9.5-in. composite drums at each wheel, 2.5-in. wide in front and 2 in. at the rear, providing a total lining area of 172.7 sq. in. in standard form. Metallic linings of 118.1 sq. in. area are available, with all shoes being self-adjusting. Five-stud steel disc 14 x 5J wheels are fitted, carrying tire sizes from 6.50 through 7.50, depending on model.

Body construction forms a sturdy, rigid shell, with major panels welded together for the passenger package but bolted together in the front fender and hood area. Roof pillars, headers and rails are box section and welded to the

roof panel. The cowl structure is a welded-up double wall affair to which the instrument panel is in turn welded. At the rear, quarter panels and rear end sheet metal are welded together to form a similarly strong section around the trunk opening. The underbody panel is heavily ribbed and formed for maximum strength and ties all the upper sheet metal together. Curved glass side windows are used, permitting a slight improvement in interior shoulder width, and windshield and rear window are bonded in place via adhesive cement rather than by weatherstripping.

As it rolls out of the showroom, the Chevelle is an admirable vehicle for the market it is intended. It must be classified as among the most handsome of the 1964 automobiles, provided the too-busy "dual cove" rear styling treatment is overlooked. With a 115-in. wheelbase and 193.9-in. overall length,

it fits the standard size class and is, in fact, quite similar in dimensions to the 1955 Chevrolet.

In operation, it has adequate power —regardless of engine—to provide easy cross-country tours and the seating and riding comfort to go with them. Brakes provide a nice, progressive action that is excellent for easy around-town travel. Steering is quite light, although at idling rpm the power assist was slow in coming on to help. The ride is almost identical to the larger Chevrolet's heavily-promoted one of "jet" smoothness. On any turnpike, it will transport up to six people and a big batch of baggage with ease, although one of the more powerful V-8 engines is needed to do the job with less strain and a consistently high velocity. For the type of driver the designers had in mind, it is an excellently tailored suit of steel.

But for the smaller group of drivers

PHANTOM VIEW of body shows rugged construction, almost as strong as an actual unit body.

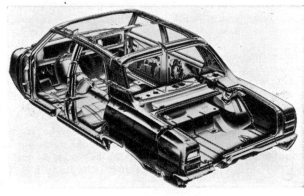

PERIMETER frame is somewhat flexible base, helps absorb road shocks before they reach passengers.

Chevelle

who take their motoring seriously, it doesn't have quite so much to offer. The fine styling and near-perfect dimensions are attractive, to be sure, as are the 4-speed transmission and power potential of the 327 Corvette engine options.

Vague and bland ride and handling, unnoticed at moderate speeds by less critical drivers, becomes pronounced during more vigorous treatment. The bump-sopping suspension turns out to be prone to wheel-flapping in front and bounce-stepping behind. The substantial understeer, compounded by the greater noseward weight bias with the V-8 engines, could only be overcome by powersliding the tail outward—a procedure more often than not helped along by rear-wheel polka on all but the smoothest of surfaces.

As expected, the Malibu handled best because of the more proper weight distribution, just as the El Camino was the biggest handful because of its lightly loaded rear (but not quite as hopeless as it might have been, since it was equipped with Air-Lift spring helpers). Such an angle is assumed by the inside front wheel under hard cor-

nering stresses that tire contact with the ground is virtually on the inside sidewall, even with increased pressures for compensation.

Heavy-duty suspension components, which are available, might go a long way toward improving this situation, of course. By the same token, the optional metallic brakes are to be recommended, since the fast-fade standard linings proved to be quite marginal for a 3500-3800 lb. car. During all-on braking from 80 mph, none of the test cars registered better than 20 ft./sec./sec. on the *Car Life* decelerometer and all experienced complete fade in doing that well. Only the Malibu sedan, however, seemed to be prone to brake lockup.

The El Camino, which imparted more of a sports car impression because of the closeness of the passenger compartment, gave a more definite demonstration of the perimeter frame's reduction in torsional rigidity. Twist and sidesway over any irregular road surface was readily evident. It was also prone to the characteristic groans and creaks of a pickup truck.

If the Chevelles tested are any indi-

cation, Chevrolet's owner relations program will be sorely tried this year. All three left something to be desired in the way they had been assembled, with a level of workmanship that had all but disappeared from the industry in recent years.

Floor carpets were poorly fitted, with gaps between sections; exterior bright work was plagued with misalignment and was pulling away from its mounts in spots; interior lights failed to work; the sedan's electric wipers refused to stop running; fuel gauge needles had a palsied flutter, particularly in the sedan; the hardtop's hood refused to latch securely and its front fenders had a 0.5-in. mismatch where they joined the cowl (as did the El Camino's); curved side windows on the El Camino and sedan wouldn't raise all the way without pressure on the outside to keep them in the lift channels; and all the rubber pedal pads continually slipped adrift from their intended moorings.

Despite all of that, the Chevelle will sell—and sell well. And in the process, it apparently is having an effect on competitors' cars in this class. Where there had been some dwindling of sales, the appearance of the Chevelle and its A-bodied brethren has apparently helped spark new interest from buyers in such things as Fairlanes and Comets.

At this writing, Chevelle accounts for 18% of Chevrolet sales and the percentage is on the rise. It is a market, as we said, that is larger than that of the enthusiasts. ∎

1964 CHEVELLE

SPECIFICATIONS	MALIBU	300	SUPER SPORT	EL CAMINO
List price	$2338	$2338	$2635	$2449
Price, as tested	2918	n.a.	3342	3090
Curb weight, lb.	3265	3100	3390	3180
Test weight	3585	3430	3720	3560
distribution, %	52/48	n.a.	56/44	58/42
Tire size	6.50-14	6.50-14	7.00-14	7.50-14
Tire capacity, lb.@ 24 psi	3520	3520	3896	4340
Brake swept area	228.6	228.6	228.6	228.6
Engine type	IL-6, ohv	IL-6, ohv	V-8, ohv	V-8, ohv
Bore & Stroke	3.875 x 3.25	3.563 x 3.25	3.875 x 3.00	3.875 x 3.00
Displacement, cu. in.	230	194	283	283
Compression ratio	8.5	8.5	9.25	9.25
Carburetion	1 x 1	1 x 1	1 x 4	1 x 4
Bhp @ rpm	155@ 4400	120@ 4400	220@ 4800	220 @ 4800
equivalent mph	101	101	123	117
Torque, lb-ft	215@ 2000	177@ 2400	295@ 3200	295@ 3200
equivalent mph	46	55	82	78

GEAR RATIOS

	MALIBU	300	SUPER SPORT	EL CAMINO
4th, overall			(1.00)3.08	
3rd			(1.48)4.56	
2nd		(1.00)3.08	(1.91)5.88	(1.00)3.36
1st		(1.68)5.17	(2.56)7.88	(1.82)6.12
1st	(1.82)5.62	(2.94)9.05		
1st	(1.82 x 2.10)11.78		(1.82 x 2.10)12.8	

DIMENSIONS

	MALIBU	300	SUPER SPORT	EL CAMINO
Wheelbase, in.	115.0	115.0	115.0	115.0
Tread, f & r	58.0	58.0	58.0	58.0
Overall length, in.	193.9	193.9	193.9	198.9
width	74.6	74.6	74.6	74.6
height	54.5	54.5	54.0	54.0
equivalent vol., cu. ft.	454	454	452	463
Frontal area, sq. ft.	22.6	22.6	22.4	22.4
Ground clearance, in.	6.0	6.0	6.0	6.5
Steering ratio, o/a	19.1	26.2	19.1	19.1
turns, lock to lock	4.1	5.5	4.1	4.1
turning circle, ft.	34	34	34	34
Hip room, front	59.9	59.9	2 x 22	2 x 22
Hip room, rear	59.8	59.8	58.7	n.a.
Pedal to seat back, max.	44	44	43	44
Floor to ground	8.5	8.5	8.5	8.5
Luggage vol., cu. ft.	16.9	16.9	16.9	n.a.
Fuel tank capacity, gal.	20.0	20.0	20.0	20.0

PERFORMANCE	MALIBU	300	SUPER SPORT	EL CAMINO
Top speed, rpm/mph	4000/92	4000/90	4300/110	4500/110
Shifts, rpm/mph	auto.	manual	manual	auto.
3rd			5500/86	
2nd		4150/65	5500/65	
1st	4050/51	4150/37	5500/50	4300/56

FUEL CONSUMPTION

	MALIBU	300	SUPER SPORT	EL CAMINO
Normal range, mpg	16-20	16-21	15-19	15-18

ACCELERATION

	MALIBU	300	SUPER SPORT	EL CAMINO
0-30 mph, sec.	4.7	5.5	3.1	4.1
0-40	6.8	7.9	4.6	5.5
0-50	9.6	10.6	6.6	7.2
0-60	13.4	14.3	8.7	9.1
0-70	18.8	20.0	11.3	11.8
0-80	26.0	27.2	14.8	15.3
0-90	38.0	n.a.	19.4	20.8
0-100	n.a.	n.a.	27.9	30.0
Standing ¼ mile, sec.	19.6	19.5	16.2	16.5
speed at end, mph	72	69	84	82

PULLING POWER

	MALIBU	300	SUPER SPORT	EL CAMINO
90 mph, max. gradient, %	n.a.	n.a.	6.5	7.0
70 mph	8.5	6.0	15.2 (3rd)	12.0 (2nd)
50	13.6	13.3	21.6 (2nd)	24.5 (1st)
30	23.8	20.0	off scale (1st)	28.8 (1st)
Total drag at 60 mph, lb.	160	n.a.	120	160

SPEEDOMETER ERROR

	MALIBU	300	SUPER SPORT	EL CAMINO
30 mph, actual	30.6	n.a.	30.2	35.5
60 mph	61.2	n.a.	61.6	63.0
90 mph	90.2	n.a.	93.0	90.0

CALCULATED DATA

	MALIBU	300	SUPER SPORT	EL CAMINO
Lb./hp test weight	23.1	28.6	16.9	16.4
Cu. ft./ton mile	97.5	85.6	102	114
Mph/1000 rpm	22.9	22.9	25.7	24.3
Engine revs/mile	2620	2620	2325	2470
Piston travel, ft./mile	1420	1420	1162	1234
Car Life wear index	37.2	37.2	27.0	30.5

NOTE: Data presented for Chevelle 300 with 3-speed manual transmission have been extrapolated from previously published test results for this power train and manufacturer's specifications.

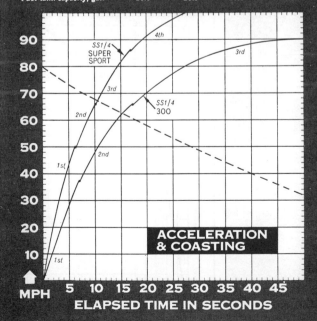

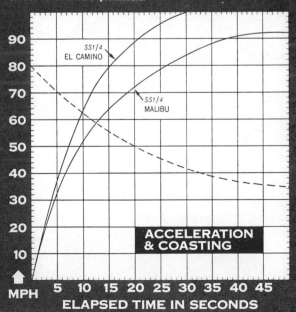

CHEVELLE MALIBU SS

Chevrolet presents a clean new transportation machine of high all-around merit. Sensible dimensions and sparkling performance augur well for its sales future.

When the largest producer in any industrial field brings out an all-new model, it is hailed as a major event. Now Chevrolet, after building 48 million cars in 52 years, has done it again. So dynamic is General Motors' junior division that after adding the Corvair (1959) and the Chevy II (1961) the Chevrolet range is again being expanded by a full line of intermediate-size cars under the model name Chevelle. The new car fits in between the Chevy II and the full-size Chevrolet, and shares the basic chassis and body shell of the B-O-P compacts, now on a 115-inch wheelbase.

The Chevelle is 11 in. longer than the Chevy II, 16 in. shorter than the Chevrolet, 3.7 in. wider than the Chevy II and 2.4 in. narrower than the Chevrolet. It undoubtedly will be argued that the Chevelle is the right size for a *big* car. In fact, it's exactly what the regular-size Chevrolet ought to have been, especially for urban areas where sheer bulk is a disadvantage and the full carrying capacity of the vehicle is rarely utilized.

Chevrolet did not have to make any new engines or transmissions to provide the Chevelle with no less than 14 "power teams." As a matter of fact the four-speed manual transmission *is* new, and manufactured by GM in a plant at Muncie, Indiana, rather than purchased from Borg-Warner. But the three-speed manual (with or without overdrive) and Powerglide transmissions are unchanged from 1963.

Chevelle engines start with the 120 bhp 194-cu. in. six of the Chevy II and go via the 155 bhp 230-cu. in. six of the Bel Air to the 195 and 220 bhp versions of the 283-cu. in. V-8 of the Impala. Cylinder dimensions are fairly well standardized, the 194 and 230 cu. in. sixes having the same 3.25-in. stroke.

The smaller six has a 3.563 in. bore. The larger one

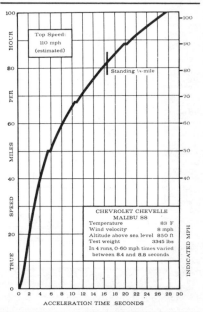

CHEVELLE MALIBU SS

Manufacturer: Chevrolet Motor Division,
           GM Building, Detroit 2, Michigan

Price as tested: To be announced

ACCELERATION

Zero to	Seconds
30 mph	3.0
40 mph	4.1
50 mph	5.6
60 mph	8.5
70 mph	11.8
80 mph	15.6
90 mph	21.1
100 mph	27.8
Standing ¼ mile	16.6

Top Speed:
110 mph
(estimated)

Standing ¼ mile

CHEVROLET CHEVELLE
MALIBU SS
Temperature   83 F
Wind velocity   8 mph
Altitude above sea level 850 ft
Test weight   3345 lbs
In 4 runs, 0-60 mph times varied
between 8.4 and 8.8 seconds

HOUR   PER   MILES   SPEED   TRUE

INDICATED MPH

ACCELERATION TIME SECONDS

ENGINE

Water-cooled 90° V-8, cast iron block, 5 main bearings
Bore x stroke......3.875 x 3.00 in, 98 x 76 mm
Displacement.................283 cu in, 4,648 cc
Compression ratio..............9.25 to one
Carburetion.........single 4-barrel Rochester
Valve gear..pushrod-operated overhead valves, hydraulic lifters
Power (SAE)............220 bhp @ 4800 rpm
Torque ....295 lb-ft @ 3200 rpm
Specific power output.........0.78 bhp per cu in, 47.5 bhp per liter
Usable range of engine speeds .1000–5000 rpm
Electrical system....12-volt, 44 amp-hr battery
Fuel recommended ....Premium
Mileage ....16–24 mpg
Range on 20-gallon tank.......320–480 miles

DRIVE TRAIN

Clutch.............10.4-inch single dry plate
Transmission .4-speed all-synchromesh gearbox

Gear	Ratio	Over-all	mph/1000 rpm	Max mph
Rev	2.64	8.12	−9.7	−48.5
1st	2.56	7.90	10.0	50.0
2nd	1.91	5.89	13.5	67.5
3rd	1.48	4.50	17.7	88.8
4th	1.00	3.08	25.8	ca. 110

Final drive ratio.................3.08 to one

CHASSIS

Perimeter frame with torque boxes
Wheelbase ....115 in
Track ....F 58, R 58 in
Length ....194 in
Width ....74.5 in
Height ....54.0 in
Ground clearance...................7.0 in
Dry weight ....3000 lbs
Curb weight......................3155 lbs
Test weight ....3345 lbs
Weight distribution front/rear %.......56/44
Pounds per bhp (test weight)...........15.2
Suspension: F: Ind., unequal-length wishbones and coil springs, anti-roll bar.
R: Rigid axle, two upper and two lower trailing arms, coil springs
Brakes.....9.5-in drums front and rear, power assist, 228.6 sq in swept area
Steering.......Recirculating ball, power assist
Turns lock to lock 4.0
Turning circle ....34 ft
Tires ....6.50 x 14
Revs per mile........................815

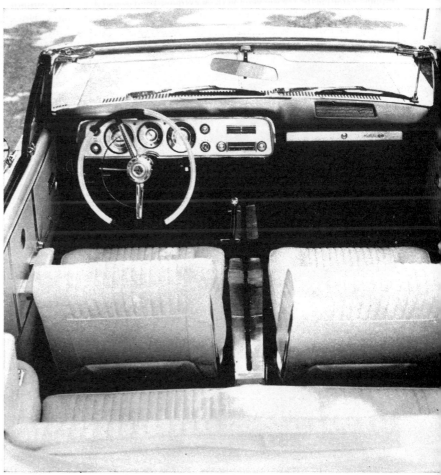

CHEVELLE

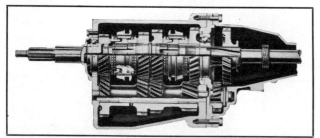

GM's new manual all-synchro four-speed transmission stands out as the most pleasant of all high-torque gearboxes in production.

Standard equipment for Chevelle is the 6-cylinder 230-cu. in. engine which also powers the larger Bel Air and Biscayne models.

The Chevelle chassis has a perimeter frame, without cross-bracing, and a well-tied-down rear axle with a one-piece drive shaft.

Pinched waist doesn't pinch passenger room; there was even a nasty rumor that the trunk is bigger than the full-sized Chevy's.

shares its 3.875-in. bore with the V-8 (which has a 3.00-in. stroke). All these engines have identical valves: intake 1.72-in. diameter, exhaust 1.50-in. diameter.

Cylinder block and head are cast iron alloy, with a forged steel crankshaft and drop-forged steel connecting rods. In the V-8 there is a chain-driven cast iron camshaft in the block (above the crankshaft) and the sixes have gear-driven camshafts in the side of the block. Valve lifters are hydraulic, with a rocker ratio of 1.5 to one in the V-8 and 1.75 to one in the sixes.

We tested the Chevelle Malibu SS with the hot V-8 and four-speed manual transmission. This model is available only as a "sport coupe" and a "convertible;" that is, no sedans. From behind the wheel the SS is easily identified by its genuine gauges for oil pressure, coolant temperature and battery charging, while the other Chevelles make do with warning lights.

The steering wheel is placed rather high up, as usual in Chevrolet products, and the steering response is slow but there's no sloppiness in the mechanism. It's just that the choice of steering ratio seems incompatible with the nature of the car. The steering has power assist and very little feedback from the road. The Saginaw power steering unit is remarkably compact and has simple connections (the control valve is integral and co-axial with the steering gear).

The whole car is well balanced, and with a forward weight bias, the directional stability is high enough to give a certain understeer characteristic and satisfactory control on turns without any disconcerting tendency to run wide. Body roll is restricted, and tire squeal sets in before the roll angle becomes objectionable. Rear end breakaway is possible on a bumpy turn, but on dry pavement the breakaway seems to be only partial, with the wheels hopping sideways rather than actually sliding. Under conditions of reduced traction, wheelspin and tailwagging occurred unless the throttle opening was so conservative as to give only modest acceleration. On dry surfaces, the car achieved excellent acceleration figures for a "compact" (see data panel).

Although the engine response is volcanic, some of the credit for the performance must go to the new gearbox which replaces the T-10 throughout the Chevrolet range. It has the same basic design but has been beefed up and made even smoother and more pleasant to use. It gives added precision of movement and greater ease of operation. It's light and quick, and certainly one of the very best transmissions now on the market. The ratios are well chosen, and the impression that they are ideal is reinforced by the flexibility of the engine.

The reaction of the sports car enthusiast to the Chevelle may be that the car is forgettable; mainly because it is so neutral in every respect. It is not the type of car that any keen driver will walk away from with strong feelings, for or against. This may be just the intention of the manufacturer, aiming for a volume, rather than an enthusiast market. Production started last September, and for the remainder of 1963 Chevelle output is scheduled to average 15% of Chevrolet production, corresponding to 30,000 units monthly. An increase is naturally expected for 1964, but it should be remembered that the car is competing in a class where it clashes head-on with the Ford Fairlane, the Mercury Comet, the Dodge Dart, and, of course, the B-O-P compacts with which it shares so many components and design features. But Chevrolet has a fine record for holding its own in any competition, and the Chevelle might do just that. With a $10 Corvair/Chevy II gap, and a $320 Chevy II/Chevrolet gap, something else was needed as a stopper. We must say, Chevelle is one of the best-looking gap-pluggers we've ever seen. **C/D**

AUTOCAR, 15 January 1965

Chevrolet Chevelle Malibu 3,769 c.c.

MOST American cars coming into Britain can be classified as "regular" models—full-sized vehicles with engines of over 4-litres. We do not get much chance to see the everyday American car—the car that Wilbur J. Oppenheimer uses to commute in, or that a company might provide for their representative. The Chevrolet Chevelle Malibu is a "senior compact," which in our terms might be called a large body with a smallish engine.

With American cars, the engine-transmission options give a generous number of permutations and our test car had the 3·8-litre in-line six-cylinder engine coupled to a two-speed Powerglide automatic transmission. Other engines are the six-cylinder 3·2-litre and the vee-8 4·6-litre; three-speed, all-synchromesh transmission is the standard offering on all models, and the four-speed can be ordered only with the vee-8 engine. There is nothing revolutionary in the design of the 3·8-litre engine; valve operation is by hydraulic tappets and the mixture is fed through a single Rochester carburettor which has an automatic choke. This is set by pressing the accelerator pedal to the floor when the engine is cold; starting is very good with a rather fast tick-over until the engine heats up. We had to make adjustments to the carburettor settings to prevent the engine

from stalling with the transmission engaged and the car stationary. At tick-over on full choke, there is a vigorous jerk as a gear is selected.

At tick-over the engine is almost inaudible; blipping the throttle results in the whole car rocking slightly in response to 220 lb.ft. of torque. There can be no doubt that the Americans like their driving to be simple—and few cars are as simple as the Chevelle. The Powerglide has a three-element torque converter and just High and Low ratios with the usual Park—Reverse—Neutral—Drive—Low positions on a steering column quadrant.

PRICES	£	s	d
Four-door saloon	1,615	0	0
Purchase Tax	338	0	5
TOTAL (in G.B.)	1,953	0	5

How the Chevrolet Chevelle Malibu compares:

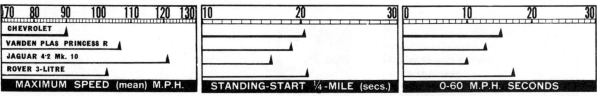

Make · CHEVROLET   Type · Chevelle Malibu (3,769 c.c.)
(Front engine, rear-wheel drive)

Manufacturer: General Motors Products of Canada Ltd., Oshawa, Canada.
U.K. Agents: General Motors Ltd., 23, Buckingham Gate, London, S.W.1.

Test Conditions
Weather .... Dull with 11-18 m.p.h. wind
Temperature ....1 deg. C. (34 deg. F.)
Barometer .... 29·9in Hg.
Dry concrete and tarmac surfaces.

Weight
Kerb weight (with oil, water and half-full fuel tank)
27·4cwt (3,071lb-1,393kg)
Front-rear distribution, per cent F, 52·5; R, 47·5
Laden as tested .... 30·4cwt (3,407lb-1,545kg)

Turning Circles
Between kerbs .... L. 39ft 5in.; R. 40ft 0in.
Between walls .... L. 42ft 6in.; R. 42ft 1in.
Turns of steering wheel lock to lock .... 5·7

FUEL CONSUMPTION

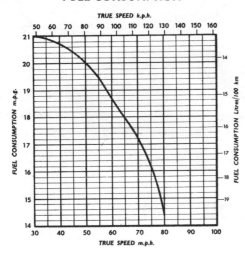

At Steady Speeds in Top:
30 m.p.h.	....	21·0 m.p.g.
40 ,,	....	20·8 ,,
50 ,,	....	20·1 ,,
60 ,,	....	18·7 ,,
70 ,,	....	17·3 ,,
80 ,,	....	14·4 ,,

Test Distance.........................	1,038 miles	
Overall Consumption	16·4 m.p.g.	
	(17·2 litres/100 km.)	
Estimated (DIN)	16·1 m.p.g.	
	(17·6 litres/100 km.)	
Normal Range	15-20 m.p.g.	
	(18·8-14·1 litres/100 km.)	
Grade...............................	Premium	
	(96–98 octane RM)	

OIL CONSUMPTION (SAE 10W30)
Negligible

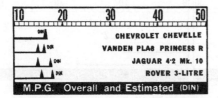

CHEVROLET CHEVELLE
VANDEN PLAS PRINCESS R
JAGUAR 4·2 Mk. 10
ROVER 3-LITRE
M.P.G. Overall and Estimated (DIN)

MAXIMUM SPEEDS AND ACCELERATION TIMES

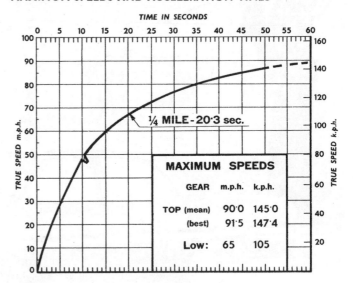

¼ MILE - 20·3 sec.

MAXIMUM SPEEDS
GEAR	m.p.h.	k.p.h.
TOP (mean)	90·0	145·0
(best)	91·5	147·4
Low:	65	105

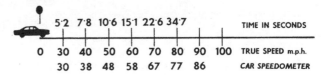

	5·2	7·8	10·6	15·1	22·6	34·7	TIME IN SECONDS
0	30	40	50	60	70	80	90	100	TRUE SPEED m.p.h.
	30	38	48	58	67	77	86			CAR SPEEDOMETER

Speed range and time in seconds
m.p.h.	Top	Low
10—30	—	3·9
20—40	7·8	6·2
30—50	9·0	—
40—60	10·9	—
50—70	13·8	—
60—80	25·0	—

BRAKES
	Pedal Load	Retardation	Equiv. distance
(from 30 m.p.h.	25lb	0·11g	275ft
in neutral)	50lb	0·58g	52ft
	75lb	0·89g	33·8ft
Handbrake		0·25g	120ft

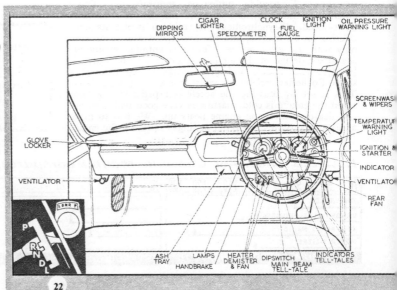

Left: Rear seat passengers have plenty of room and the doors open to nearly 90 deg. for easy entry and exit. Right: Lap-strap seat belts are used; the rather basic heater unit and odd position of the dip switch can be seen

For normal use, the transmission is put into Drive and left there. Using full throttle, the change from Low to High takes place at around 48 m.p.h.; by holding the transmission in Low, the speed can be taken up to 65 m.p.h., but there is no safety change into High nor any governing to prevent the engine being over-revved. Kick-down from High to Low will operate at below about 44 m.p.h.—kickdown being the right word for the Chevelle, for the accelerator had to be given a hard thump into the carpet to trip the linkage from the carburettor to the gearbox. On a light throttle, the automatic change takes place at around 12 m.p.h. with a slight jerk. All other changes are made with commendable smoothness, especially on about half throttle. Incidentally, the gate between the forward and reverse ratios is not effective, so that it is quite possible to select reverse at speed if one goes the "wrong" way from Drive—with possibly expensive results.

There is a good deal of creep with the engine idling and while this has its uses when parking, the need for using the brakes to keep the car stationary can dazzle following drivers in traffic after dark.

As with all automatics, the Chevelle can be one of the first away from traffic lights; we tried both fully automatic and manually over-ridden acceleration runs, but there was very little variation in the recorded times, even when taken as high as 60 m.p.h. in Low. It seems that Chevrolet have chosen just the right change-point. There is little engine braking in High, but when required Low can be selected manually at any speed.

Drum brakes are used all round; they are of the Bendix self-adjusting type, any wear being taken up when the car is stopped in reverse. At low speeds the brakes have characteristic American viciousness and unless the driver is careful, passengers can become unseated.

At higher speeds the brakes are not particularly sensitive and are quite prone to fade. During a series of tests we carried out from 70 m.p.h., the pedal pressure required to give a 0·5g stop rose from 48lb when cold to over 140lb after seven stops at roughly 1min intervals. On maximum pressure stops, the back wheels locked first. An efficient but rather awkward-to-reach handbrake is located under the facia; it held the car firmly on a 1-in-3 hill, whence the car

moved off very easily. The brakes were badly affected by flood water, and dried out unevenly.

The Chevelle is a very "American" car and is not really at home on our rolling English roads. The steering requires 5·7 turns to get from lock to lock and the turning circle is in the region of 42ft. Such low-geared steering makes it exceedingly difficult to drive fast on twisting roads, especially if the going is slippery. In town driving the fairly strong self-centring action, which allows the wheel to spin back on its own, helps a great deal—although this is not a technique approved by the pundits.

Understeer predominates and on fast curves, the car must be "set up" well in advance if the line through is to be maintained accurately. On motorways and other high-speed main roads the lost movement in the straight-ahead position calls for concentration, making the car tiring to drive at over 80 m.p.h. It wanders from lane to lane in gusty weather. The car's best cruising speed seems to be 70 m.p.h.—the maximum speed allowed on most American freeways—and up to this speed directional instability is not marked. In the dry, the roadholding was quite good; when cornered fast the tyres howled and there was a lot of roll but we did not reach breakaway. In the wet and on icy roads the Chevelle had to be treated with more respect, the low-geared steering making inadvertent slides

The front part of the boot is left uncarpeted and the spare wheel takes up a lot of useful room; the boot lid is counterbalanced

Smooth lines are rather spoiled by the unnecessary use of bright metal trim. The bumpers are really massive and are designed to withstand hard knocks

Chevrolet Chevelle Malibu . . .

difficult to control. Despite the Positraction limited-slip differential, the car was difficult to get away on icy or slushy roads without an excess of wheelspin.

The Americans have made great progress at keeping travellers insulated from road shocks; in common with the majority of other transatlantic cars, the Chevelle now has a perimeter frame chassis, with the bodywork attached through sturdy rubber mountings. On our *pavé* and washboard test tracks the car was outstandingly good, the passenger being able to write notes while almost oblivious of the terrible surfaces over which the car was travelling. This type of body-mounting also contributes towards keeping the noise inside the car down to very low levels and effectively insulates the occupants from the engine and transmission.

Damping is good for everyday driving, smoothing out humps before they can develop into wallows; only on a series of waves taken fast does the suspension get caught out and the car tries to become airborne.

To British eyes, American trim still tends to look rather garish; the test car's interior was in a pale metallic blue p.v.c. and the plastic moulding of the facia had a ribbed aluminium instrument panel set into it. Instrumentation itself is minimal—a slightly pessimistic speedometer, with just a total mileage recorder, a clock which stopped when the ignition was turned off, and a third dial containing the fuel gauge (which never moved from "full") and warning lamps for low oil pressure, high water temperature and lack of alternator charge. Bright metal push-pull knobs control the lamps, screenwipers and washers and cigarette lighter. The screenwiper switch has a small stud in its centre which, when pushed, operates the washers as well as twisting the wiper knob to the "on" position; two-speed wipers are fitted and the blades kept their pressure on the screen up to 80 m.p.h. Ventilation in hot weather is looked after by two vents in the side panels under the facia.

On the Chevelle a bench front seat is used; it gave no lateral support. Furthermore, the position of the front seat is such that the driver, by our standards, sits too close to the steering wheel although the attitude of the wheel is good otherwise. If the long steering column could be shortened three or four inches, there would be a better relationship between arms and legs and the switches. A curious feature is the positioning of the dip-switch under the large brake pedal; if one is dipping the headlamps and brakes at the same time, the left foot gets squashed.

A four-headlamp system is used for the Chevelle; on main beam there was a good flood of light both along and across the road. On dipped beam the sharp cut off was biased too much to the left, but this was probably more a matter of adjustment than basic design.

The fuel tank holds 16·75 gallons and, with the overall fuel consumption figure of 16·4 m.p.g., the useful range is around 250 miles. The filler cap is behind the spring-loaded rear number plate and the tank took the full flow of a modern pump without blowing back.

General Motors in Britain had fitted the heater unit, which was rather a crude affair under the facia. A small sub-panel held three controls, for fresh air, temperature and the two-speed booster fan. The air and temperature controls seemed to be permanently set at "on," regardless of where the control knobs were put. Distribution was controlled by two flaps at each end of the matrix unit, so that to change from demist to interior heating meant stopping and then groping under the facia. On full speed the booster fan was noisy and very powerful.

Rear window demisting is looked after by a fan set into

All parts of the engine are easily reached and the underbonnet space kept very clean during the test

the rear shelf and operated by a switch under the facia. This fan is recirculatory and does not have a heating element, drawing warm air from the interior and then blowing it over the glass. Set to fast, the gale of air and the noise were rather excessive but the rear window kept clear. No specific provision is made for getting heat to the rear passengers.

With all these heating and ventilation fans going, plus, at night, the current used by the driving lamps, one can see the need for an alternator; that on the Chevelle has a maximum output of 44 amp at 1,000 engine r.p.m., which is more than adequate for the maximum possible load.

Boot space is enormous, but the spare wheel is stowed horizontally on the right-hand side, with the jack and wheelbrace underneath it, where they take up an awkward amount of room. The jack itself is a really sensible design, working on the bumpers. The boot lid cannot be opened unless the key is used.

The bonnet has no interior release, the catch being reached from under the chromium-plated grille. Looking surprisingly small in the great steel cavern, the orange-painted six-cylinder engine is very easy to get at. The oil filter is a screw-on unit which does not even require a spanner for fitting, and there is also a special holder for a bottle of screen-washer anti-freeze. In the lower part of the radiator is a heat exchanger for the automatic transmission fluid. It is interesting to note that, for the American market, with the terrific variations in temperature, only one thermostat is fitted, a 183deg. F. unit. This would be considered a winter one in Britain.

Externally the Chevelle might be considered to have too much bright metal trim; the wheel discs fitted to export cars make it virtually impossible to inflate the tyres with a standard service station air line.

One can understand why Americans buy cars like the Chevelle. For their wide roads, 70 m.p.h.-odd speed limits and cheap petrol it is an ideal machine to get from A to B in with the very minimum of fuss or bother. But to British eyes the car has a curiously machine-made look—almost "untouched by human hand" until the moment the driver gets in. In character it resembles a refrigerator or gas stove —efficient, reliable and built for a purpose. But in the same way one thinks of it as a domestic machine rather than a cherished possession.

Specification : Chevrolet Chevelle Malibu

PERFORMANCE DATA
Top gear m.p.h. per 1,000 r.p.m.....................20·8
Mean piston speed at max. power........2,377 ft/min
Engine revs. at mean max. speed............4,327 r.p.m.
B.h.p. per ton laden 128

ENGINE
Cylinders ... ... 6-in-line, water-cooled
Bore ... ... 98·4mm (3·86in.)
Stroke ... ... 82·5mm (3·25in.)
Displacement ... ... 3,769 c.c. (230 cu. in.)
Valve gear ...... Overhead, hydraulic tappets
Compression ratio 8·5-to-1
Carburettor ... Rochester
Fuel pump ... AC mechanical
Oil filter ... Full-flow, renewable element
Max. power ... 140 b.h.p. (net) at 4,400 r.p.m.
Max. torque ... 220lb. ft. at 1,600 r.p.m.

TRANSMISSION
Gearbox ... ... Powerglide two-speed automatic with torque converter
Gearbox ratios ... Top 1·0-1·82. Low 1·82-2·10. Reverse 1·82-2·10
Final drive ... Hypoid bevel, with limited-slip differential

CHASSIS
Construction ... Perimeter chassis, with steel bodywork

SUSPENSION
Front ... ... Independent, coil springs and wishbones, telescopic dampers
Rear ... ... Live axle, trailing arms and coil springs, telescopic dampers
Steering ... ... Recirculating ball
Wheel dia. ... 16·5in.

BRAKES
Type ... ... Bendix self-adjusting, drums front and rear
Dimensions ... F, 9·5in. dia., 2·5in. wide shoes R, 9·5in. dia., 2·0in. wide shoes
Swept area ... F, 113·5 sq. in.; R, 142·0 sq. in. Total: 255·5 sq. in. (187·0 sq. in. per ton laden)

WHEELS
Type ... Pressed steel discs, 5 studs, 5in. wide rim
Tyres ... 6·95—14in. Firestone tubeless

EQUIPMENT
Battery ... 12-volt 44-amp hr.
Headlamps Four lamp system, 37·5-55 watt
Reversing lamp ... Two, standard
Electric fuses Four
Screen wipers ... Two speed, self-parking
Screen washer ... Standard, electric
Interior heater Standard, two speed booster fan
Safety belts Extra, anchorages provided
Interior trim P.v.c.
Floor covering ... Carpet
Starting handle ... No provision
Jack ... Screw pillar
Jacking points Four, under front and rear bumpers
Other bodies Convertible, Estate car, Coupé

MAINTENANCE
Fuel tank ... 16·75 Imp. gallons (no reserve)
Cooling system 20 pints (inc. heater)
Engine sump 8 pints SAE 10W30 Change oil every 2,000 miles; change filter element every 6,000 miles
Gearbox ... 3 pints SAE AQ-ATF. Change oil every 24,000 miles
Final drive 3·5 pints SAE80. No change needed
Grease ... 12 points every 6,000 miles
Tyre pressures F and R, 24 p.s.i. (normal driving) F and R, 29 p.s.i. (fast driving)

▼ Scale: 0·3in. to 1ft. Cushions uncompressed.

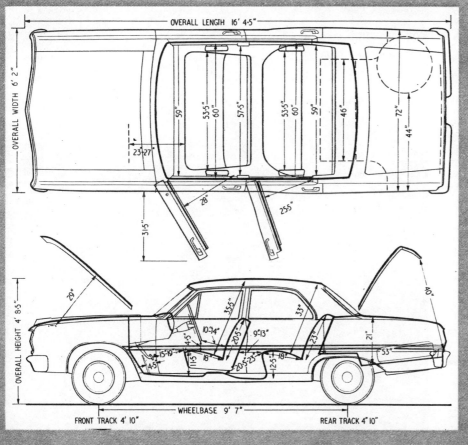

375-hp "396" puts Chevelle at the

top of the list of hot ones

Almighty Malibu!

by John Ethridge, *Technical Editor*

WHEN CHEVROLET Motor Division makes up its mind to do something, it never goes *half*way. As you'll see, an excellent case in point is the Chevelle Malibu Super Sport with RPO Z16 (we'll call it the Chevelle "396" to get the message across in the fewest words).

While awaiting its new engine, Chevrolet had a chance to watch other divisions' and competitors' hot performance cars. All were doing well, and some were selling like skateboards, so Chevy decided to come out with one of their own. Not merely an engine swap, the Chevelle "396" was re-engineered from the ground up to take Chevy's hot new engine. The wait evidently paid off, because the Chevelle "396" is without a doubt the hottest and finest car of its type ever made.

The engine chosen, the 375-hp "396," is very much like the 425-hp version. In fact, their only real difference is in the cam and valve gear. The 425-hp engine uses solid lifters, while the 375-hp job comes with hydraulic lifters. So far, this engine's available only as part of the RPO Z16 package for the Malibu SS. This engine has all the goodies the more powerful one has: impact-extruded pistons, molybdenum-coated rings, special-alloy con rods, and four-bolt main caps.

Specially designed for high revs, the hydraulic valve gear on our test car permitted as many as 6000 rpm without complaint. We didn't try taking it beyond this, because we felt there was no need. This is well beyond where most hydraulic setups will cry "calf rope." Valve timing for this cam is: Intake opens 56 degrees BTC and closes 106 degrees ABC for 342 degrees duration. Exhaust opens 110 degrees BBC, closes 66 degrees ATC for 356 degrees

---

(RIGHT) *Charging off line with both rear tires smoking got lowest times. New suspension makes this possible without limited-slip differential or locked rear end.*

duration. Valve overlap is 122 degrees, with intake lift .461 and exhaust .500 inch. Single valve springs with internal dampers close the valves.

A big Holley 4150 carb with 1.69-inch barrels squats on the intake manifold. A large, oil-wetted, paper-element air cleaner with two intake pipes tops it off.

There's a dual exhaust system to get rid of the burned gases. The exhaust manifolds lead into huge, 2.50-inch laminated pipes. Twin reverse-flow mufflers and 2.25-inch-diameter tailpipes, which exit underneath each rear fender, complete the job. These emit an authoritative sound, but you wouldn't say they're noisy.

A large, thick radiator and a staggered, five-bladed fan with thermo-modulated cutout take care of the increased cooling chores imposed by the big "396."

An 11-inch, centrifugally assisted diaphragm-type clutch with 2300-2600 pounds' plate pressure carries the torque and power to the Chevy four-speed manual transmission. This box uses the 2.56 low (instead of 2.20), with the other ratios being 1.91, 1.48, 1.00, plus 2.64 reverse. A single-piece, 3.25-inch-diameter propeller shaft connects the transmission and the heavy-duty rear end. This uses a large, 8.88-inch-diameter ring gear and a *non*-limited-slip differential. Standard ratio is 3.31—the only one listed at present.

In designing the rear suspension, Chevy engineers made a massive assault on the problems inherent in live-axle designs, and it looks like they've carried the day. They use a total of four

control arms to locate the rear-axle assembly. The two short upper ones attach near the differential, with two long lower ones attached outboard near the coil springs and shocks. The inboard pair are angled outward as they go forward to take care of axle tramp. Together they pretty much eliminate any tendency for the rear axle to twist on its own axis or to steer the car.

There was still one problem left for the engineers to work out, however. When the propeller shaft twists the final drive gears, the whole axle assembly wants to rotate in the opposite direction, lifting the right rear wheel. Chevy's antidote for this is a big, fat anti-roll bar attached between the lower control arms and passing below the differential housing. *Now* when a wheel tries to lift, this bar exerts a torque on the opposite wheel linkage trying to lift it, too. But the weight of the car is holding that one down, so the first wheel is held firmly in place. The fact that you can light *both* rear tires on acceleration without benefit of a limited-slip differential is ample proof that the principle works. They needed something sturdy to attach the suspension to, so they used the reinforced convertible frame with some extra beefing at suspension tie points.

The front got its share of attention, too. Besides a 1.06-inch-diameter anti-roll bar, it got cast-steel wheel hubs and shot-peened ball studs. A fast car like

this has to be able to change directions quickly, so it got fast, 15-to-1 power-assisted steering.

The standard Chevelle brakes had to go, and big-Chevy 11-inch brakes took their place. Stiffer springs and shocks all around finished the suspension. Six-inch-wide wheels and 7.75 x 14 improved nylon gold-stripe tires were the final touch (made by Goodyear). These tires stick like glue and are an important part of the package. A trip to the proving grounds convinced the engineers that what they'd done was good.

And on the seventh day, they rested . . . while the styling people took over. Besides the usual emblems and identification, these boys came up with one of the most handsome and authentic-looking simulated custom wheels we've seen. You have to get on your hands and knees and pick at them with your fingernail to tell they're not the real thing.

We'd anxiously been awaiting arrival of our test car for what seemed like a long time, but it was more like a couple of weeks when we heard the good news: Chevy had finally turned its Kansas City plant into an arsenal of sorts and produced 200 of these bombs for distribution to strategic locations. Our Chevelle "396" was the first deployed to the Los Angeles area.

While we were putting some miles on the car before performance testing, we had a chance to get acquainted with it and to get some general driving impressions. The engine's docile in traffic, idling at 800 rpm. It's a quiet car, and

you won't have any trouble enjoying the AM-FM with multiplex stereo that's thrown in as part of the $1501.05 RPO Z16 package. Even when using maximum power, engine and gear noise are still at a low level.

The way horsepower figures are bandied about nowadays, we never know what to expect. But this one's got it—from idle to red line, it's definitely got it. There's no brief range where it feels like it comes on the cam. It puts out gobs of romping, stomping torque throughout the entire range of useful rpm.

Performance figures in our spec panel are extremely impressive, but they're inadequate inasmuch as they don't tell the story of how this car will accelerate over 100 mph. The needle doesn't hang there, but goes on wiping the face of the 160-mph speedo until the engine red-lines. With proper gearing, we wouldn't be at all surprised to see the Chevelle "396" peg its speedometer.

With all that power on tap, we were surprised when gasoline mileage didn't fall below 10 mpg during performance testing. Our high was 13.8 mpg, which we got when soft-pedaling on freeways. Average for the entire 942-mile test was 11.1 mpg.

We expect the demand for copies of our test car to exceed the supply for quite a while. Expect to wait and expect to pay sticker price when yours does arrive. It's the hottest of the hot intermediates. In fact, it's king of the road.   /MT

(ABOVE) *Inflating the front tires to 42 psi and rears to 35 psi produced nearly neutral steering in tight turns. Grab of improved nylon gold-stripes made for pleasant going at all times.*

(LEFT) *Stamped-steel simulated wheel, actually a wheel cover, exclusively adorns Chevelles with "396" powerplant. Somebody's sure to put a lug wrench on false nuts, because they look so real.*

Not actually an anti-roll bar, stabilizer bar between lower control arms comes into play only when rear wheel tries to lift.

Upper control arms (arrow points to right one) locate rear axle assembly laterally, as well as helping to prevent axle wind-up.

160-mph speedometer, on left, isn't there just for window dressing (see text). Easy-to-see tach occupies the center slot.

CHEVELLE MALIBU SS "396"

2-door, 4-passenger hardtop

OPTIONS ON TEST CAR: RPO Z16 package, power windows, vinyl roof, bumper guards, tilting steering wheel, tinted glass
BASE PRICE: $2647
PRICE AS TESTED: $4586.40 (plus tax and license)
ODOMETER READING AT START OF TEST: 857 miles
RECOMMENDED ENGINE RED LINE: 5800 rpm

PERFORMANCE

ACCELERATION (2 aboard)
0-30 mph	2.9 secs.
0-45 mph	4.5
0-60 mph	6.7

PASSING TIMES AND DISTANCES
40-60 mph	2.7 secs., 198 ft.
50-70 mph	3.7 secs., 326 ft.

Standing start ¼-mile 15.3 secs. and 96 mph.
Speeds in gears @ 5800 rpm

1st .... 53 mph		3rd .... 93 mph	
2nd .... 69 mph		4th ....135 mph (observed)	

Speedometer Error on Test Car

Car's speedometer reading	30	45	50	60	71	81
Weston electric speedometer ...	30	45	50	60	70	80

Observed mph per 1000 rpm in top gear .... 23.2 mph
Stopping Distances — from 30 mph., 32 ft.; from 60 mph., 150 ft.

SPECIFICATIONS FROM MANUFACTURER

Engine
Ohv V-8
Bore: 4.09 ins.
Stroke: 3.76 ins.
Displacement: 396 cu. ins.
Compression ratio: 11.0:1
Horsepower: 375 @ 5600 rpm
Horsepower per cubic inch: 0.95
Torque: 420 lbs.-ft. @ 3600 rpm
Carburetion: 1 4-bbl.
Ignition: 12-volt coil

Gearbox
4-speed manual, all synchro;
floorshift

Driveshaft
1-piece, open tube

Differential
Hypoid, semi-floating
Standard ratio: 3.31:1

Suspension
Front: Independent SLA, with coil springs, double-acting tubular shocks, and anti-roll bar
Rear: Live axle with 4-link control arms—2 upper and 2 lower —with stabilizer bar between lower control arms, coil springs and double-acting tubular shocks

Steering
Semi-reversible, recirculating ball nut, with coaxial power assist
Turning diameter: 41.9 feet
Turns lock to door: 3.5

Wheels and Tires
14x6 5-lug, short-spoke steel disc wheels
7.75x14 2-ply gold-stripe nylon tires

Brakes
Hydraulic, duo-servo, with integral vacuum power assist; cast-iron rim, steel-web drum
Front: 11-in. dia. x 2.75 ins. wide
Rear: 11-in.dia. x 2.00 ins. wide
Effective lining area: 183.4 sq. ins.
Swept drum area: 328.3 sq. ins.

Body and Frame
Welded perimeter frame with 3 crossmembers, reinforced between upper and lower control arm pivots
Wheelbase 115.0 ins.
Track: front, 58.0 ins.; rear, 58.0 ins.
Overall length: 196.6 ins.
Overall width: 74.6 ins.
Overall height: 52.8 ins.
Curb weight: 3720 lbs.

CHEVELLE 396

WHEN OLDSMOBILE and Buick jumped onto the big-engine, small-car bandwagon with Pontiac, it was pretty certain that Chevrolet wouldn't be far behind. The only surprising part was that Chevrolet wasn't among the leaders in this scheme; after all, Chevy has been a respected member of the high-performance club for 10 years now, even if it isn't allowed to say so publicly.

Pontiac led the way with its GTO, a combination of Tempest chassis and styling with 389-cu. in. engine; Oldsmobile brought along its 442, an F-85 with a hot 330-cu. in., and later a 400-cu. in. V-8; then, last spring Buick announced the Gran Sport, a 401-cu. in. V-8 powered Special. The question remained, what could Chevrolet do?

The answer wasn't long in coming. The Chevelle, which shares its basic structure with its GM A-body counterparts (Tempest, F-85 and Special), obviously only needed a whopping big engine and some trimwork to be competitive. When Chevrolet unveiled its new 396-cu. in. V-8 early in 1965 the whopper was available. Presto! Change-O! The Chevelle 396 Supercar!

The surprise was that it wasn't instantly made available to the general public. Certainly Chevrolet management must recognize the demand potential inherent in runaway GTO, 442 and GS sales. However, because of some obscure problem, such as the unavailability of large quantities of 396 blocks, the Chevelle 396 is at present a limited edition. Only 200 have been produced and these went into what the zone men call "Brass Hat" service; i.e., they are being driven (and tested) by the press, shown and clucked over by various VIPs, and, in a few cases, run in dragstrip competition. The general car enthusiast can't buy one—yet.

There's little doubt that Chevrolet will produce Chevelle 396s in sufficient quantity during the 1966 model-year. There's also little doubt that it will differ much from the package examined here; there may be slight styling changes, of course, but the mechanical format will be the same. And there is no doubt that a long line will form for these particular cars at Chevrolet dealerships: The things that make the car appealing probably outweigh the things that detract.

As it stands, ready to streak the street with burnt rubber marks, the Chevelle 396 is a Malibu SS hardtop coupe equipped with a 375-bhp variation of Chevrolet's new 396-cu. in. V-8 engine, a 4-speed manual shift transmission, much larger than normal power brakes, better springing and a rear-end anti-roll stabilizer, quickened power steering, an am/fm/stereophonic radio system, wide-base wheels and Firestone Super Sport tires, and a set of the homeliest, phony "mag-wheel" hubcaps imaginable.

As an image-builder it should serve Chevrolet well. Box-boys at the local supermarkets (you know the type—drop-outs who have to wrestle grocery-sacks to make their new-model car payments) fell down in awe at the sight of the "396" labels on the Malibu's flanks. "Wot'll-She-Do-in-the-Quarter!" was their favorite question and one told us he'd already tried to order a 396 Chevelle only to have the dealer tell him it couldn't be done; so he was buying a 327 Chevelle. None of the other Supercars CL tested (May issue) drew as much attention, but then there are infinitely more Chevrolet fans around. When the 396 Chevelle

Both a Prototype and an Image-Builder, This is the First of the Red-Hot Malibus!

is entered in serious competition at the dragstrip, it should further add to the performance image. The engine potential is enormous and, this, after all, is the most important factor in straight-line competition.

As a car, it suffers from the same banality of bigness that afflicts its GM cousins. It seems to accomplish things more by brute force than by sophistication of its systems. It is strong on straightaway performance but only mediocre at covering curving roads at velocities more than 40% of its potential. In short, it does what others of its ilk do, not much better nor much worse.

The 396/375 engine in this series Chevelle is directly related to two other 396s tested by CL in recent months. The 396/325 which powered a Caprice (July issue) and the 396/425 in a Corvette (August) are essentially the same engine in different stages of tune. It would seem that this new engine line is particularly responsive to the normal pepping up techniques, and is big and beefy enough to be bored and stroked to well beyond the next increment of 427 cu. in. (these are already competing on NASCAR

circuits); maximum displacement from the current blocks appears to be nearly 470 cu. in.

COMPARATIVE SPECIFICATIONS

Bhp @ rpm	325 @ 4800	375 @ 5600	425 @ 6400
Torque @ rpm	410 @ 3200	420 @ 3600	415 @ 4000
Comp. ratio	10.25	11.00	11.00
Carburetion	1x4 Holley or Rochester	1x4 Holley	1x4 Holley
Primaries, dia.	H-1.388 R-1.562	1.686	1.686
Secondaries, dia.	H-2.25 R-1.562	1.686	1.686
Valve lifters	hydraulic	hydraulic	mechanical
Intake valve dia.	2.07	2.19	2.19
Exhaust valve dia.	1.72	1.72	1.72
Valve timing	42-98, 89-51	56-106, 110-66	61-107, 102-66
duration	320°	342/346°	348°
overlap	93°	122°	127°
Timing, initial	6°	8°	10°
Dist. centr. adv.	24°	28°	28°
vacuum adv.	15°	15°	15°
Exhaust system	single	dual	dual
Exh. pipe dia.	2.5	2.5	2.5
Tailpipe dia.	2.0	2.25	2.0

The 396 was examined in considerable detail in *Car Life's* March '65 issue and outside of the few details in tuning outlined in the preceding specification table, the information in that article would still apply. Note, however, that the 375 version is the best, at least theoretically, of the two worlds. It combines the flexibility and quiet operation of hydraulic lifters

from the 325 with the long, strong camshaft, bigger intake valves and Holley carburetor of the 425. Although horsepower is less, torque is greater and the engine is less fussy about which rpm range it is being driven in. Where the 325 will rev to 5000 rpm, the 375 runs up to 6000 before lifter pump-up; however the mechanical-lifter 425 tops 7000 rpm without damage.

As installed, the 375 begins to run out of power at just about its rated rpm, so that further flogging to a higher rpm gains naught in acceleration. This, of course, is due to the restrictions of air cleaner and exhaust system, without which the power rating is achieved in the dynamometer room. The addition of a nice set of extractor headers and a cold-air duct to the carburetor should measurably improve the 375's performance, if such is desired. We found no pressing need for additional power as the car's over-the-road capabilities are impressive enough as is. Quarter-mile acceleration to nearly 100 mph in just under 15 sec., and a top speed of double the allowed highway speeds of most states should suffice everyone but the lunatic fringe.

The initial series of Chevelle 396

31

CHEVELLE 396

was produced with a 4-speed manual-shift transmission only; no automatic nor 3-speed manual. Doubtlessly, the GM 3-speed automatic and the new Warner Gear all-synchromesh 3-speed manual will be offered when the car goes on sale to the general public (they already are available with the 396/325); after all, the GTO, 442 and Gran Sport have such options. The transmission in the test car was the "Muncie" gearbox of late Chevrolet design, with the 2.56 first gearset. Although the close-ratio 2.20 first set might provide better dragstrip gearing, the 2.56 is ideal for the 396 Chevelle's all-around performance characteristics. Shift points for optimum acceleration work out to 50, 70 and 90 mph (before speedo correction) with the 3.31:1 rear axle ratio.

Power is transmitted through a significantly larger clutch when the car is 396-equipped. Where the normal Chevelle V-8 (283 cu. in.) with 4-speed transmission has a 10.4 in. clutch disc (103.5 sq. in. effective area) and a 2100-2300 lb. pressure plate, the 396 V-8 needs an 11-in. disc (123.7 sq. in.) and a 2300-2600 lb. pressure plate. Both are a diaphragm, bent-finger type of clutch with centrifugal action to increase plate pressure as rpm increases. Release bearings are single row ball and clutch operation is smooth and positive. Pedal pressure tends to be on the stiff side, although not objectionably so from an enthusiast's standpoint.

Linkage to the transmission is an-other matter—at least on this particular test car. Somewhat stiff and sticky, it would hang up in neutral whenever full-on shifts werc attempted. The problem was particularly severe in the 2-3 shift—which was when we found the engine would rev to 6000 rpm without damage. Chevrolet has rid itself of the characteristic buzzing linkage rattle apparent in all older design 4-speeds, but in the process has made the shifting process more difficult—a tragedy for such a fine 4-speed transmission. Another point of criticism is the long throw between gates. Perhaps both situations could be rectified with the installation of one of the better commercial shifter systems, such as Hurst or Drag-Fast.

Along with the more sturdy clutch and transmission, for the 396 Chevelle, a far stronger rear end was obviously needed. Where the normal Chevelle has a 8.125-in. ring gear, the 396 has the 8.875-in. gear out of the larger Chevrolets. As the 396 Chevelle maintains its standard-model 58-in. track (both front and rear), complete rear axles are not interchangeable, only the third members. Doubtlessly any ratio available for the larger Chevrolet —2.73, 3.07, 3:55, 3.73, 4.11, 4.56— could be substituted to further adapt the Chevelle to specialized performance usage.

Larger brakes are borrowed from the big Chevrolet, too, and here the Chevelle 396 rises yards above its GM cousins and its own more mundane counterparts: This Chevelle has brakes! They are the 11-in. diameter drums, with 2.75-in. wide shoes in front, 2.00-in. shoes in the rear, from the big

Chevrolet. Their swept area is 328.3 sq. in., as compared with the normal Chevelle's 268.6 sq. in. from 9.5-in. drums. A vacuum-boosted power assist is included in the 396 package option, and this provides 717 lb. of pressure to the 1.00-in. master cylinder for 100 lb. of pressure on the brake pedal.

Subjecting these brakes to *Car Life's* usual series of stops produced normal-rate decelerations. Braking as hard as possible, without skidding the tires, we achieved three consecutive stops at 21 ft./sec./sec. deceleration from 100 mph, with only a minute or so of cool-off time between. The fourth such stop produced considerable fade and a greatly reduced rate of deceleration; however, few cars we test survive more than two all-on stops from 75% of their maximum speed. Chevrolet rates a chromium-plated medal for making bigger, better brakes part of *its* performance package.

It should be mentioned that Chevrolet continues to offer sintered iron brake linings for both Chevelle and big Chevrolet. These are in both drum sizes, so that the enthusiast seeking optimum braking for his Chevelle 396 could make a switch from organic to metallic linings and thereby achieve virtually fade-free operation. Of course, Chevrolet also has the best domestic braking system yet produced on its Corvette, but conversion of the production sedans to the Corvette's all-disc set-up might be prohibitively expensive. Until the discs are available for the sedans, the power-boosted sintered iron remains the best, and safest, compromise for the hard driver.

The 396 Chevelle's suspension layout is basically the same as the other Chevelles, with two noteworthy changes. One, of course, is the substitution of stiffer springs to take care of the increased vehicle weight; the other is the placement of an anti-roll stabilizer at the rear end as well as the front. The normal Chevelle V-8 has spring rates of 250 lb./in. front and 100 lb./in. at the rear; the 396 calls for 320 front, 120 rear. Both front and rear anti-roll bars are 1.06 in. diameter HR steel; the standard Chevelle has a 0.812-in. bar in front only. The two bars give considerably more roll stiffness to the chassis, without the use of unduly harsh springing. Added roll resistance helps maintain optimum traction under cornering conditions as it keeps the chassis-tire-pavement geometry in better relationship; that is, the tires can better be kept perpendicular to the road surface, thus retaining their maximum effectiveness, when the body

does not roll too much on the suspension. It also helps combat the torque reaction "unloading" of the right rear tire, and subsequent slippage, under hard acceleration.

The Chevelle's rear anti-roll stabilizer follows the pattern established for the Olds 442. It is a simple piece of bar-stock steel, shaped in a large U, with ends flattened and drilled so that they may be bolted to the horizontal, lower suspension links. The middle of the U passes directly under the differential case.

The effect of this roll stiffness is to ameliorate, to some degree, the detrimental effect on good handling that the very front-heavy chassis must have. It makes cornering seem, because of the lack of body roll and its attendant "plowing" sensation, much more stable than it really is. Despite some 58% of the vehicle's weight on its front wheels, which produces a strong

understeering condition, the disguising effect of power steering and the lack of body roll make low-speed cornering seem positively nimble. It is when less than smooth roadway is encountered that the instability becomes apparent. When cornering is attempted on a rippling pavement, the rear wheels hop, skip and jump toward the outside of the roadway in their own sort of non-track meet; the front, of course, stays anchored by that preponderance of weight.

The gross inequity of the weight distribution manifests itself in yet another manner: Pitching. When the car is driven down a secondary road, the front and rear ends pitch up and down in dissimilar cycles. This is caused by the widely differing spring rates and shock absorber valving necessary because of the weight imbalance. This vertical oscillating, if not totally objectionable, is at least annoying. To be

INSTRUMENT PANEL features full set of gauges, tachometer in middle. Stereo controls are just above shift-lever.

CHROMED COVERS over rockers and air cleaner dress up the 396 installation. Big engine fills all of the compartment.

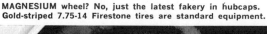

MAGNESIUM wheel? No, just the latest fakery in hubcaps. Gold-striped 7.75-14 Firestone tires are standard equipment.

GENEROUS-SIZED trunk of Chevelle could be equipped with a concrete floormat to counterbalance over-heavy front end.

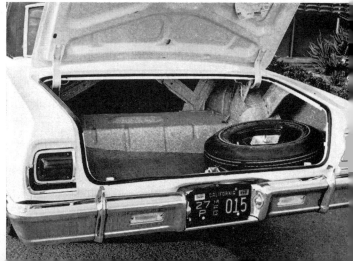

CHEVELLE 396

fair, we must cite similar motions in the 442 and Gran Sport, caused by the same condition.

Heart of this weight problem is the engine; it weighs 690 lb., where the 283-cu. in. V-8 is a good 100 lb. less and the standard 6-cyl. another 100 or so under that. Such items as the heavy-duty radiator, larger battery and power accessories all add weight to the end where it is least needed. Hence, the curb weight of this test Malibu hardtop is 385 lb. greater than that of a 6-cyl. Malibu tested when CL first evaluated the Chevelle line (March '64), and all of it is on the front wheels. That Six had a 52/48 distribution of 3265 lb. (curb weight), a 283 Malibu had a 56/44 spread of 3390 lb., this one has a 58/42 of 3650. A CL editorial last spring likened such distribution to a "10-lb. sledge on a 3-ft. handle" and warned against the advisability of the design of such cars. The driver, we feel, should be aware of these things *before* he buys the car.

That the car does as well as it does on curving roads is due in good part to the tire/wheel combination speci-

fied. This is a 7.75-14 Firestone Super Sport high-speed nylon cord tire on a 6.00 x 14 rim. These rims are an inch wider than would normally be used and this width helps increase tire sidewall stability, although, the tiremen say, at the expense of a slightly harsher ride. CL's testers applied additional inflation, to 28 psi front, 24 psi rear, to compensate for the weight differential, (normal inflation is 24/24) and this, we thought, also slightly improved the handling. We had the opportunity to drive these tires on rain-slickened streets and they were surprisingly good—unlike certain other "high-speed" tires which are pretty "low-speed" in the wet! Wide-base wheels and suitable tires should be the first items on everyone's list of chassis improvements.

This Chevelle also has speeded-up steering which uses 15:1 gearing rather than the normal 17.5:1 in the coaxial power system. Steering wheel turns required to move the road wheels from lock to lock are reduced from 4.0 to approximately 3.5. Along with power steering, the equipment included the Saginaw tilting steering wheel, which gives a choice of seven positions over a 5 in. arc; we would have preferred

another Saginaw development, the telescoping wheel, which can be better adjusted to suit the driver's armlength.

Other interior equipment included bucket seats, the usual, useless, chrome-plated between-seat, tunnel-top console, a full set of instruments, a tachometer and that fabulous am/fm/stereo radio system offered by Chevrolet and Delco. CL's editors raved over this electronic marvel in the Caprice Road Test and further exposure to it only heightened our enthusiasm. "There's nothing in this world, Charlie, like slipping down the turnpike being belted in the back by 375 horsepower and in the ear by 4-speaker Bach-power!" to quote our old friend Tom McMolehill.

Criticism of the interior centers on two points: The size and readability of the tachometer and instruments. The tachometer has a 90° needle sweep on a relatively small face. Although it is located high enough to be readable, the markings are close together; and accurate, quick-glance reading is impossible. The substitution of a 270° sweep instrument should be the first order of business. All instruments are glass-covered and these faces are so angled that they become excellent reflectors of ambient light. Consequently, the instruments are particularly difficult to read on anything but the dullest day.

The exterior differences between the 396 Chevelle and the 194, 283 or 327-equipped car are minor. Outside of the small "Malibu SS 396" nametag on the rear and the crossed-flag "396 Turbo-Jet" insignia just ahead of the front wheel-wells, nothing distinguishes it from the more mundane.

Perhaps Chevrolet could re-name the package-equipped cars, such as Pontiac *et al* have done. Since "Super Sports" has already been usurped, Chevrolet nomenclature experts might simply resort to the option code of "Z-16." After all, the fellow who puts out the kind of money this equipment costs wants something that shows it; what's the use of buying it if no one can tell it from the neighbors' Powerslide Slick-Six? It has to say, "I'm a Z-16 Chevy, and king of the road," or the name may not be worth the game.

The price of our test car is misleading. The special package for this series is listed at $1501 extra and includes all those previously mentioned. Without power equipment, special radio and those grotesque hubcaps, the price probably could be cut in half. As reference points, consider that the 396/425 adds only $292.70 to the price of a Corvette but $376.60 to a big Chevrolet while the 396/325 costs about $300 more than a Six in the standard sedan. It would appear that the basic horsepower is pretty cheap—it's all that modification necessary to make it usable that costs. ∎

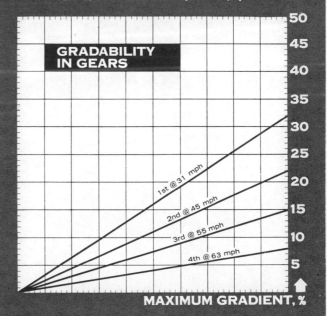

CAR LIFE ROAD TEST

1965 CHEVROLET
Chevelle Malibu 396

SPECIFICATIONS

List price	$2647
Price, as tested	4586
Curb weight, lb.	3650
Test weight	3990
distribution, %	58/42
Tire size	7.75-14
Tire capacity, lb. @ 24 psi.	4480
Brake swept area	328.3
Engine type	V-8, ohv
Bore & stroke	4.09 x 3.76
Displacement, cu. in.	396
Compression ratio	11:1
Carburetion	1 x 4
Bhp @ rpm	375 @ 5600
equivalent mph	130
Torque, lb.-ft.	420 @ 3600
equivalent mph	83

EXTRA-COST OPTIONS

Special Z-16 option (engine, power steering, 4-speed, special suspension & wheel covers, power brakes, am/fm stereo radio), tinted glass, tilt wheel.

DIMENSIONS

Wheelbase, in.	115.0
Tread, f & r.	58.0
Overall length, in.	196.6
width	74.6
height	52.8
equivalent vol., cu. ft.	448
Frontal area, sq. ft.	21.9
Ground clearance, in.	4.7
Steering ratio, gear	15:1
turns, lock to lock	3.5
turning circle, ft.	44.7
Hip room, front	2 x 22
Hip room, rear	58.7
Pedal to seat back, max.	44.0
Floor to ground	8.5
Luggage vol., cu. ft.	16.7
Fuel tank capacity, gal.	20.0

GEAR RATIOS

4th (1.00) overall	3.31
3rd (1.48)	4.88
2nd (1.91)	6.32
1st (2.56)	8.47

CALCULATED DATA

Lb./bhp (test wt.)	10.6
Cu. ft./ton mile	149
Mph/1000 rpm.	23.1
Engine revs/mile	2600
Piston travel, ft./mile	1630
Car Life wear index	42.3

SPEEDOMETER ERROR

30 mph, actual	29.8
60 mph	59.3
90 mph	87.4

FUEL CONSUMPTION

Normal range, mpg	11-14

PERFORMANCE

Top speed (5600), mph	130
Shifts @ mph (manual)	
3rd (5600)	88
2nd (5600)	68
1st (5600)	51
Total drag at 60 mph, lb.	140

ACCELERATION

0-40 mph, sec.	3.8
0-50	4.8
0-60	6.5
0-70	8.4
0-80	10.3
0-90	12.7
0-100	15.4
Standing ¼ mile, sec.	14.9
speed at end, mph	98

ACCELERATION & COASTING

GRADABILITY IN GEARS

1st @ 31 mph
2nd @ 45 mph
3rd @ 55 mph
4th @ 63 mph

MPH 5 10 15 20 25 30 35 40 45
ELAPSED TIME IN SECONDS

MAXIMUM GRADIENT, %

a STORMER & A STROKER FROM CHEVELLE

A dual test of the potent 396 SS and a genteel Malibu 283

OUR CHOICE of the Chevelle Super Sport 396 as the subject of a test is fairly obvious. Anyone with a drop of red blood in his veins would have some natural curiosity when it comes to a potent performer like this. But there are lots of 1966 Chevelles on the road—and most are not Super Sports. Consequently for a companion test car, we requested the kind of Chevelle the average buyer would end up with after all the haggling and head-scratching.

This one turned out to be a Malibu Sport Coupe equipped as indicated in the spec panel. The Chevy people stressed that this was *about* what the average buyer would choose, but with all the options available, possible choices could literally number in the thousands.

This year's production Super Sport is quite different from the special, limited-production 1965¾ Malibu SS 396 we tested in the July, 1965, issue. The 1966 model uses standard Chevelle brakes and suspension parts throughout, except

COMPOUND USED IN WIDE RED-LINE TIRES MAKES THEM SUPER-SMOKERS. REAR SUSPENSION DOES CREDITABLE JOB OF CONTROLLING WHEEL HOP.

SPECTATORS AT JUAREZ, MEXICO GRAND PRIX WERE TREATED TO THEIR FIRST GLIMPSE OF SUPER SPORT WHEN WE TOURED CITY-STREET CIRCUIT.

the springs are about 30% stiffer, the shocks have heavy-duty valving with a different calibration, and a stiffer front stabilizer bar is used. There is no rear stabilizer bar.

You have a choice of red-stripe NF nylon tires or whitewalls to go on the 6-inch rims. (By all means, take the red-stripes — they're far more suited to a car like this.) The rear axle has a sturdier differential carrier with a larger 8.875-inch-diameter ring gear to take the extra torque of the 396 engine.

There are only two engines available for the SS: the standard 325-hp 396 and the test car's optional 396 with a higher-lift, longer-duration cam that puts out 360 hp. Transmissions start with a heavy-duty 3-speed and go on to optional street and close-ratio 4-speeds, plus a water-cooled Powerglide.

Standard axle ratio for the base engine is 3.31, with 3.55, 3.73, and 4.10 as options. The 3.73 ratio is standard with the 360-hp engine and 3-speed, street 4-speed, or Powerglide, with the other listed ratios optional. When the close-ratio 4-speed is ordered, 3.31, 3.55, 4.10, 4.56, or 4.88 can be specified. The last three come with Positraction limited-slip differential standard, and it can be ordered with the others.

The nice thing about the SS is that there are very few package deals on accessories. You can choose pretty much what you please, according to your taste or the money you have to spend. While we feel the test car certainly was reasonably priced with all the options it had, several hundred dollars can be pared off the price by foregoing some of the add-ons. If it came down to it, we might give up the console, but we would have to be pretty strapped to give up the buckets.

Our other test car, the Malibu Sport Coupe, had the buckets, too. In our opinion, they're just as desirable here as on the higher-performing SS. The Malibu and SS Coupes, except for trim and identification, share the same body. This includes the flat rear window, which affords some of the clearest, undistorted rearward vision we've experienced in a long time.

The Powerglide-equipped Malibu had an improperly adjusted throttle transmission/linkage as delivered. It upshifted at only 30 mph with the throttle wide open and wouldn't downshift until the car was brought to a halt. We got 18 mpg around town and a severe case of frustration driving it this way. After having it set up correctly, mileage dropped to just under 15, but our spirits rose considerably.

DISTINCTIVE TRIM AROUND WINDOWS AND LOWER BODY ADORNS SUPER SPORT ONLY. BLACK-PAINTED WHEEL WELLS EMPHASIZE FANCY COVERS.

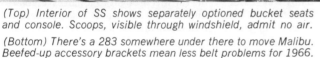

(Top) Interior of SS shows separately optioned bucket seats and console. Scoops, visible through windshield, admit no air.

(Bottom) There's a 283 somewhere under there to move Malibu. Beefed-up accessory brackets mean less belt problems for 1966.

(Top) Super Sport gets a pair of frame reinforcement members between suspension tie-points. (Arrow points to left one.)

(Bottom) Big 360-hp 396 breathes through open-all-around air cleaner. Black grille with big emblem sets Super Sport apart.

CHEVELLES

The 195-hp 283 V-8 in our Malibu comes from the middle of a list of engines that includes two other V-8s and two 6s that range from 120 to 275 hp. This engine with the Powerglide transmission is by no stretch of the imagination a neck-snapper, but performance is entirely adequate for any normal need. This version of the tried-and-true 283 provides an excellent balance between performance and economy with ability to handle air conditioning and other power accessories. It also motors along happily on regular gasoline — an important but often overlooked money-saving feature.

Handling of the SS was, naturally, better than that of the Malibu, which is itself a well-mannered car. Contrary to what some who haven't tried it may think, the doctored suspension on the SS hardly takes anything away from the ride. We took an extended trip in the SS that was mostly on highways but did include some rough stretches where construction was underway. It neither bores nor beats you to death. It's the kind of car in which you'll find yourself stopping only for food and gas, because it somehow never ceases to be a pleasure to slip behind the wheel and drive. Outstanding directional control and stability, reserve passing power, and the very comfortable bucket seats contribute to this feeling.

The speedometer tended to dispel some of our euphoria, though. About the only unequivocal reading is 60 mph, when the needle is straight up and coincides with both a mark and the numeral. Elsewhere they don't jibe, necessitating a lot of guesswork.

Once while buying gas for the Malibu, we were busily engaged in an attempt to decipher this druid sundial when a couple in an older Chevelle drove up.

Looking inside our car, the wife exclaimed, "What a beautiful instrument panel!" This is as perfect an example as you'd want to find of the triumph of art over reason.

When we were seated in the normal driving position, the tachometer on the SS, part of an optional instrument package, was obscured by a steering-wheel spoke. However, there's not much danger of over-revving, since the hydraulic lifters won't allow revs to rise much higher than 5400 rpm. Without the instrument package, the SS comes with a speedometer, gas gauge, and warning lamps for temperature, oil pressure, and alternator — same as other Chevelles.

The Malibu got between 13 and 18 mpg on regular for the test. Not surprisingly, the SS ranged between 10.4 and 14 on super-premium.

John Ethridge

Popular Malibu Sports Coupe, a sort of personalized Chevelle, is well balanced, handles very well with normal suspension.

More-than-adequate interior room with reduced overall dimensions and weight makes Chevelles comfortable, easy to drive.

CHEVELLE SS 396

2-door, 5-passenger sport coupe

ACCESSORY PRICE LIST

*Engine options: 360 hp	$105.35
Automatic transmission	115.90
*4-speed transmission	105.35
Overdrive	—
Limited-slip differential	36.90
*Heavy-duty suspension	4.75
Whitewall tires	53.60
Disc brakes	—
*Power brakes	42.15
*Power steering	84.30
*Power windows	100.10
*Power seat	69.55
*Radio AM	57.40
Radio AM/FM	157.00
Air conditioning	355.95
*Tinted glass	30.55
*Bucket seats	110.60
*Adjustable steering wheel	42.15
*Clock	79.00
(incl. w/spec. instr. pkg.)	
*Tachometer	part of spec. instr. pkg.
Automatic headlight dimmer	—
Automatic speed regulator	76.40
*Vinyl roof cover	73.75
Head rests	52.70
*On test car	
Dash (—) — Not offered	

MANUFACTURER'S SUGGESTED LIST PRICE: $2776
(incl. taxes, safety equip't & PCV device)

PRICE OF CAR TESTED: $3888.10 (incl. excise tax, delivery & get-ready charges, but not local tax & license)

MANUFACTURER'S WARRANTY: 24,000 miles and/or 24 months

SPECIFICATIONS FROM MANUFACTURER

ENGINE IN TEST CAR: Ohv V-8
Bore and stroke: 4.09 x 3.76 ins.
Displacement: 396 cu. ins.
Advertised horsepower: 360 @ 5200 rpm
Max. torque: 420 lbs.-ft. @ 3600 rpm
Compression ratio: 10.25:1
Carburetion: 1 4-bbl.

TRANSMISSION TYPE & FINAL DRIVE RATIO: 4-speed manual, all-synchromesh; single-disc diaphragm clutch. 3.31:1

SUSPENSION: Steel coil springs with direct, double-acting shocks at each wheel. Heavy-duty stabilizer bar optional.

STEERING: Coaxial, recirculating ball-nut gear
Turning diameter: 40.3 ft., curb to curb
Turns lock to lock: 3.98

WHEELS: Short-spoke disc; steel

TIRES: 7.75 x 14 red-line tubeless, nylon

BRAKES: Duo-servo 4-wheel hydraulic; self-adjusting
Diameter of drum: front, 9.5 ins.; rear, 9.5 ins.

SERVICE:
Type of fuel recommended: Premium
Fuel capacity: 20 gals.

Oil capacity: 4 qts.; with filter, 5 qts.
Shortest lubrication interval: 6000 mi.
Oil- and filter-change interval: 6000 mi.

BODY & FRAME: All-welded steel perimeter frame
Wheelbase: 115.0 ins.
Track: front, 58.0 ins.; rear, 58.0 ins.
Overall: length, 197.0 ins.; width, 75.0 ins.; height, 51.9 ins.
Min. ground clearance: NA
Usable trunk capacity: NA
Curb weight: 3800 lbs.

PERFORMANCE

ACCELERATION (2 aboard)

0-30 mph	3.2 secs.
0-45 mph	5.0 secs.
0-60 mph	7.9 secs.

TIME & DISTANCE TO ATTAIN PASSING SPEEDS

40-60 mph	3.8 secs., 278 ft.
50-70 mph	4.1 secs., 360 ft.

STANDING-START QUARTER-MILE: 15.5 secs. and 89 mph

BEST SPEEDS IN GEARS @ SHIFT POINTS

1st	35 mph @ 4000 rpm
2nd	49 mph @ 4000 rpm
3rd	63 mph @ 4000 rpm
4th	94 mph @ 4000 rpm

MPH PER 1000 RPM: 23 mph.

SPEEDOMETER ERROR AT 60 MPH: 10%

STOPPING DISTANCES: from 30 mph, 42 ft.; from 60 mph, 162 ft.

CHEVELLE MALIBU

2-door, 5-passenger sport coupe

ACCESSORY PRICE LIST

Engine options: 140 hp	$ 26.30
to 275 hp	92.70
*Automatic transmission	194.85
4-speed transmission	105.35
Overdrive	105.00
Limited-slip differential	36.85
Heavy-duty suspension	4.70
*Whitewall tires	28.15
Disc brakes	—
*Power brakes	42.15
*Power steering	84.30
Power windows	100.10
Power seat	63.20
*Radio AM	57.50
Radio AM/FM	157.00
*Air conditioning	355.95
*Tinted glass	37.50
*Bucket seats	110.60
Adjustable steering wheel	42.15
*Clock	NA
Tachometer	47.40
Automatic headlight dimmer	—
Automatic speed regulator	76.40
Vinyl roof cover	73.75
Head rests	52.70
*On test car	
Dash (—) — Not offered	
NA — Information not available at presstime	

MANUFACTURER'S SUGGESTED LIST PRICE: $2618.75
(incl. taxes, safety equip't & PCV device)

PRICE OF CAR TESTED: $3561.15 (incl. excise tax, delivery & get-ready charges, but not local tax & license)

MANUFACTURER'S WARRANTY: 24,000 miles and/or 24 months

SPECIFICATIONS FROM MANUFACTURER

ENGINE IN TEST CAR: Ohv V-8
Bore and stroke: 3.875 x 3.00 ins.
Displacement: 283 cu. ins.
Advertised horsepower: 195 @ 4800 rpm
Max. torque: 284 lbs.-ft. @ 2400 rpm
Compression ratio: 9.25:1
Carburetion: 1 2-bbl.

TRANSMISSION TYPE & FINAL DRIVE RATIO: Automatic, 2-speed torque-converter; Powerglide. 3.08:1

SUSPENSION: Steel coil springs at each wheel, with direct double-acting shocks

STEERING: Coaxial, recirculating ball-nut gear
Turning diameter: 40.3 ft., curb to curb
Turns lock to lock: 3.98

WHEELS: Short-spoke disc; steel

TIRES: 7.35 x 14 tubeless; rayon

BRAKES: Duo-servo 4-wheel hydraulic; self adjusting
Diameter of drum: front, 9.5 ins.; rear, 9.5 ins.

SERVICE:
Type of fuel recommended: Regular

Fuel capacity: 20 gals
Oil capacity: 4 qts.; with filter, 5 qts.
Shortest lubrication interval: 6000 mi.
Oil- and filter-change interval: 6000 mi.

BODY & FRAME: All-welded perimeter frame, attached body
Wheelbase: 115.0 ins.
Track: front, 58.0 ins.; rear, 58.0 ins.
Overall: length, 197 ins.; width, 75.0 ins.; height, 51.9 ins.
Min. ground clearance: NA
Usable trunk capacity: NA
Curb weight: 3540 lbs.

PERFORMANCE

ACCELERATION (2 aboard)

0-30 mph	3.1 secs.
0-45 mph	7.0 secs.
0-60 mph	14 secs.

TIME & DISTANCE TO ATTAIN PASSING SPEEDS

40-60 mph	11.5 secs., 841 ft.
50-70 mph	9.5 secs., 559 ft.

STANDING-START QUARTER-MILE: 19.5 secs. and 75 mph

BEST SPEEDS IN GEARS @ SHIFT POINTS
1st ....*NA
*Throttle control rod improperly adjusted. Car shifted manually at 4800 rpm for acceleration test

SPEEDOMETER ERROR AT 60 MPH: 1%

STOPPING DISTANCES: from 30 mph, 36 ft.; from 60 mph, 158 ft.

CHEVELLE 396 SS
Take your brave pills before you set forth in this one.

ROAD TEST has been accused of everything from "being in the pay of Chrysler" through "favoring foreign cars" to being "little old ladies from Pasadena who believe all cars should be equipped with governors" by irate readers who don't appreciate the editorial attitude we express toward the Pontiac GTO class of automobile.

Being not guilty on any of the counts but rather only concerned that whatever abilities to build better cars for driving pleasure and necessity Detroit possesses should be utilized for the full benefit of the consumer, we feel that in building the high-performance (meaning high-powered) intermediates, the manufacturers are short-changing us.

As enthusiasts, people who have spent years in competition and driving for fun, we would like to see some good chassis engineering brought to bear on the Chevelle 396, Pontiac GTO, Buick Skylark GS and Olds 442 instead of the perpetration of a snow job on the public through advertising and propaganda while continuing to fob off 1936-type cars with unlimited-displacement engines.

Let's take the Chevelle 396SS.

Last year the car was announced as a limited production model, presumably built only for drag strip competition. Acceptance caused more than the original number to be produced and it was set up as a regular production option for 1966 (RPO L-34), made part of the line and a considerable ad campaign worked up to get it to the public generally.

And here's the crime. As long as you are selling these cars to the informed enthusiast for a special purpose, fine. When you run full page ads in color in newspapers and magazines indicating that the 396-SS is just any businessman's virility pill, you've placed it in another classification entirely. The enthusiast presumably knows enough to correct the car's faults or how to handle them. Joe Average may know where the sparkplugs are and has no special driving skill.

Viewed in this light, the 396SS, as it is being huckstered, is definitely the dirty end of the stick.

The initial batch of cars (1965) were strictly an engine-swap concept which could have been engineered by your 18 year old neighborhood hot rod addict. This year, a bundle has been spent on restyling and fixing-up and precious few dollars on mechanical changes — most of which fall far short of the mark.

The flaws aren't in the 396 cubic inch engine (obtainable in either 320 or 360 horsepower ratings), the four-speed transmissions (normal or close-ratio gearing), the multiplicity of final drive ratios or even the wheels (six-inch base) and tires (7.75 x 14). But in that horse-latitude region where 1936 chassis design has been frozen by some asinine directive that every GM car must ride like a Cadillac, regardless.

Although the ads tell us that the Chevelle 396 is a flat-cornering wonder, we have not been able to discover an example which fits that description. Our favorite hot rod magazine also assured us that the

Acceleration potential of 360 horsepower 396 is tremendous, but is limited by poor traction of stock model. Limited slip differential helps, but even in this car so equipped, wheelspin is excessive.

car has "30% heavier-than-normal front and rear coil springs, larger-valved, shocks, 15/16-inch front sway bar and neat things like front ball joints that are shot-peened to frustrate the development of cracks." We can't vouch for the shot-peening, but if the other assets are present in the stock Chevelle 396SS, then Chevy's AMA Specifications don't reveal it and we can't detect them.

You can bury the front end of this handsome machine at even moderate speed on a moderate curve. The rear end bottoms on almost the slightest dip and it understeers so badly that the term "handling" can hardly be applied.

This is with the regular suspension.

There is an optional heavy duty suspension which will give you some help. It cures these problems by about 30%, which leaves 70% to go. No, you don't have to have the extra-cost options to make the car driveable, but what's the point in having all the power in the world if you can't drive the car in any more of a sporting manner than your rich uncle can in his Chrysler Imperial?

It isn't up to ROAD TEST to give advice to the world's most efficient corporation and the world's largest engineering group, but nobody on the staff would own a Chevelle without substantially better shock absorbers than those available from Chevy. And, they aren't about to get this suspension to work without strengthening the frame. Many 1965 Chevelle 396s have been in the shop for frame crack welding, usually discovered when the enthusiast has it on the rack to change the exhaust system.

Brakes, if you can call the stock units that, are nowhere — if the potential top speed of this car is taken into account. Even the generally-laudatory hot rod magazine mentioned earlier pointed out that they are useless when wet and that a cleverly-devised water shield actually succeeds in holding water inside the brake drums where it can keep brakes wet for a long period.

Oh, yes, there's a cure, and its a pretty satisfactory one, but why in the name of Louis Chevrolet, isn't it standard, so that Joe Average, who believes those full-color ads, will get it automatically? We mean metallic brake linings, of course, whose fade and water resistance is infinitely superior to the compressed rags which Chevrolet fits in production.

Even with the metallics, the 396 isn't going to set any international records for deceleration. About 23 feet per second/per second from 60 mph is all we can get because of rear end lock-up. This is considerably less than the Dodge Charger (26 ft./sec.^{2}). If the two cars were hurtling toward the same object 150 feet away at the same time, the Charger wouldn't hit it, but the Chevelle would go 15 feet through it. This might give you a clue as to why this group of little old ladies from Pasadena who favor foreign cars

Braking capability is also limited by rear end suspension and weight transfer during deceleration. Metallic brakes proved to have good fade resistance, but car required 165 feet for panic stop from 60 mph at rate of 23 ft./sec.². Deviation from straight line was not excessive.

and are in the pay of Chrysler can't become too thrilled about this "spirited new model from Chevy designed for those who LIKE to drive."

If it was impossible to make these cars any better than they are, we wouldn't be quite so derogatory. But the fact that police departments can buy Chevies and Oldsmobiles and Fords and so on which have got some stopping and handling power to match the acceleration and top speed potential, makes it abundantly clear that the factories could do better for the guy who does LIKE to drive. Even if the masses wouldn't cotton to the harsh ride now necessary to get stability, it is not impossible to make a better handling, safer car in this configuration at no more extra cost than you pay for styling changes.

From the practical ownership aspect, the Chevelle 396SS, particularly the 360 horsepower model, should be a pretty good investment. The prospects for high resale value in the next two or three years are excellent. It will cost more for fuel — on a good day you can get 12 mpg — but you should not expect any additional repair or maintenance problems with normal driving.

Drag racing is something else, and regardless of the fact that the SS is being pushed as something for everyone, certainly a high percentage of those sold will go to people who want to at least try it at the strip. This will get you in deeper right off. The 396SS has lots of engine, but it still takes some chassis work and a lot of rear rubber to make it turn anything exceptional in the quarter-mile. The amount of wheelspin (on a car equipped with Positraction) caused by a regular out-of-the-chute start can be seen in the accompanying photos.

Because of its size, styling and other appeals, the Chevelle will probably be bought by a number of ROAD TEST readers. Our only advice is to buy one from a dealer who understands the need for optional equipment, such as Harry Mann Chevrolet in Los Angeles, whose experience with Corvettes has made them performance conscious. Then treat it with respect.

Position of brake and accelerator pedals is not conducive to hard driving. Shift lever action is quick, positive.

Bucket seats in SS offer better support than previous design. Head room is ample for over-six-footer.

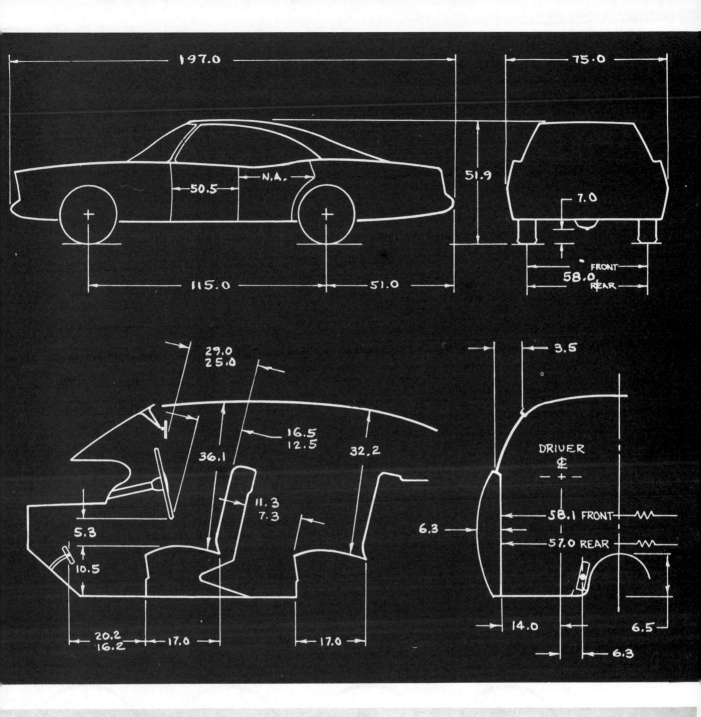

GENERAL SPECIFICATIONS

		ENGINE		Optional trans.:	
Curb weight	3841	Type	90° OHV V-8	4th	1.00:1
Weight dist.	56/44	Bore	4.094	3rd	1.46:1
Brake type	drum	Stroke	3.76	2nd	1.88:1
Swept area, sq. in.	268.6	Disp. cu. in.	396	1st	2.52:1
Tire size	7.75 x 14	Comp. ratio	10.25	Automatic:	
Steering turns:		BHP @ rpm.	360 @ 5200	Drive	
Manual	5.48	Torque @ rpm	420 @ 3600	Drive	1.00:1
Power	3.98	Clutch dia.	11.4	Low	1.76:1
Turning circle	40.3				

HOW THEY COMPARE

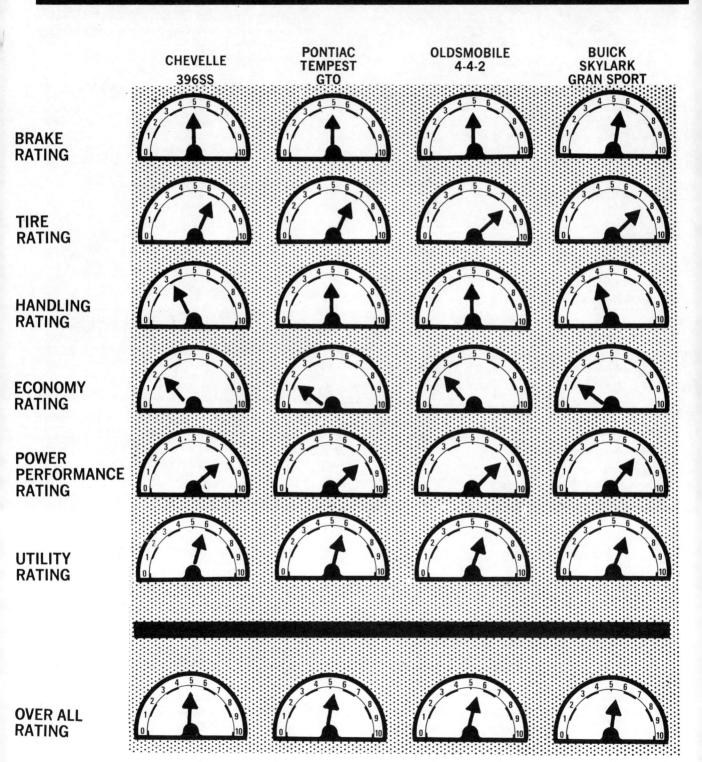

	CHEVELLE 396SS	PONTIAC TEMPEST GTO	OLDSMOBILE 4-4-2	BUICK SKYLARK GRAN SPORT
BRAKE RATING				
TIRE RATING				
HANDLING RATING				
ECONOMY RATING				
POWER PERFORMANCE RATING				
UTILITY RATING				
OVER ALL RATING				

SS 396: More than just a straight-line machine.

Personally, we don't like the idea of a car that goes like a bird when the road's like a ruler, and then turns chicken every time it has to change direction. What's more, we don't think you do either. Be assured, we gave every SS 396 an engine — a 325-hp 396-cu.-in. Turbo-Jet V8, with 360- and 375-hp versions on order. That wasn't all. We gave it a suspension, too.

Stiffer coil springs and shocks at all four corners came first. Next, a stiffer anti-sway bar at the front and special frame reinforcements at the back. Then a set of 7.75 x 14 red stripe tires and a fully synchronized 3-speed transmission with floor-mounted shift.

By the time we were finished, we knew we had your kind of machine; a machine that you could use to demonstrate the techniques of safe precision driving to others. The final touch was to paint the grillework black and add two businesslike scoops to the hood. After all, this was a machine with a purpose. What we did was give it a purposeful look.

'66 CHEVELLE SS 396 by CHEVROLET

Chevrolet Division of General Motors, Detroit, Michigan.

45

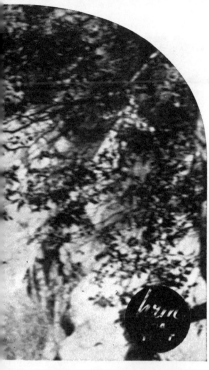

by Eric Dahlquist/*technical editor*

'66 SS 396—These are the call letters
of a spirited new model from Chevy,
designed for those who LIKE to drive

Super Street CHEVELLE

"Have any trouble keeping it on the ground?" The question came at us through a grey wall of water, which was part of the pre-Thanksgiving deluge that engulfed Southern California and put our 396 Chevelle Super Sport test car through a wet set of paces during the thousand miles we had it. Our interrogator was everybody's idea of how a young American male should look, outfitted in a yellow Nantucket slicker with a stream of water cascading off the brim. He knew it was a 396 because it said so on the front fender and had those "wiggy" air ducts on the hood. He also wanted to know if we had taken it to the strip yet and how it compared with the 4-4-2's and GTO's and how much it cost (because he was going to buy one) and if we had had our parking ticket validated. All this in the middle of a parking lot in a pouring down rain yet!

Chevrolet has been kind of out of it for the last couple of years, as far as having their own hottest hot dog, but after the parking lot caper, it's apparent that guys still remember when she was real fine, that 409, and how Dyno Don Nicholson and Frank Sanders put 'em back on their heels at the drags in '61 with their first demonstrations of what a stocker could do. The wave of enthusiasm that the 409 created carried stovebolt-maniacs along, and the Beach Boys helped with their dragging ballad (Giddy-Up 409). So did the Daytona

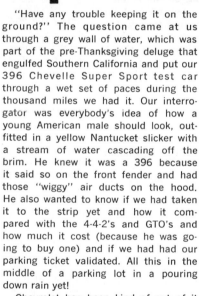

Going or coming, the Chevelle 396 SS
stood up to the challenge of the wide
country, not losing its footing even on
the serpentine mountain trails. Heel-
over was contained in marked degree,
due mostly to 30 percent stiffer springs
and shocks, as well as fat anti-sway bar.

"Mystery 427" which some of the executives back at the plant still say is a mystery to them as a misty look comes to their eyes with recall of how those '63's set the track on fire.

So this is what it had all boiled down to: the semi-hemi, porcupine top, 4.094 x 3.76-inch 396, like the one HRM broke the story on last year, plunked into a 115-inch wheelbase Chevelle with a black vinyl top and a lower body color known as Aztec Bronze, reminiscent of something called Titian Red from the mid-'50's. The two-door hardtop has those "in" for this season "struts" or "sail panels" (or just plain extensions), emphasizing that desirable fastback silhouette from the side, but embodying the practicality of a more vertical, recessed (in relation to the extension) back window. Then, too, this negates the manufacture of a special glass piece just for fastbacks, which, considering the volume Chevy sells, makes for a fair budgetary chunk.

Those in the know can spot the '66 SS 396 from its earlier counterpart because there has been a concerted effort made so that they can. Little changed since it was first introduced in '63, the new Chevelle has undergone such style transformation as to resemble more closely the full-sized Chevy, which it does, most handsomely. As another play to identification, all the grille bars in the SS have been blacked out except for the top and bottom, which is an inexpensive way that any Chevelle owner can escape the "I'm from Detroit-fluorescent light grating" look. All 396ers come with the red line 7.75 x 14 NF nylon tires (U.S. Royal) on wide-base 6-inch rims. Our test machine also had the benefit of a set of the optional mag-spoke hubcaps which, from anything be-

SS CHEVELLE

yond twenty feet, appear more real than what they're imitating. But probably the easiest way to know that you've just been or are about to be passed by one is by reading the SS 396 signs that are hung on, as is mentioned at the beginning of the story. Since the factory has gone to all this trouble to advertise, the enterprising "Bondish" type will no doubt derive endless hours of delight by swapping his 396 emblems for 327 or, sly dog, 283 counterparts—but that's another story.

After originally announcing last year, with the inception of the new engine, that only about

ABOVE LEFT — Bold face in a bold land is one facet of the Chevelle's front. Spoke hubcaps and blacked-out grille add style — bumper slots vent air. LEFT — Shapely between-the-buckets console ends in neat, electric 24-hour clock. Inland shifter is swift and positive. BELOW — Almost enough to make a man abandon his horse, this "bonanza" of sleek silhouette corralling stallion's spirit.

ABOVE LEFT — Under the spreading bonnet the mighty 3 holds court to continual audience of interested onlookers who wa to know things like horsepower (360), gas consumption (14 mpg.

ABOVE RIGHT — Any way you look at it there's somethi. special about the Chevelle. Take the keen outline of the pseud fastback roof or the hood ventilators or everything — it's gre

200 of the 396-equipped Chevelles would be available, quite a good number more than this were run off. Although one of those original SS's was not included in our testing program, we drove a representative sample and found it to be quite interesting although a trifle noseheavy. In '66, this negative trait has been cured to a point that even our 360 hp version with optional cam (322-degree duration and 0.3983-inch lift compared to 340 and 0.4614) and Muncie 4-speed was a totally pleasant vehicle, just the ticket for a quiet Sunday drive or drag. Helping toward this goal are the 30%-heavier-than-normal front and rear coil springs, larger-valved shocks, 15/16-inch diameter front sway bar and neat things like front ball joints that are shotpeened to frustrate the development of cracks.

It has been felt in some quarters, especially after breaking an axle, that Chevelle rear housing stabilization left a bit to be desired when it came under hard usage. Now a good part of this deficiency has been rectified. It is also quite obvious that a great deal of attention has been given to the hind quarters in general. To begin with, the stiffer rate rear coil springs and shocks will go a long way toward controlling wheel hop under acceleration or hard braking. In addition, there is a new frame reinforcement

strut between each rear upp and lower control arm piv point which will solidify t rear section considerably. T axles themselves have a stur differential carrier with a b 8.875-inch diameter ring gea which means, in practical term that it is a full ¾-inch larg than the common run-of-the-li unit.

The axle ratio standard wi our 360 hp model was 3.73 but, unlike some years with easy recall, there is a veritab myriad of gear combination from which to select. If you g for the baseline 325 model, 3.31 ratio is standard, wi 3.55, 3.73 and 4.10 on th shelf if specified. In 360-lan when the machine is equippe with 3-speed manual, Powe glide or street-type 4-speed choices are identical to the one just enumerated. Howeve should a close-ratio four-hole be beneath-the-boards, yo could opt among 3.31, 3.5 4.10, 4.56 and 4.88—the las three being Positraction as pa of the deal. Limited slips ca also be had in any of the othe gear sets as well. Viewing th whole rear scene in perspective it looks as though all base are pretty much covered.

At the other end of the ship things are not out of shap either. For your motivation, it' an either/or proposition—eithe the standard 325 pony packag or the several-hands-higher 360 That's it—no sixes or smalle

ABOVE LEFT — *Underneath it all, things are stiffened up a bit with hearty springs and shocks and a new reinforcement strut (light colored) between each upper and lower control arm pivot.*

ABOVE RIGHT — *As you slip behind the burnished-spoke, wood-rimmed wheel (imitation, that is), all gauges and switch knobs fall into logical order. "Strato"-buckets are reformed and comfy.*

ights to muddy up the water or drag down the car's reputaion. Just two brands of hairong and longer. But not quite s long as last year when the ated power pegged out at 375, nd the machine had more of a last effect. Why? Well, supericially at least, the '66 cam iming is less exotic, for one hing. As for the upper level lecision to retrench from last ear, one can only guess that he original 396 just didn't fill he bill as a machine that a reat number of people would ke to be married to for 36 ayments. And after all, image or no, this is why the thing is n the market.

We could go into gales of pecifications on the 396 enine, but this has already been lone in copious form in HRM, tarting with the original 396 tory back in March of '65 and ontinued varyingly in the reent Bill Thomas and Smokey 'unick pieces. Enough research as been done on the powerlant to answer just about any uestion of maintenance or nodification.

Today's breed of box is dentified by the numerical ratio of its first gear, such as 2.52 or 2.20, the latter being most lesirable and the former being vhat our SS came equipped vith. These two transmissions are the only 4-speeds that are offered with the Chevelle 396, and both are listed as heavyluty. For the wide-ratio transmission (2.52, 1.88, 1.46 and 1.00), as opposed to the closeratio (2.20, 1.64, 1.27, 1.00), numerous improvements have found their way into the design. Specifically, the teeth of

the clutch gear and meshing member of the counter gear have a coarser pitch for increased durability. In addition, the new counter gear incorporates a damper to virtually eliminate backlash. Both transmissions, wide- and close-ratio, feature a larger diameter counter gear shift and reinforced synchronizer blocker rings.

Another choice heretofore not available in any Chevy product is an all-synchro three-speed. This configuration has now been added to the 396 SS line and, like the 4-speeds, is considered a heavy-duty option. With ratios of 2.41, 1.57, and 1.00, it represents a sturdy assembly that incorporates wide, constant-mesh gears. Probably most interesting of all Chevy transmissions is the one which isn't even being offered in the Chevelle line at all— the 3-speed Turbo Hydra-Matic. The outfit is decently light and responsive but for some reason it has been withheld as an option from the "A"-bodied series. We recently had the opportunity to drive a former 2-speed Chevelle which had been converted over to Turbo action and the gain in performance, seemingly at no sacrifice to economy or dependability, is startling. This is one instance where the Division is missing a good bet, and competition being what it is, little will be gained by dallying.

So now that we've surveyed the salient properties that combine to form the character of the SS 396, let's drive the thing to work for a while, bend it into a few corners at speed, ridgerun a mountain road or two, and play an odd hand at the drags. Foremost in our minds,

as indicated above, the 396 is an especially nice package to get from point to point and to have a measure of fun while doing it. The 360 hp version's 3.73 final drive ratio is a happy compromise in union with the 4-speed which you can row along on its Inland shift linkage. Action with the 11-inch centrifugal clutch was generally smooth, but now and again a slight amount of shudder was evident when hot, after stop-and-go driving.

The one area we did get to examine carefully was the adequateness of water sealing. For most of the time the car was ours, the rains came with sickening regularity, day in and day out, to break all records, seasonal or otherwise. During this dampish phase, the car never sprang a leak in spite of many "river crossings" and the 2-speed electric wipers could not be faulted. However, something that does need alteration is the brakes, or rather lack of them, judging from their performance after wading through an intersection pond 6-8 inches deep in water. It is quite understandable that with a drum-type arrangement, 268.6 square inches worth, in fact, that the binders will tend to become ineffective for a short period, but more than once it was necessary to drag the pedal for several long blocks to dry them out. We put the car on a hoist to survey the

situation and it appears that the shield Chevrolet Engineering has devised to keep water out of the drum also serves as a dam to hold it in. In other portions of the water world, like heavy rain or the normal shallow puddles, no problem was encountered.

While the 9.5 x 2.5 molded asbestos binders are at least equal to the task of everyday traffic, successive stops from over sixty are not their forte as pedal effort increased and the right front wheel (on our car) tended to lock up. Fortunately, there is a cure within the RPO list — a nifty set of welded sintered iron brakes that rise to fill the breach. Although we did not have the opportunity to try the iron anchors, several owners reported that this is the way to fly — there is no warm-up problem, the things wear forever, and they stop on a dime over and over again without temperamental displays. We inquired further and learned from area dealers that, speaking for Southern California, a goodly number of SS's are sold with the metallics, so at least a portion of the buyers are playing it safe for any contingency.

We noted that even in the wet the Chevelle was admirably sure-footed when in traffic, and when the rainmaker did finally close up shop, a definite date

CONTINUED ON PAGE 85

SUPER
SPORT(Y)
396
CHEVELLE

Test Team — Prowlers Car Club, San Diego, California

BY DICK SCRITCHFIELD ☐ ACTION IS THE word when you see the Chevelle 396 Super Sport. It *looks* fast . . . and on the street or strip, it *is* fast! Whether you grab it with the fully synchronized 3-speed, 4-speed (there are two), or automatic Powerglide, the Super Sport comes alive at the touch of the throttle pushing you back into the seat. ☐ Our test car came equipped with the 360-horsepower Turbo-Jet 396 V8, 4-speed transmission, and the standard 3.73 positraction rear axle. Extra good stuff included bucket front seats with head rests, tachometer, center console, push button radio, power brakes, power steering, air conditioning, and of course, that "neat" California "Air Injection Reactor (Smog device)." Nothing like it! 396-cubic inches produce 420 pounds of torque and, as we mentioned earlier, 360 or 325 horsepower depending on which camshaft is installed. A bore of 4.001 and stroke of 3.25 give you the 396 inches. The 360 horsepower engine is listed under RPO-L34 and holds a high lift camshaft with .4614 inches lift and 340° duration as opposed to .3983 inches and 322° duration. 35 horsepower right there. ☐ Sitting atop all this is a 4 hole Holly or Rochester Quadra-Jet. The test car this month was equipped with the Holly which was fine for the street but possibly lacking for the strip. Eye appeal in the engine compartment is provided by chrome air cleaner and valve covers, which comes standard on the Super Sport models. ☐ A car club long familiar in Southern California is the San Diego Prowlers who are well-known for their very clean show and street ma-

chinery. While working on a story in the San Diego area we started checking around in hopes of locating a member of the club. We were finally able to reach Norm Urquhart, a past president, and together set up a meeting between the club and the test car at Carlsbad Drag Strip located roughly 30 miles north of San Diego. The management of the Carlsbad strip was instituting a new procedure which started the day of our tests. They decided to have the strip open the Saturday before each Sunday meet to allow racers to get in a full day of running and tuning. Everything was in full operation, timing lights, "Xmas tree," and public address system. We therefore felt this was the perfect place to make our car tests as we would have both the drag strip for clocking times and the rolling hills and back roads to check the handling of the Super Sport. ☐ While talking with Norm on the telephone, he gave us a lot of background on the "Prowlers." It seems they are one of the oldest clubs still in existence in Southern California having been organized in 1947. At that time, you had to have a '40 or earlier Ford to be a member, but now, all that's changed. You have to have a '48 or earlier Ford! Too bad about that, Chevy owners! So, who other than Ford owners could better check out a Chevelle? ☐ The Prowlers met us early on a Saturday morning, arriving in Bob Wolin's '29 roadster and Norm's beautiful '47 pickup. The red Super Sport really lit up their eyes upon first inspection. Bob was quick to express his views. **"The 396 really comes on with the wild simulated air scoops**

50

Popular with young guys since it hit the market, the Chevelle series gets another shot in the arm for '66 with the addition of the "SS 396." A machine that's rated as an agile handler, a strong runner and good looker. Topping it off, name an option of any kind and you can get it.

mounted on top of the hood. If they could be made operable, you might pick up a couple of extra miles on top end. It adds much to the appearance and makes the car easily recognizable if you miss the blacked out center grill and SS 396 emblems scattered about. I like the chrome arrangement on the sides. Keeping it scarce except around the wheel openings and along the rocker panels below the "hip hugger" belt line doesn't distract your eyes from the sculptured lines. The recessed rear window is another feature I like. The way the roof side panels extend, gives the Super Sport that 'fast' Continental look. From the side it looks just like a fastback, but from the rear, a completely different appearance with the deck panel going right in under the back glass." □ Only two models are available in the Super Sport line. The 2-door hard top and the convertible. An interesting addition to the convertible, is the anti-ballooning construction of the top which has a hidden fabric strip fastening it to the top bow. This keeps the top from looking like a big bubble as you cruise down the highway at 60 mph. □ On the inside, our "Sport" was equipped with the optional "strato-bucket" seats and head rests, which look like a one piece unit when the "rest" is not raised. They slide in and out of the seat back so that none of the hardware is visible. The center floor console, another extra, mounts a 24 hour "rally-type" clock with sweep second hands. Fine for the "navigator" but too far away from

the windshield for the driver to get the time while driving. A special instrumentation package is available which includes water temperature and oil pressure gauges which replace a clock or filler panel in the right instrument cluster bezel and a fuel gauge and ammeter, replacing the single fuel gauge in the left bezel. An 8000 rpm tachometer, mounting on the lower dash next to the steering, and a parking brake lamp, finish off the group. □ Curt Holmquist was the interior specialist for the Prowlers so he loaded everyone in and went for a drive to check out comfort, instrument placing, and wind noise. Upon returning, Curt explained: **The seats are firm but comfortable, however I like a bucket that fits around your sides more, giving additional support. These seem quite narrow, more like Fords than General Motors. The head rests are really kind of a waste. They supposedly were designed and installed to prevent neck injuries to passengers should the car be struck in the rear, but these are so far away from the back of your head that you would have reached the strain point long before your head ever reached the rest! They were very**  much in the way when it came time to back up. Most people can turn farther around, to look through the back window, by putting their arm along the top edge of the seat. With the head rest, it's impossible and really limits your vision. It's definitely a four passenger car. I only weigh about 150-pounds and I bottom just sitting in the center of the rear seat. And on bumps, forget it! You can't go down because you're already there, on the drive shaft hump, and you can't go up because your head is brushing the top. At the sides of the hump it's not so bad but it is still a little short on head room. Besides that, there just isn't any place to put your feet to get your knees out from under your chin, when sitting in the center. So, I'd say it was strictly a four passenger vehicle. One thing that did impress me favorably was the absence of wind noise. This is something that almost anyone who buys a hardtop complains about. I should know, working for a dealership, we're always fiddling with it trying to get it quiet. This shows up more in hardtops for two reasons. One, you don't have

Prowler members really checked out the trunk on this one! Found the spare tire mounted flat on the right rear section of the floor where it would take up usable luggage space.

Far left — Ernie Blanchard indicated closeness of the top while Norm Urquhart displays how far his head would have to move before it would reach the head rests. Little protection afforded.

Lower left — With a person in the normal driving position, their head would have to move approximately 5 inches before it would start to be cushioned by the head rests, when it's fully extended.

Below — The back roads adjoining the Carlsbad Drag Strip proved a perfect place to find out if the Super Sport had handling qualities young people want. Everyone agreed it was the greatest!

Lower left — According to drag champion Tommy Johnson, Delco "Super-Lift" air-type shock absorbers are the only changes necessary to the rear suspension to gain better than average times.

97.82 isn't bad for a street equipped stocker...

the rear post as a support for the backside of the glass. You therefore usually get a lot of wind noise between the quarter glass and the front door glass. Secondly, this type of car is more subject to jars. With the windows rolled up, it's only supported at the forward edge of the glass. The Super Sport appears to be a pretty sturdy car.99 Most of the test members got their handling and driving practice dragging the 396 through the Carlsbad quarter. Norm was the first to go through and set the low elapsed time of 14.98, which held for all our runs. This was straight off the street, running stock 7.75 x 14 Firestone Champion tires with about 30-pounds air pressure, and standard air cleaner. Best time for the quarter was 97.82 which isn't too bad for a *complete* street equipped stocker. Under the floor panel we were lucky to have the "Muncie" close ratio 4-speed which has ratios of: 2.20, 1.64, 1.27, and 1.00, first to fourth. The street 4-speed has 2.52, 1.88, 1.46, and 1.00. Standard axle ratio for the 360 horsepower is 3.73 to 1 with ratios of 3.55, 4.10, 4.56, and 4.88 to 1 available. All of this works through an 11" clutch. □ Several chassis refinements have been made this year with the main being a frame reinforcement between each rear upper and lower control arm pivot point which provides greater strength and rigidity. Shock absorbers were recalibrated to compliment the higher rate springs which are 30% heavier than normal. Coils are mounted all around and control wheel hop on acceleration and braking. Ball joints have shot peened studs providing greater durability and the front stabilizer bar's diameter has been increased to maintain stability. □ After a few good runs down the strip, Ernie Blanchard had these comments: 66The shifting mechanism is really an improvement over some of the past models I've driven. There is no hanging in the gears and everything

works real nice and smooth. Coming out of the hole was real nice, but top end just wasn't there. Possibly a 4.56 or 4.88 rear gear would correct that. Another point I felt needed improving, is the location of the tachometer. If you should ever have a front end collision, your right knee is in such close proximity that both would most likely be badly damaged. As far as an all around car, it handles real great . . . and it's a comfortable car too. I noticed on the power steering and power brakes it's pretty touchy. Mostly the brakes though, 'cause they're just right there. The tires are a decent size (7.75 x 14), but you could probably go to a 15 inch rim without looking a little odd. It would undoubtedly give the car a better bite in order to use the car for weekend dragging and week day transportation. Surprisingly enough, you get pretty poor bite with the street tires that are on it, considering the high gear that it has.99 □ The "Prowler" member to really put the Super Sport through its paces was Norm Urquhart who has had much experience in handling hot iron whether it be motorcycles or fast cars. With Norm at the wheel we headed out along the back roads surrounding the strip. Here we were able to test the car over dips, banked and unbanked corners and dirt roads. There was certainly no disagreement on one point. The Super Sport could hold its own on any type of road, whether it be the tight corners of mountain switch-backs or gentle rolling hills of the plains. Norm remarked: 66It handles fantastic for a standard production car without any special

handling package being it's right off the show room floor. Even with four people in the car you don't have the feeling that it's rocking around. I don't feel the ride is too harsh, seems about right. Of course it depends a lot on what you're used to. If you were used to a good road holding roadster, it would feel about comparable. Considering what Chevrolet has had in the past with their piece of chrome spaghetti sticking out of the four speed, that you couldn't get into gear, this new linkage is excellent. It's real positive and goes in there everytime. Access to the rear seat, while someone is sitting in the right front bucket is a chore, because of the head rests. With the seat higher, it doesn't fold far enough forward. It's pretty much impossible for anyone to enter or leave the back seat with a person sitting in the front. I'm glad to see instruments in a car for a change. The position of the tachometer is kind of poor. It should be mounted up somewhere near your line of vision. If you're using it for racing, you can't be looking down at the floor and hunting around for it when you're going at excess of 60 mph. It should be where you could focus your eyes without moving your head. Possibly it could be mounted near the right side of the speedometer as you don't need the 120 mile per hour area on the street anyway.99 □ To get a comparison and find out just what the potential of the 396 might be, we asked Tom Johnson of

Test car was equipped with special instrument package which included fuel gauge and ammeter, water temperature and oil pressure replacing warning lights. Tachometer, parking brake lamp.

Console package mounted electric 24-hour clock and additional storage space. Tachometer mounting on dash was considered too low to be read safely and a possible hazard to your knee.

Lancaster, California, to bring his Starksen Chevrolet sponsored Chevelle to the Carlsbad strip to make some runs and explain just what it takes to make the Super Sport into a class winner. ☐ Tom is somewhat of a newcomer in drag racing having gotten his first taste of active participation in 1963 when he started running a 327 Chevy. Now a "Get-ready Technician" at Starksen Chevrolet, he decided to replace the 327 with the new 396 SS. He ordered the car with the 360 horsepower engine and two days after taking possession, headed for the Fontana drag strip. The first Sunday out netted him 13.66 seconds and 103 in the quarter, running the standard 3.73 with positraction and 900 x 15 Goodyear slicks. During the next two weeks Tom was busy changing to 4.88 gears and getting a set of headers installed by Jerry Jardine of Garden Grove, Calif. Back at Fontana he went to 107 in 13.25 seconds. As the American Hot Rod Association allows factory experimental cams, Tom ordered the latest factory 427/396 experimental grind and started preparing for their Winter Championships. This cam was purchased right over the counter at Starksen's and came in kit form, complete with springs and retainers. With this cam installed, the Super Sport went to 12.43 and 114.94 mph for the record, using 7-inch tires. Adding larger tires, Tom charged through in 12.20 seconds but it was too late in the meet to mark it as a record run. ☐ Tom felt a few modifications were necessary to put the suspension in race shape so he installed heavier duty Chevelle

CONTINUED ON PAGE 59

Norm, Burt, and Ernie inspect the simulated air scoops in the hopes of finding a method of making them functional.

Prowler Curt Holmquist stands on it burning both rear tires as he gets the green light from Tom Johnson of Starksen Chevrolet. 396 Super Sport turned 97.82 mph with 14.98 elapsed time.

Above right — Crew checks out Johnson/Starkson Chevelle on the scales. Weighed 3380-lbs. compared to 3725-lbs. of test car. With 325 h.p. engine, Johnson cars run C/S, turning 12.94, 110.02.

Right — Prowlers inspect the modified air cleaner that Johnson runs at AHRA meets. Tubing brings cool air from ducts behind the grill direct to carburetor. Change is not allowed by NHRA.

Below — Engine of test car is almost entirely hidden by maze of tubing connected to the Air Injector Reactor system (Smog device to Californians). The Quadra-Jet Carburetor is optional.

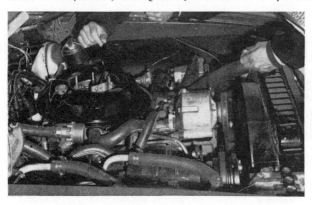

SS

Supercar or just another Chevelle?

Chevy bucks the "in racing" boys with a 396 cube "Semi-Hemi" middleweight loaded with gobs and gobs of goodies

CHEVROLET DIVISION of General Motors maintains a most unique position in the wild and woolly race for supercar supremacy. Because of the stand General Motors took when the market crashed (performance market, that is) a few years ago and the continuance of this position to the present, Chevrolet is just one of many of GM's divisions that refuses to admit any connection with horsepower, racing or high performance in general. Because of tremendous brand loyalty, however, independent performance-minded enthusiasts have been carrying the ball for GM in the big race.

Over the past couple of years the GM *dropouts* have been dabbling in performance, without really infringing on the decision made by chiefs. If you call up Olds Division in the quest of information on its 442 model you'll get all the data that's available. The same holds true for Pontiac, especially if you want info on their hot-to-trot line of tempestuous tigers. However, Chevy's engineering men have taken a different approach to the Division's relationship with anyone who wants performance information. Here are some examples of answers given to "yours truly" when he called up Chevy Engineering for some pictures of high performance products: "Z-11 427 Mystery engine, what's that? I've never heard of that one!; Action shots of a Sting Ray? No, we don't take pictures like that, it might look as though the car is being raced!; 396 or 427 engine shots taken in a car? Sorry, we don't have pictures like that around. We wouldn't want people to think we build cars for racing!" If these answers hadn't come from one of the top men I would have taken it for granted that he was either sniffing fumes or had never bothered to read his Division's advertisements for 427 engine options, 396 SS Chevelles, 350 hp Chevy II Super Sports or the 425 hp Sting Rays which appear in performance magazines. I guess Chevy's advertising agency is not bound by the Division's feelings on racing!

Interested in learning just where Chevrolet fit into the performance race, we queried their New York office for a 396 SS Chevelle for road testing purposes. More than a month and six phone calls later, we were invited to drive their prime contender for honors—that is if we didn't keep it more than five days. It seems that the car was in great demand for testing and editors were waiting in line to write performance reports about this little battlewagon. Since there are only four publishers of high performance automotive enthusiast publications in the New York area, we can't imagine where all these waiting editors were from!

The Chevelle SS turned over to us for testing was graced with just about all the performance and dress-up items listed in Chevy's extensive catalog. Because of its strut-like roof extensions, which give that ultra fast-back appearance without any appreciable loss of visibility, the car could easily be mistaken for any of its GM brothers which share the same basic 115-inch wheelbase chassis.

The SS 396 is a pleasant looking, clean cut automobile, but our test model suffered obviously from a lack of quality control. The scoop-type trim on the hood was surrounded by poorly applied paint, as were portions of the rear deck and front fenders. Panel fit was not of the same quality that is prevalent among the bigger brothers who share the same basic shell and chassis. The black-faced grille with centered 396 SS trim set off the yellow body color and neatly matched the vinyl roof topping.

Below, gussied-up 396 SS mill is rated at 360 hp at 5200 rpm. Rating seems ultra-high considering car's performance on the asphalt. Bottom, strut-like roof extensions account for car's long, low look. Vinyl roof topping is optional.

Top, Holley quad with vacuum-controlled secondaries offers compromise street-strip carburetion. Above, left, ultra comfortable vinyl buckets and a wood-type tiller dress up the cockpit. Above, right, because of its mounting position and small face, tach is less than desirable.

not as quick as comparable GTO's and 442's

The interior of this top-line Chevy middleweight was packed full of the little goodies that seem to help sell cars in this hectic market. Plush comfortable front buckets, a "geegawed" center console with built-in shifting controls and a sunken clock (no one seems to know what it's doing down there!) a black non-reflecting dash with *extra cost* instrumentation, a "mickey mouse" tach which does little more than interfere with right knee travel and a wood *type* steering wheel are there to justify the SS model designation. Although the buckets were probably the most comfortable offered in any middleweight car, they did very little in the line of serving the functional purpose that bucket seats were designed for. Knobs and interior trim stood out as being "not the highest quality" and had a cheapening effect on the appearance of the interior. With the buckets set up for serious driving, the rear seating was not exactly adequate for two adults.

Lurking under the scooped-*type* hood of all SS 396 models is the 396 cubic inch street adaptation of the race bred "semi-hemi" engine. Chevy started on this line last year, making 396's available in a limited quantity of Corvettes, Impalas and Z-16 Chevelles. Standard engine for the SS 396 is a 325 hp at 4800 rpm version rated at 410 foot pounds of torque at 3200 rpm. Our test Chevelle was outfitted at the factory with what was the hottest engine option listed at that time, a 360 hp at 5200 rpm version rated at 420 foot pounds of torque at 3600 rpm. Chevrolet, in

their never ending quest to kill any references between their hallowed division and the performance race, recently announced the availability of a 375 hp option for 396 SS models.

We were most surprised at the "semi-hemi" 360 hp 396 in our test car as it was extremely smooth, responsive, easy to start in the coldest weather and a most tractable all-around street engine. Because of past experiences with 425 hp versions in special Sting Rays and 425 hp 427 versions in new Sting Rays, we had expected to find the 360 hp version sort of on the ragged edge between street and strip.

The use of compromise internal and external engine components is responsible for the car's tractable behavior on the street and fairly respectable performance on the asphalt. Internal action is by a hydraulic lifter camshaft tagged at .4615-.4800 inches lift and 350-352 degrees of duration. Resting in the "porcupine" heads are 2.07-inch intake and 1.72-inch exhaust valves with special aluminumized facings. The high quality aluminum pistons, which make for a 10.25-to-1 compression ratio are decked out with special cast alloy iron rings with moly-filled grooves. The moly rings, which are similar to speed type parts, insure long cylinder wall and piston life because of the lubrication qualities of the moly filling.

Since we didn't have too much time allotted to us on this test we had Charlie Dodge and George Snizek tune the 396 to strict factory specifications

1966 CHEVELLE SS 396
SPECIFICATIONS

ENGINE

Type	OHV V-8
Displacement	396 cubic inches
Compression Ratio	10.25-to-1
Carburetion	Single Holley four-barrel
Camshaft	Hydraulic, .460-.480-inch lift
Horsepower	360 @ 5200 rpm
Torque	420 foot/pounds @ 3600 rpm
Exhaust	Dual headers, dual pipes
Ignition	Standard vacuum advance

TRANSMISSION

Make	Muncie four speed
Control	Inland Steel floor shift
Ratios	Standard ratio 2.52, 1.88, 1.46, 1.00

REAR END

Type	Positraction
Ratio	3.73-to-1

BRAKES

Type	Drums, asbestos linings
Swept Area	268.6 square inches

SUSPENSION

Front	Independent, HD coil springs, HD shocks, sway bar (special order)
Rear	HD coil springs, HD shocks (special order)
Steering	Optional power assist
Overall Ratio	20-to-1

GENERAL

List Price	$2776
Price As Tested	$3800
Weight	3700 pounds
Wheelbase	115 inches
Overall Length	197 inches
Tire Size	7.75 x 14-inch U.S. Royal "Redlines"

PERFORMANCE

0 to 30 mph	3.3 seconds
0 to 60 mph	8.0 seconds
Standing ¼ mile mph	91 mph
Elapsed Time	15.85 seconds
Top Speed	120 mph (est)
Economy	12.8 mpg

disc or metallic-lined drum brakes should be standard on a car of this type

Below, left, heavier than stock front sway bar is part of $4.25 optional HD suspension package. Below, right, phoney scoops and distinctive trim set SS 396 off from standard Malibu models. Bottom, Charlie Starter of Pacers Auto displays one of the Goodyear cheater slicks used during performance runs. Super-bite slicks caused engine to bog!

at Pacers Auto and off we went to the track. We were most surprised when we received the results of our acceleration tests. The car seemed extremely quick on the street, but the Chrondeks and stop watches related a different tale. Running with the standard SS 396 7.75x14-inch US Royal "redlines" dropped to 24 psi at the rear and pumped to 30 psi up front and standard 3.73-to-1 Posi-Traction gears, our best quarter-mile time was a most disappointing 91 mph in 15.85 seconds. Most of the runs were in the high 16's! We figured on paper that a car weighing in at 3700 pounds with a 2.52 to 1 low gear four-speed, 3.73-to-1 Positraction rear, heavy duty suspension, high performance street tires and 360 ponies under the hood should go through the "eyes" pretty close to 100 mph with ets in the neighborhood of 14.80 to 14.90 seconds. Other acceleration tests produced results that led us to believe that Chevy highly overrates its "semi hemi" 396 package. The best 0 to 30 and 60 mph runs netted us with 3.3 and 8.0 second time slips respectively. We had expected to negotiate the 0 to 60 mph bash in no more than 7.2 to 7.5 seconds.

Stock 360 hp GTO's, which weigh a slight bit more than the Chevelle, run faster and quicker than the times posted by our 360 hp SS 396. The only real fault we found with the operation of the 396 engine, except, of course, for its lack of real horsepower, was the less than desirable vacuum-operated secondaries on the Holley quad. All 360 hp models are fitted with Holley 3886087 quads with 1.562-inch primaries and secondaries. For maximum response the vacuum mechanism should be disconnected to prevent late opening of the secondaries when the stops are pulled out. Mechanical kits are available from speed shops for this simple conversion.

The big job of getting the power to the ground in the Chevelle is delegated to basic Chevy big-car component parts. Backing up the 396 is an 11-inch diaphragm bent finger type clutch and a Muncie all-synchro four-speed transmission with 2.52,

CARS ROAD TEST

1.88, 1.46 and 1.00 gear ratios. At the receiving end is a Chevy rear (not of the original type designed for the 115-inch GM models in 1964) with a dual disc type Positraction locker and respectable 3.73-to-1 final gears. This setup is standard on all 360 hp models and as far as we can see is near ideal for all around street and strip use. Since the new 375 hp package has been announced, however, a new listing for gears with ratios up to 4.56 has been added to the option list. Along with the new gears is a close-ratio four-speed listed for use with the two tallest gear ratios.

Although the four speed in our test car was silky smooth, the Inland Steel reverse lockout linkage performed flawlessly and the 3.73 cogs were pretty much ideal, we experienced mucho trouble getting the horses to the ground. Even with the reinforced frame members and the so called heavy duty suspension (optional at $4.75) we experienced tremendous fishtailing and freewheeling when we really got on it. Our car was

equipped with the optional "Redline" tires which are supposed to be the ticket for high performance use. We tried a set of Goodyear cheater slicks on Crager mag wheels, but all they did was bog the engine!

The Mickey Mouse tach in our SS was redlined at 5500 rpm, approximately 300 rpm more than the maximum horsepower point as calculated by the factory engineers. We tried pulling our shifts at 6000 rpm, but were hampered by flying power steering belts that become expensive.

The front end was far too mushy even though the front coils are supposed to be 30% beefier than the stockers and the sway bar is almost 1-inch thick. On rough roads under full power we experienced bottoming meaning that the jounce-rebound control (shocks) was far from heavy duty. Tracking was also rather poor and the car tended to drift out of its line of action at speed. Steering response and accuracy was rather good, as our car was equipped with the optional power steering with an overall ratio of 20.4-to-1.

Since Chevy does pack quite a few cubes between the rails of its 115-inch Chevelles, we had expected disc brakes or at least oversize drums to be mandatory with this package. Small 9.5-inch drums are used all around and the only braking option is metallic linings. Our test car was not equipped with the optional linings and it required a full 170 feet to bring from 60 mph panic stopping to a full halt. The metallic brakes should be standard, and discs should be listed as optional on *all* 396 models.

After spending a few days with the SS 396 Chevelle on the drag strip, ride and handling course and street, we feel that it's far from being an ultimate performance package. It is not as quick as a GTO or an Olds 442 and it doesn't handle nearly as well as the 442 does. It's not a true integrated package, mainly because the HD suspension, tachometer and basic instruments, good brake linings are optional at extra cost. We feel that any middleweight that can be bought with up to 375 hp should be equipped with the above mentioned component parts as standard. Both for reasons of maximum safety and maximum performance.

Just about the only saving graces we could find with the SS 396 were the ultra comfortable bucket seats (not much room for rear seat passengers, however) , the docile engine and the maximum fuel economy of 14.5 mpg logged during our five day "shakedown cruise."

springs in the front which raised the 3200-pound Chevelle to where the "A" frame bumps the rubber bumpers on the frame itself. Delco "Super-Lift" shock absorbers, which are an air type, were installed in the rear. The right shock·is filled to about 6-pounds and the left to 3. With 45-pounds of air in the front tires and 12 to 25, depending on the strip, in the rear, the chassis was ready to go.

No major changes were made to the ignition other than changing the springs to gain a quicker advance curve and the disconnecting of the vacuum advance. It was then set on the engine with an initial 12° advance and moves up to a total of 38° maximum. Wiring and plugs remained stock as did the Holly carburetor. Closer jetting would possibly be of some value but as yet it hasn't been touched.

The National Hot Rod Association does not allow factory "Experimental" cams nor any cylinder head modification such as polishing or matching of the intake ports. You are only able to "CC" the heads and perform a racing valve grind. One item to be watched closely is the valve spring tension. If the car is operated on the street, it will weaken the valve springs due to the prolonged heating of the engine. In just quarter mile runs they normally will not get hot enough to lose any tension. Main thing to do is to make sure that springs are at maximum factory recommended pressure.

If you're wondering about this "experimental" equipment, all dealers should have the special parts list from the factory on how to up date the 396 which explains the availability of this equipment. Tom mentioned that over half of the twelve mechanics at Starksens' are hot rodders so handle most of the high performance work in the area.

What about gas mileage? As with most high performance cars, mileage takes a back seat. No matter how you work it, you can't have go-power without sacrificing mileage. With the 3.73 gear, GM has come up with a fair compromise. At the drags we averaged slightly over 8 miles to the gallon. Street driving was in the 11 mpg bracket. No Economy Run favorite; but it runs good!

Chevrolet has given you a great start with their 396 Super Sport. There's no doubt about it, as it comes from the factory it's a going concern. You can leave it the way it is and probably grab your share of the drag trophies or you can benefit from Tom Johnson's experience and move into the "inner circle." It's a beautiful performing street machine with agility and class if you just like to feel that power. It's all up to you. Wail! . . . 🅒

TRES chevelles

two for the road and one
more for the load

El Camino sedan-pickup, hot and cool Chevelles all used the SS 396 "porcupine head" engine, but personalities differed.

Breathes there a man with soul so dead that never has he taken sides in the age-old Chevrolet versus Ford partisanship? Last month we tested a trio of Ford Fairlanes, including the Ranchero, and rather liked them. Rather than suffer the slings and arrows (or even irate letters) of outraged stovebolt lovers, we decided to take an equally searching look at three corresponding Chevelles.

Our three Chevrolet intermediates did not have the range or displacement or horsepower that the Fairlanes did, all being 396-cubic-inchers, the biggest options in the Chevelle arsenal, standard on our 396 SS models and optional on the El Camino. One hardtop had the 325-hp version with a 2-speed Powerglide automatic. Another hardtop mated the 375-hp option to a 4-speed do-it-yourself box. The El Camino pickup also had the 325 horse mill, but with the 3-speed Turbo Hydra-Matic.

Engines & Transmissions

A funny thing happened when we went to weigh the cars; they all weighed the same, or virtually so. Despite two different body styles and several different combinations of transmissions, engines, brakes, etc., the certified truck scale with 20-pound gradiations that we used showed no difference. This was especially surprising since Chevrolet Division's own specs indicate an 80-pound difference between the SS 396 and the El Camino.

With this knowledge in mind, it didn't take the logic of Star Trek's Mr. Spock to tell us that the car with the most horsepower would go fastest. Sure enough, the hot SS 396 was about a full second faster than the 325-hp car in both the 0-60 and quarter. The difference in potential was actually greater than the figures indicate, for the "little 396" was tested on a surface that was drier than a WCTU banquet while the 375 was tested on the first clear day after a week of liquid sunshine. The strip was reasonably clear (meaning none of the puddles was deep enough to drown in), but there was still some moisture to cause wheelspin.

Mileage was quite good on the El Camino, including a 200-mile run that netted about 19 mpg. With the hot SS 396 we found out that what power corrupts is gas mileage as the spec chart shows.

The El Camino was also tested on the damp track, but performed slightly better than the SS 396 with the same engine. Here the difference was the

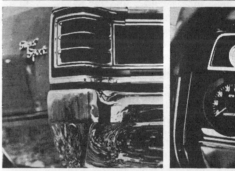

The 325-hp SS 396 was tamest of the trio, but still fast. The 375-hp is dealer option on 350-hp engine. Tail lights are connected by simulated wood grain strip on Custom version of El Camino. Tach option has left turn indicator light, but covers gas gauge. El Camino had plushest interior of three cars.

El Camino's Turbo Hydra-Matic. The extra forward speed gives it a distinct edge over the 2-speed Powerglide, although the PeeGee wound tighter before shifting. Turbo Hydra-Matic is available only with the 396s in the Chevelle series. The "ohs" and "ahs" of the gas station rubbernecks when they looked at the 396 engine (or even the emblem) changed from major to minor key when they realized that the car had Powerglide. The 4-speed and Turbo Hydra-Matic brought favorable comment everywhere. Perhaps some of the marketing people from Chevrolet should go forth with tape recorders among the service station people to capture some of these very sophisticated responses before they finalize the powertrain combinations next time around. With both the automatics we got the best results using "Drive" rather than shifting. With the 4-speed, we found that downshifting into 3rd improved the 40-60 passing test by more than a second compared with trying to pull in 4th.

Handling, Steering & Stopping

One of the pluses that goes with the SS 396 option is an improved suspension. Other than this, there is no suspension option or kit, but none is really necessary. The SS 396s were the first GM intermediates we've driven that were free of the rear-end jello-roll blues that make life so hard for back-seat passengers, and give the driver a few "moments" as well. This phenomenon, caused by coil springs, inadequate rear axle location, and poor shock absorbers is the bane of the owners of both intermediate and full-size Chevy wagons when they carry full loads or pull trailers. All the devices meant to cope with such usage solve only part of the problem. The SS 396 breaks away from this negative image and is

far and away the best handling and riding GM product we've driven — aside from the luxury specialty cars — in a long time.

Everything the 325-hp SS could do, the 375-hp car could do better, thanks, in no small measure, to its Firestone Wide Oval tires. Both cars have identical power steering units, but the car with the Hot Rocks felt more agile and inspired more confidence in tight spots in traffic and crowded parking lots. We were concerned about how these would work in the wet, being aware that the wide-tread, low-profile rubber now in vogue for race cars tends to aquaplane over puddles with consequent loss of steering control. No sooner had the question occurred to us than the weatherman arranged just such a test. A long one. The sun was out just often and long enough to create the half wet/half dry/very greasy condition that is even more treacherous than the downpour itself. When a week of this had passed and we hadn't found it necessary to back the Chevelle out of any store windows or strange living rooms, we were ready to allow as how the Wide Ovals were an all-weather improvement for car handling.

The El Camino has its own set of handling conditions due to a rear suspension designed to cope with a half-ton payload. We had no chance to test the El Camino, which is officially described as a "sedan pickup" by the manufacturer, with the bed loaded, but even empty the ride and handling were excellent. The bias between front and rear spring rates is less apparent than it was with the Ranchero, and it did not dip the outside front corner in sharp bends. The real acid test came when a crash program was necessary to put enough mileage on the car over a weekend to be ready to test on Monday morning. Therefore, the author,

singlehandedly, made an 800-mile round-trip to nowhere, leaving one Saturday morning and returning the same evening still fresh enough to stay up for the Late Late Show on the boob tube. Except for the lack of seating capacity, we found this to be as satisfactory a transportation vehicle as any of the three and in some ways better than the SS 396s.

By the time we were ready to do the stopping tests, the sun had pretty well dried out the drag strip at Irwindale, giving the El Camino and 375-hp car an even shake with the 325-hp SS that was tested at an earlier date. We had had enough time in all the cars, in rain and shine, to know how they handled and hadn't had any bad surprises when stopping in a hurry, so no great excitement was anticipated. Ho! Ho!

It seemed likely that because of the equal weights, the only difference in stopping distance between the SS 396s would be due to the disc brakes on the hot car. The difference at 30 mph was negligible — one foot — but at 60 mph the edge, slight as it was, belonged to the drum-braked car. This was pretty nominal — only four feet — and would probably disappear after several runs when the fade resistance of the discs came into play. For the one, desperate stop that saves your neck, there was little to choose between them, but we still regard disc brakes as a bargain option.

The El Camino gave us one of those moments that makes us wonder about the fine print in our Blue Cross policy. At 30 mph the drums pulled us up nice and straight with the engine still running, though the stop took a half-car length or so more than the SS 396s. On the 60-mph run, however, we thought we'd bought the whole ranch as the light rear end kept trying to pass the heavy front end. Some tip-toeing, worthy of Fred Astaire, kept us from spinning, but each time we tried the brakes again, the back-end locked up and tried to go one way or the other, but not straight. The distance was so ridiculous we didn't even bother to measure, but revived our passenger, screwed our courage to the sticking place, and determined to try it again with even more judicious pressure on the brake pedal. Same game. At such times we wonder if we shouldn't have found a safer occupation — selling "Fiddler on the Roof" albums in Cairo, perhaps. Stopping power was no problem on the trip home from the strip, but we were more than usually alert for perilous situations before we got close to them.

Comfort & Convenience

As already mentioned, riding qualities were better than for any of the other GM products of recent memory. Seating was also excellent both on the bench-seated 325-hp car and the bucket seats of the 375-hp car and El Camino. Comfort was also satisfactory in the back seat, but until more people become educated about using seatback safety latches, access will be a problem.

Though TV commercials tout stainless steel razor blades as "spoilers," cars with adjustable steering columns (fore and aft) and wheel angles have done more to spoil the non-adjustables for us than anything connected with our tonsorial needs. Human beings aren't all built alike (as we are prone to observe at the beach) and the Chevelle steering wheel set-up, while satisfactory for many people, is far from universal. We found that we kept looking for the latch to tip it lower, but there wasn't any.

With less space to heat, it wasn't surprising that the heater in the El Camino was the most effective. In all of the cars we were impressed with the sensitivity of the heater adjustment which made it possible to achieve a comfort level that let us forget that the heater was on until we got out into the cold, cold night.

Luggage space in the SS 396s was plentiful, but much of it is pirated by the spare tire. In the El Camino, the spare is behind the passenger seat, upright, under a boot. Trunk space isn't likely to get bigger, so the more plausible route is for spare tires to get smaller. A collapsible spare such as that used in the Camaro would seem to be in order. Aside from the exposed bed, the only place to safeguard your things in the El Camino is the space behind the driver's seat. It's okay for hiding a camera case or small suitcase, but not much more. In the bucket-seat cars with a console there is a compartment for small objects that is handier

than the glove compartment and about as large. It proved to be more trouble than useful as we often either bumped or rested something on the latch button so that it sprung open.

Best & Worst Features

Power, or the lack of it, is usually the most obvious feature of a car outside of looks, and these Chevelles were no exception. All had bigger engines than the biggest of the Fairlanes tested in the June issue. Even the tamest had nearly as much power as the 335-hp Fairlane GT and one had much more. In all of them something really happens when the loud pedal is applied. The El Camino's Turbo Hydra-Matic was the most impressive transmission with a very reassuring kickdown for passing that could be timed so that it had the car really moving just the instant that we had to commit ourselves to the other side of the road.

All the cars had excellent stopping power, despite adventure with the El Camino which was caused by weight distribution rather than brake efficiency. Given our druthers, though, we would still go along with the discs.

The only better heater or control system we've seen is the automatic Climate Control on the Cadillac Eldorado, but lots of things are very impressive about a car like that, especially the price tag.

Instrumentation left a lot to be desired. The speedometer could stand to be bigger, for example, and the markings were often confusing, especially in the range where 5 mph is liable to make the difference between cruising along and seeing a red light in the rearview mirror. The tach, which was only installed in the hot one, is better located than it was last year — at the left of the dash rather than near your right knee — but Chevrolet had better keep looking. With our hands in the quarter-to-three position, our left fist was in the way, but this was the smallest of our complaints. The tach obscures the gas gauge, which nearly resulted in a very embarrassing moment on the expressway during rush hour. A look at the gas gauge should be accomplished casually, not as a deliberate project as is necessary when it is so hidden. The tach also covers the left turn indicator light, but another is provided on the tach face itself, showing that someone at Chevy is thinking.

We'd have probably enjoyed the 4-speed more if the stick hadn't jammed our thumb against the edge of the seat every time we grabbed 2nd. We finally learned to hold the chrome shift knob differently; however, that shouldn't be necessary.

So if you dig power along with posh you can pay your money and take your choice of the 396 Chevelles. /MT

performance . . .

	SS 396 (325-hp)	SS 396 (375-hp)	El Camino
ACCELERATION (2 aboard):			
0-30 mph (secs.)	3.1	2.4	3.0
0-45 mph (secs.)	5.1	3.9	5.2
0-60 mph (secs.)	7.5	6.5	7.4
0-75 mph (secs.)	10.9	9.6	11.8
¼-mile from rest (secs.) & (mph)	15.9 & 89.5	14.9 & 96.5	15.7 & 90
TIME & DISTANCE TO ATTAIN			
PASSING SPEEDS: 40-60 (secs.) & (feet) 50-70	3.6 & 263.5 3.9 & 343.2	4.0 & 292.8 4.7 & 413.6	4.2 & 307.4 5.0 & 440.0
SPEEDS IN GEARS:			
1st (mph) @ (rpm)	68 @ 5000	50 @ 5000	52 @ 4800
2nd (mph) @ (rpm)		66 @ 5000	88 @ 4800
3rd (mph) @ (rpm)		85 @ 5000	
MPH PER 1000 RPM:	22.7	21.3	25.3
STOPPING DISTANCES:			
From 30 mph (feet)	37	36	44
From 60 mph (feet)	165	169	234
SPEEDOMETER ERROR:			
Calibrated speedometer	30 45 50 60 70 80		
SS 396 (325-hp)	30 45 50 61 71 82		
SS 396 (375-hp)	31 46 50 60 71 82		
El Camino	31 46 51 61 72 82		

specifications . . .

ENGINE:
Bore & Stroke (ins.): 4.094 x 3.76
Displacement (cu. ins.): 396

Horsepower:	325 @ 4800 rpm	375 @ 5200 rpm	325 @ 4800 rpm
Torque (lbs.-ft.):	410 @ 3200 rpm	NA	410 @ 3200 rpm
Compression ratio:	10.25:1	11.0:1	10.25:1
Carburetion:	Rochester 4V	Holley 4V	Rochester 4V
TRANSMISSION:	2-spd. Powerglide	4-spd. all-synchro	3 spd. Turbo Hydra-Matic

FINAL DRIVE
RATIO:	3.07:1	3.73:1	2.73:1

STEERING:
Type: Semi-reversible, re-circulating ball & nut, power assisted
Turning dia., curb-to-curb: 40.3
Turns lock-to-lock: 3.98

WHEELS:
Type: Short spoke disc
Size:	14 x 6JK	14 x 6JK	14 x 5J

TIRES:
Type:	Nylon Wide Ovals	Nylon Wide Ovals	Rayon 2-ply 4PR
Size:	F70-14	F70-14	7.75 x 14

BRAKES:
Type:	Duo-Servo hydraulic self-adjusting, power-assisted	Disc front, drum rear, power-assisted	Duo-Servo hydraulic self-adjusting, power-assisted
Front dia. (ins):	9.5	11.375	9.5
Rear dia. (ins):	9.5	9.5	9.5
Effective lining area (sq. ins.):	168.9	235.5	168.9

FUEL CAPACITY:
(gals.): 20
MILEAGE RANGE (mpg):	11.2-17.8	8.8-13.0	12.5-19.0
USABLE TRUNK CAPACITY (cu. ft.):	17.1	17.1	—

WHEELBASE (ins.): 115.0
FRONT TRACK (ins.): 58.0
REAR TRACK (ins.): 58.0
LENGTH (ins.):	197.0	197.0	199.9
WIDTH (ins.): 75.0
HEIGHT (ins.):	51.9	51.9	54.6

SUSPENSION: Independent front with coil springs. One piece rear axle with longitudinal leaf springs.
BODY & FRAME: All welded perimeter frame.

prices and accessories . . .

MANUFACTURER'S SUGGESTED RETAIL: (includes federal excise tax, but excludes state and local taxes, license, options, accessories, and transportation) Chevelle SS 396 2-door hardtop: $2875. El Camino Custom V-8: $2615.

OPTIONS & ACCESSORIES	SS 396	El Camino
396-cu.-in., 325-hp V-8 engine	std.	182.95
396-cu.-in., 350-hp V-8 engine	105.35	290.55
396-cu.-in., 375-hp V-8 engine	475.80*	
Powerglide automatic transmission	115.90	194.85
Turbo Hydra-Matic	231.35	231.35
4-speed manual transmission	105.35	184.35
F70-14 Wide Oval tires	std.	64.10
Power steering	84.30	86.10
Power brakes	42.15	43.05
Disc brakes	79.00	80.70
Positraction differential	42.15	43.05
Bucket Seats	113.00	113.00
Radio AM	57.40	58.65
Air conditioning	356.00	363.70

*Total cost of parts to convert 350-hp engine.

SS 396 CHEVELLE

Can a beautiful 375-hp street performer find happiness on the drag strip? Well now, that all depends...

BY JOHN RAFFA

As THE LIGHTS come down, you squeeze the engine towards six grand, slide your left foot off the clutch, stab the loud pedal between the last yellow and the green, and *bang!* — 375 horses (a 425 Performance Rating via NHRA's new system) launch you off the line for a near record run. Right? Wrong! At least that's the way it was on every run we made with this month's drag test vehicle, a '68 Chevrolet SS 396 Chevelle hardtop. Oh, the horses are there, all right (just witness that "drive-in idle" of the L-78 engine option), but somebody back in Detroit forgot to couple 'em up to the drive train in the properly prescribed quarter-mile manner; so, instead of a clean break away from the line and solid punch from the green on, we got a big jump, then a letdown — like "Bog City." But don't despair, 'cause once you get the gears you're going to need in this model, you'll have a bear on your hands! ☐ Let's get back out of the driver's seat for a second and take a look around the '68 Chevelle, then come back to the gearing problems. The wheelbase on our coupe is 112 inches, actually down three inches from last year's 115 (overall length remains 197 inches, however), but the all-new body will fool you — it *looks* like a bigger car than the '67. We suspect that much of the illusion of growth comes from the rakish fastback rear roofline treatment; it gives the car a very massive and impressive look. The silver blue exterior finish on our car was excellent and nicely complemented by the all-black interior motif. Opening and closing of the doors gave us the nice solid sound and feel too often lacking in much of today's "Detroit Iron" and made us wonder a bit about the weight of the car. A preliminary check with the AMA spec book told us that our model SS 396 carried a shipping weight of 3550 pounds, a bit heavier than we'd supposed, even with the power brakes and steering options our "guinea pig" had. Next, we wanted to know where the Chevelle fit into NHRA's 1968 plans, so we put in a call to NHRA headquarters. Since our test car was equipped with a pair of Casler eight-inch slicks (not the "cheater" variety), the car as tested would have to be placed in the Super Stock

Photos by Dick Scritchfield

brackets. NHRA informed us that our car, with slicks, would run in SS/D, while it would fall into A/S if prepared for the Stock classes. (NHRA's 1968 rule book classifies Stocks, Super Stocks and Sports cars via the aforementioned Performance Rating method, not ac- cording to weight and advertised horse- power figures as in the past.) The old SS/D e.t. record was held by Wally Booth's outstanding Camaro at 11.70, but a more meaningful figure for our purposes is the old SS/E record, since its factor figures are much closer to the '68 SS/D class than were the old SS/D marks. Another Camaro, that of Volpe- Pizzi-Rose of Philadelphia, held that record at the end of the '67 season at 11.98. (Due to the gearing in our test car, all quarter-mile trial runs were made in the first three gears only;

therefore, any comparison of top end figures on the test car with the listed standards would be meaningless. Top speeds for our Irwindale Raceway trials were in the 102-104 mph category *in third gear*.)

Okay, let's climb back in and take a look around. The thing that pleased us most after getting situated behind the wheel was the vision — forward, to the rear and to the sides. It's superb — no unexpected protruberances jumped at you from the dash or windshield, and glare was at a minimum.

Seat belts fastened? Okay, crank it up! Plenty of guts there (once we carefully slipped our fingers around the key recess in front of us — no mean feat if you've got "fat fingers") — with the idle at about a grand. The new tach may take a little getting used to, but we think it's a real winner. The tach "face" is printed vertically in 500 rpm increments from zero to 7000 (yellow line at 5800, red at 6,000), and the horizontal needle moves vertically from bottom to top as you rev the engine. We found it quite legible in its position directly in our line of sight, and not in any way obtrusive.

On the first run, I took it to 4800 and popped the clutch. Immediately, it felt great, torquing the rear slightly to the right. Just as I corrected for the torque, however, the bog came. The tach needle dipped deeply, then began to climb

slowly back toward the top of the dial. I shifted easily into second and let the tach needle run into the yellow, shifted to third and saw the traps beginning to approach. Just as I was thinking about going for high gear, I cleared the traps, wondering at this point just what kind of cross-country number I had in the rear. Later inspection at the nearest Chevrolet agency revealed that we'd been testing with a 3.08 gear in the Salisbury rear! No wonder we had that bog off the line and a seemingly interminable wait between gear changes.

I planned my "attack" a little differently for the next run. Taking the tach all the way into the yellow zone, I popped the clutch hard and hoped the bog would be overcome. No dice. Casler's tires were just too much for that blankety-blank gear in the rear, so it was bog time again. I let the needle go all the way to the red line, set for my best Ronnie Sox-type "git a hat" shift and banged hard. Nothing. The shift hung between first and second, in neutral. I had to get almost all the way off the power before I could make the shift. Second to third met with a little less resistance with the power shift method, but it was still there — definitely. Through the traps and back to the line again. This time I came off again in the six grand neighborhood, waited out the bog and shifted a lot easier — kind of a compromise between

my version of the Sox "explosion shift" and your grandmother's handling of the same apparatus. I got second this time, but not without a lot of effort spent. Third came quite easily using this method and the Chevelle's time felt fairly respectable making it through the traps (still in third).

Checking with Steve Gibbs, track manager at Irwindale, who'd been recording the times in the tower, I found the clockings on the three runs read 14.32, 14.27 and 14.02, respectively. We were a bit disappointed, especially when compared to the '67 SS/E record of 11.98, but upon reflection and weighing all factors involved, they don't seem really bad at all. First, consider our "big hangup" — the one between gear changes. Now, when you first look at the Chevy shifting mechanism in this year's four-speed models, you get a very confident feeling. Nestled there between the seats is a most familiar looking sight — the flat handle that has come to mean "Hurst" in the minds of most do-it-yourself drivers. There's even the familiar block lettering on the handle, only here it spells "Muncie." Too bad. But a handle only controls the action, so we had to look a little further. Let's glance under the floor. Gadzooks, zounds, and holy mackerel, Andy! Look at *that* action. What we'd found was one of the wildest mazes of linkage it

CONTINUED ON PAGE 91

ABOVE—*Factory rear suspension does great job of preventing rearend windup and keeps power going to the ground.*
RIGHT — *Tie to crossmember dampens road noise effectively, but raises havoc with quarter-mile shifting tactics.*

ABOVE — *Casler slicks did great job of launching 396's 375 horses off the line, but 3.08 "bog" gear pulled rpm way down just off line.*
RIGHT — *Full power was delivered after disconnecting smog devices (visible above headers) and installing a set of tubular Hooker headers.*

CHEVELLE MALIBU 327

A careful combination of options
adds up to an unusually satisfactory car

WE BECAME INTERESTED in this Chevelle Malibu because the engineering editor went to Palm Springs in it one day. Riding with his opposite number from *Car Life* over California 74, a pleasant back road that crosses some good back country, then winds down through the Santa Rosa mountains to reach Palm Springs by the back door, so to speak, he was impressed by the low noise level, comfortable ride, good performance characteristics, lack of tire squeal and absence of body roll. On the return trip, the e.e. drove it himself, hard, and was sufficiently impressed to suggest a road test, saying it was a car that *Road & Track* readers should know about. The rest of us were skeptical but once we'd tried it, we too couldn't help being impressed. For a reasonably unpretentious American car—no high-pressure promises of sports car handling or sly suggestions of eternal virility—it's not bad at all. What it does is what it's supposed to do and if that weren't so unusual in a typical Detroit-built sedan, it wouldn't be worth mentioning at all.

First, let's see what it is. It's a Chevelle, which is one of the six lines built by Chevrolet, and this particular model package is known as the Malibu 2-door sports coupe. It's what you might call a light heavyweight, in the Detroit sense, as it has a wheelbase of 112 in., an overall length of 197 and a curb weight of 3590 lb. In many ways, it's a typical product of the system. For example, it starts with a low basic list price and everything you really want on it costs extra. The basic, stripped Malibu with 6-cyl engine and 3-speed manual gearbox lists at less than $2800. But the "as tested" price of our car equipped as it was (275-bhp 327-cu-in V-8 engine, Powerglide, disc brakes in front, power steering, power

brakes, air conditioning, radio, wide tires and wheels, etc., etc.) added up to a nice fat $3992. And it is possible to go even further with such things as 396-cu-in engines and push the price tag well over $4000.

Where our Malibu wasn't typical was in balance. It seemed to have exactly the right assortment of options. The 327-cu-in, 275-bhp V-8 engine seemed altogether appropriate to the car; handled its weight and bulk without sweat or strain and yet didn't overpower everything else the way the 396-cu-in engine did in another Malibu we tried. This 327 engine is one of the two oldest V-8 designs still in production in the U.S. It's still smoother and quieter than anything the competition offers in the same bracket and now they've even been able to control its emissions (with automatic transmission) without using the infamous smog pump. With the 327 in the Malibu, you get the 2-speed Powerglide automatic transmission and Chevrolet must be nearly alone in using a

ROAD & TRACK ROAD TEST

CHEVELLE MALIBU 327
AT A GLANCE

Price as tested	$3992
Engine	ohv V-8, 5356 cc, 275 bhp
Curb weight, lb	3590
Top speed, mph	115
Acceleration, 0–¼ mi, sec	17.1
Average fuel consumption, mpg	12.2

Summary: Excessively large but handles and rides very well . . . smooth, quiet and effortless performance . . . could use 3-speed transmission . . . disc brakes need better proportioning.

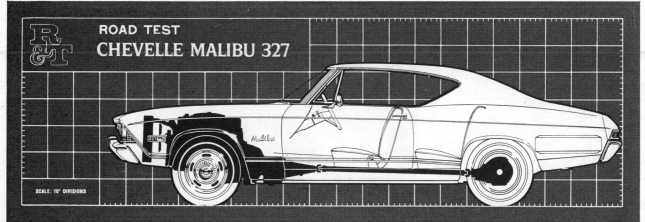

SCALE: 10" DIVISIONS

PRICE

Basic list.................$2788
As tested.................$3992

ENGINE

Type.......,.........ohv V-8
Bore x stroke, mm....101.6 x 82.6
    Equivalent in.......4.00 x 3.25
Displacement, cc/cu in..5356/327
Compression ratio.........10.0:1
Bhp @ rpm.........275 @ 4800
    Equivalent mph...........104
Torque @ rpm, lb-ft..355 @ 3200
    Equivalent mph............69
Carburetion.....one 4V Rochester
Type fuel required......premium

DRIVE TRAIN

Transmission: Powerglide auto-
    matic (torque converter with 2-
    speed planetary gearbox)
Gear ratios: D (1.00)......3.36:1
    L (1.76)..............5.91:1
    L (2.1 x 1.76)........12.41:1
Final drive ratio.........3.36:1
Optional ratios....2.73 to 4.88:1

CHASSIS & BODY

Body/frame...........perimeter
    frame, separate steel body.
Brake type: 11.0 vented disc
    front/9.5 x 2.0 drum-rear;
    power assisted.
    Swept area, sq in.........332
Wheel steel disc,.......14 x 6JK
Tires...........Firestone F70-14
Steering type.........power
    Overall ratio...........20.4:1
    Turns, lock-to-lock.........4.0
    Turning circle, ft........39.4
Front suspension: unequal-length
    A-arms, coil springs, tube
    shocks, anti-roll bar.
Rear suspension: live axle with
    trailing arms, upper control
    arms, coil springs, tube shocks.

OPTIONAL EQUIPMENT

Included in "as tested" price: 275-
    bhp V-8 engine, automatic
    transmission, power steering,
    power brakes, front disc brakes,
    wide tires, whitewalls, radio, air
    conditioning, numerous trim
    items, "handling" package.
Other: typical wide range of engine
    options from 140 to 415 bhp plus
    attendant drivetrain choices.

ACCOMMODATION

Seating capacity, persons.......6
Seat width, front/rear...51.5/53.5
Head room, front/rear.....41/37
Seat back adjustment, deg......0
Driver comfort rating (scale of 100):
    Driver 69 in. tall...........95
    Driver 72 in. tall...........90
    Driver 75 in. tall...........85

INSTRUMENTATION

Instruments: 120-mph speedome-
    ter, 99,999.9 odometer, fuel
    level.
Warning lights: water temperature,
    oil pressure, ignition, high beam,
    directionals.

MAINTENANCE

Engine oil capacity, qt.........5
    Change interval, mi.......6000
Filter change interval, mi.....6000
Chassis lube interval, mi.....6000
Tire pressures, psi.......22/26

MISCELLANEOUS

Body styles available: 2-door
    coupe (as tested), convertible
    or sedan pickup; 4-door sedan,
    2-door sedan, station wagon.
Warranty period, mo/mi. 60/50,000

GENERAL

Curb weight, lb..........3590
Test weight...............3960
Weight distribution (with
    driver), front/rear, %....56/44
Wheelbase, in............112.0
Track, front/rear......59.0/59.0
Overall length..........196.8
    Width................76.0
    Height...............52.8
Frontal area, sq ft.........22.2
Ground clearance, in.........5.9
Overhang, front/rear...37.5/47.3
Usable trunk space, cu ft.....13.6
Fuel tank capacity, gal........20

CALCULATED DATA

Lb/hp (test wt)..............14.4
Mph/1000 rpm ("D" gear)....20.6
Engine revs/mi (60 mph).....2805
Piston travel, ft/mi........1520
Rpm @ 2500 ft/min.....4610
    Equivalent mph..........100
Cu ft/ton mi..............134
R&T wear index.............44
Brake swept area sq in/ton....178

ROAD TEST RESULTS

ACCELERATION

Time to distance, sec:
0–100 ft................3.7
0–250 ft................6.4
0–500 ft................9.6
0–750 ft...............12.1
0–1000 ft..............14.4
0–1320 ft (¼ mi).........17.1
Speed at end of ¼ mi, mph....82
Time to speed, sec:
0–30 mph................3.9
0–40 mph................5.3
0–50 mph................7.1
0–60 mph................9.3
0–70 mph...............12.3
0–80 mph...............16.2
0–100 mph..............26.6
Passing exposure time, sec:
    To pass car going 50 mph....5.1

FUEL CONSUMPTION

Normal driving, mpg.......11–13
Cruising range, mi.......220–260

SPEEDS IN GEARS

D gear (5300 rpm), mph......115
L (5300).....................65

BRAKES

Panic stop from 80 mph:
    Deceleration, % g..........68
    Control..................poor
Fade test: percent of increase in
    pedal effort required to main-
    tain 50%-g deceleration rate in
    six stops from 60 mph.......43
Parking brake: hold 30% grade. yes
Overall brake rating.........fair

SPEEDOMETER ERROR

30 mph indicated.....actual 29.0
40 mph...............actual 38.8
60 mph...............actual 57.4
80 mph...............actual 77.0
100 mph..............actual 95.6
Odometer, 10.0 mi....actual 9.86

ACCELERATION & COASTING

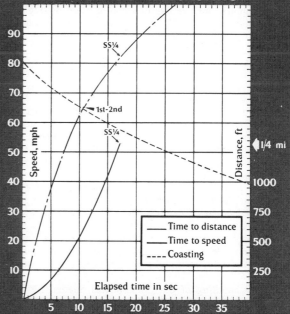

Legend: Time to distance — Time to speed — Coasting

Elapsed time in sec

CHEVELLE MALIBU 327

2-speed automatic. But when you drive it, you understand how they can get away with it—the 327 V-8 is that flexible, quiet and satisfactory.

Most outstanding of all was the level of ride and handling. It had what our local Chevrolet contact man calls the "$4.75 handling package" (Part no. 06F40HH, in case you want it for your Malibu) which results in a combination of ride and handling about equal to that of an Alfa Romeo sedan we drove recently. Really. And it should, actually, as the suspension is very much the same—independent at front and with a live axle with trailing arms, upper control arms, coil springs and tube shocks at the rear. With our 275-bhp combination, the rear axle stayed where it was supposed to and neither hopped nor juddered on hard starts. On a smooth, winding road the tires stay on the ground—not all American cars can make that statement—and it's possible to toss it around corners, twitching the front wheels as needed to catch the slide very much as it's done in the Alfa. Even the power steering isn't bad and though it was a bit lighter than we prefer, some "feel" still does get through to the driver.

Even on poor road surfaces, the handling doesn't deteriorate completely. In fact, compared to the "no-give" springing that comes with most Detroit handling packages, the Malibu is excellent. Rough roads also demonstrated a freedom from rattles that is uncommon if not unique among perimeter-frame designs. The overall shape of the body must be aerodynamically good, too, as the wind noise level is very low.

The good handling of our Malibu was abetted by tires and wheels that are *big*. Mounted on 6-in. rims are wide F70-14 Firestones and these are generously sticky. In spite of these, though, the brakes on our car turned out no better than fair. During our panic stop from 80 mph, a maximum deceleration of 0.68g was all that could be recorded because of rear tire lockup and breakaway. In our 6-stops-from-60 fade test, there was a 43% increase in pedal pressure required to make the final half-g stop. Front discs or not, these are scarcely better than typical American car brakes—that is to say, not really very good—but could be greatly improved by closer attention to proportioning the pressure to the front and rear brakes.

The exterior styling of the Malibu shows why General Motors is the styling leader in the U.S. Without making it look far-out and thereby scaring away the more conservative, there are some fairly bold departures from previous models. GM took the lead in getting rid of the definite separation between upper body and lower body with the introduction of the Toronado; now the current A-body series, which includes the Malibu, is the first to offer this in the medium-price category.

The performance of our test car was what you might call better than adequate for any circumstances. It did 0-60 mph in 9.3 sec, the standing quarter-mi in 17.1, had a top speed of 115 mph and did it all without fuss or bother.

We're almost resigned to such things as minimal instrumentation (not even a resettable trip odometer on a $4000 car!) but there were things that disappointed us. The front bench seat seemed to fall off at the edges and was no better than marginally acceptable for comfort when occupied for more than a few minutes. The entire instrument panel/facia, though padded and round-knobbed, is reminiscent of a plastic toy. And we would feel slightly immoral to drive a "sensible" car—even one costing $4000—and yet only get between 11 and 13 miles per gallon of premium fuel.

What we ultimately concluded about our Chevelle Malibu test car was that it had just exactly the right combination of options to add up to an unusually satisfactory American car. Try one before you sneer.

Sam Posey and the C/D staff
Compare Detroit's 1970 Performance Cars
SS454 CHEVELLE • DUSTER 340
MUSTANG BOSS 302
To The Ultimate of the '60s
SHELBY AC COBRA

Through the windshield the horizon is tilted. Neck muscles strain against G-forces to support the weight of a crash helmet. Senses are bombarded with sounds—the painful scream of tires against asphalt, the belligerent roar of a 289 Ford—and smells; good British leather and traces of gasoline vapor. We are halfway through the Hook, Lime Rock's unforgiving hairpin that is conquered with two carefully chosen apexes or not at all. The black Cobra snorts and bellows against an unseen force as Sam Posey works on the huge wooden steering wheel, correcting minute slides before they become malignant. He shouts over the auditory assault, "No doubt about it, this has the feel of a real racing car—very, very serious."

His description couldn't have been more accurate. The Shelby Cobra was as menacing as its name from the very first. With malice aforethought it attacked and annihilated the Corvettes in SCCA's A/production, and after that taste of blood a coupe-bodied version went on to win its class at Le Mans in 1964. So successful was it as a racer that it was the first car to break Ferrari's hold on the World Manufacturers Championship in the years after that title became based on competition among production automobiles. It is a single purpose car—a powerful, high-winding V-8 in a stark, lightweight English AC chassis—for men who equate truth with speed and agility, and ask for nothing more. Production ceased in 1966 but the Cobra's performance still stands as a high water mark for all to see. It is the yardstick by which all other performance cars must be measured.

Today a yardstick (and a long one at that) is essential if we are to comprehend the improvements Detroit is engineering into its performance cars. The need became obvious this past summer as we previewed the 1970 models. Small cars are being outfitted with big engines—medium-size cars have engines that are enormous. Wheels and tires are now as wide as what you would have found on pure racing cars a few years ago, and truly sophisticated handling packages (many with rear anti-sway bars) are standard equipment. The point was forcefully pounded home at the GM proving grounds when we discovered that a Buick GS455 (of all things), loaded down to 4300 pounds with every conceivable comfort option, would still drive circles around an Opel GT, a "sports car," on the handling course. Detroit is building some very athletic automobiles, not just in acceleration but in handling and braking as well. Urged on by our natural curiosity about the sporting side of these devices we set out to ascertain the state of the art in Detroit.

Thanks to model proliferation, testing every one of Detroit's super cars is out of the question—it would take about five years for the task. Instead, we would take a sample, one car from each of the three distinct performance car categories, and see how they measured up to the Cobra yardstick. Which cars? Well, there had to be an intermediate sedan because that is what Detroit's super cars have been since the beginning. Chevrolet is fixing to sell a 450-horsepower SS454 Chevelle—the highest advertised horsepower rating in all of Detroit—and that is reason enough that it should be in the test. Walter Mackenzie, a gray-haired veteran of Chevrolet's diplomatic corps, was up for the idea as soon as we phoned him. He remembered the Cobra ("You mean that low, skinny, lightweight thing?") and what it had done to the Corvettes and he wanted just one more chance. Production of the 450-hp Chevelle wasn't scheduled until January—but there were engines and there were cars—it was just a matter of putting the two together. Not to worry—there would be an SS454 Chevelle for the test.

Of course, there had to be a sporty car. These scrappy coupes have hyped up the Trans-Am Series popularity to the point where it threatens to eclipse the Can-Am. Deciding on a representative from this class was more difficult. Eventually, all the big engine versions were dismissed in favor of the 5-liter, Trans-Am-inspired models because they specialize in carefully tailored overall performance rather than merely dazzling acceleration. We finally settled on the Boss 302 Mustang for the most straightforward of all reasons—we just like to drive it. We've been enchanted by its capabilities since we drove the first prototype in Dearborn (C/D, June '69) and Brock Yates has proven that a mildly modified Boss can be competitive in SCCA regional racing (C/D, January '69) while still remaining streetable. After all of this favorable experience we wanted to see how an absolutely stock Boss ranked on Cobra yardstick.

That left one category to be filled—a category that we feel is the start of a trend. For a long time we've been questioning Detroit's logic in concentrating its performance efforts on the heavy intermediate-size cars when there were lighter models around which could do the same job but with smaller engines and, ultimately, less expense to the customer. Plymouth's junior Road Runner, the Duster 340, is a giant step in this sensible direction. By including a Duster in the test we could get an early reading on the validity of the concept and perhaps even encourage its growth. But in Detroit our motives were not so transparent. Plymouth felt picked upon. Remembering past C/D comparison tests designed to ferret out the most capable car in a given class, Plymouth figured it had been singled out for the booby prize. "What are you guys trying to do? How can a Duster compete against a 454 Chevelle?" The Cobra was obviously beyond comprehension. "Let us bring a Hemi Cuda. That'll show those bastids." But we finally convinced Plymouth that this wasn't the apples-to-pumpkins comparison test that it appeared to be. In fact, it wasn't a comparison test in the conventional sense at all. Rather, it was to be the definitive statement on the whole range of Detroit performance cars, using as reference what most enthusiasts consider to be the world's fastest production car, the Shelby Cobra.

And, of course, we had to have a Cobra. Because it was the 289 that established the Cobra's all conquering reputation we chose that model. The 427 is faster, to be certain, but in reality it only made the Cobra legend burn a bit more brightly. Besides, classifying the big-engined brute as a production car is something of a dubious practice since only about 200 of them were built.

Cobras are where you find them. Walter Perkins, a bright young engineer with a bumper crop of red hot corpuscles, had a well-oiled 1965 model—bright, shiny, and unmodified—that he figured was more than a match for any Chevelle, 454 or otherwise. We would find out. So would Sam Posey, our consulting arbitrator, who can be counted upon to hand down a decision in effusive pear-shaped tones. Posey is perfect for the job. That he is an intrepid

Front lock-up on the Chevelle makes for a straight, if smokey, stop while rear lock-up aims the Mustang at the guard rail.

competition driver is merely a proven fact, but his ability to drive to the ragged edge in anything with wheels *and* coolly describe its behavior in detail at the same time is a source of wonderment. And no one knows the way around Lime Rock better than he does. Any lingering doubts about that should have been erased by his two professional-series victories there in this past season alone; one in a Shelby-prepared Trans-Am Mustang and the other in his Formula A McLaren-Chevrolet. With this kind of background our 4-car road test couldn't help but be revealing.

A varied group converged at Lime Rock on the appointed day—a handful of escapees from the *C/D* office; Posey and his stopwatch expert, John Whitman; Bill Howell, an engineering wizard from Chevrolet who can always be found stalking around in the pits at Trans-Ams making sure that Chevrolet isn't racing; Don

Wahrman from Ford, one of Jacque Passino's disciples; and a couple of Detroit-owned PR men whose job is always to influence the outcome if possible. Plymouth had planned to send an engineering-type but the one chosen fell off a motorcycle at the last minute and couldn't make it. Perkins and Mrs. Perkins arrived with the Cobra and everything was set.

The cars had arranged themselves as to straight-line performance the day before at New York National. Perkins had kept the Cobra reputation alive by charging his machine through the quarter at 101.58 mph in 13.73 seconds—a scant 0.08 seconds ahead of the Chevelle—proving that there is no substitute for weight distribution. The Chevelle was decidedly more powerful, pushing its 3885-pound bulk through the traps at 103.80 mph, but with 57.1% of its weight on the front wheels it just couldn't quite get a good enough

grip on the asphalt to move out ahead of the Cobra. The big 454 did prove itself however. It is a fairly straightforward derivative of the 435-hp Corvette 427 with a 0.24-inch longer stroke and a single 780 cubic-feet-per-minute Holley 4-bbl. instead of the Corvette's three 2-bbls. Because its solid-lifter valve train is very stable at high engine speeds, Howell felt that 6500 rpm wasn't an unreasonable redline—even though the Chevelle seemed to go just as quickly when shifted at 6000.

Just behind the Cobra and Chevelle in acceleration was the Duster. At 3368 pounds it was the lightest of the Detroit cars—though still 1046 pounds heavier than the Cobra. It also had the best weight distribution of all the Detroit iron with exactly 55% on the front. Its quarter-mile performance of 14.39 seconds at 97.2 was hampered by a balky shift mechanism but, even so, the Duster speaks well for the compact super car concept.

The Mustang turned out to be a disappointment. It was only a bit heavier than the Duster, 3415 pounds with a full tank, but it was significantly less powerful, something we hadn't expected from an engine that was developed specifically for racing. When our best efforts were no better than 14.93 seconds at 93.45 mph we asked Wahrman to try, just to see if the factory knew something about driving Boss 302s that we didn't. In the best drag racer, gas-pedal-flat-to-the-floor tradition, he made two runs but neither bettered the Mustang's standings. The real point to be made here is that small displacement, high specific output engines suffer mightily in passing the exhaust emission and exhaust noise standards. Now that the SCCA allows production engines to be destroked down to the 5-liter maximum for the Trans-Am, the high performance 302s will soon disappear as a production option. In fact, the Boss 302 is the only one left right now.

That the acceleration portion of the test was out of the way meant that we had the whole day to evaluate handling and breaking at Lime Rock with Posey. Braking distances and cornering speeds would be measured, and to understand the behavior of each car as it approached the limit, one of the staff would ride along on all but the fastest laps to record Posey's observations. In the lead-off spot was the Chevelle.

We could have predicted Posey's first comment, which came within 100 feet after pulling onto the track.

"Oh, look at that little louver. Whenever I accelerate a little trapdoor on the hood opens."

It is a great piece of entertainment. With the "Cowl Induction" option, Chevrolet's version of a hood scoop, a little backwards-facing hatch at the rear of the hood opens whenever manifold vacuum drops below a predetermined value. In goes cold air and up goes horsepower or something like that. But Posey's next observation was far more serious.

"The rear view mirror is placed exactly where I want to look for a right turn. I have to scrunch down if I want to see."

This has been a problem in many Detroit cars since the federal safety standards requiring larger rear view mirrors went into effect. Now you have a blind spot in front instead of behind, which is a most unsatisfactory trade-out. And there were more comments about the interior.

"The driving position is really quite good but I can't brace my knees against the side panel—it is too far away. I just have to hold on to the steering wheel."

The observations continued in a calm, analytic flow, but there was absolutely nothing calm about what he was doing with the Chevelle. Three-digit numbers on the speedometer, airborne over the brow of the hill, 6000 rpm on the tach— the straights were now brief bursts of

SHELBY AC COBRA

Price as tested: $6167.00

Options on test car: dress-up group, $172.00 (price does not include chrome wire wheels or hardtop).

ENGINE
Bore x stroke.................4.00 x 2.87 in
Displacement.....................289 cu in
Compression ratio...............10.5 to one
Carburetion.................1 x 4-bbl Autolite
Power (SAE)...........271 hp @ 6000 rpm
Torque (SAE).......312 lbs-ft @ 3400 rpm

DRIVE TRAIN
Final drive ratio...................3.77 to one

DIMENSIONS AND CAPACITIES
Wheelbase........................90.0 in
Track...........F: 51.5 in, R: 52.5 in
Length..........................151.5 in
Width.............................61.0 in
Height............................49.0 in
Curb weight.....................2322 lbs
Weight distribution, F/R.........48.5/51.5%

SUSPENSION
F: Ind., lower wishbones, upper transverse leaf spring
R: Ind., lower wishbones, upper transverse leaf spring

STEERING
Type....................Rack and pinion
Turns lock-to-lock.....................2.75
Turning circle.....................34.0 ft

BRAKES
F:.........................11.6-in disc
R:.........................10.8-in disc

WHEELS AND TIRES
Wheel size........................15 x 6.0-in
Tire make and size.........Goodyear F70-15, polyester
Test inflation pressure....F: 30 psi, R: 30 psi

PERFORMANCE
Zero to	Seconds
40 mph	2.7
60 mph	5.2
80 mph	8.5
100 mph	13.4

Standing ¼-mile.....13.73 sec @ 101.58 mph
80–0 mph panic stop..........256 ft (0.84 G)

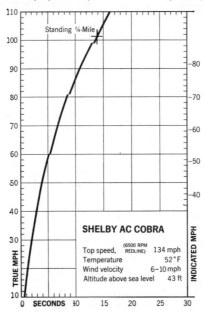

SHELBY AC COBRA

Top speed, (6500 RPM REDLINE) 134 mph
Temperature 52°F
Wind velocity 6–10 mph
Altitude above sea level 43 ft

MUSTANG BOSS 302

Price as tested: $4318.45

Options on test car: fastback coupe with Boss package (includes: 290-hp engine, bucket seats, 4-speed transmission, front disc brakes, racing mirrors, collapsible spare, quick-ratio steering, competition suspension, front spoiler, carpets, gauges, fiberglass belted tires), $3720.00; rear spoiler, $20.00; limited-slip differential, $43.00; 3.91 rear axle, $13.00; convenience check group, $32.00; sport slats, $65.00; AM/FM stereo radio, $214.00; decor group, $78.00; tinted glass, $32.00; deluxe belts, $15.00; HD battery, $13.00; tachometer $54.00.

ENGINE
Bore x stroke....................4.00 x 3.00 in
Displacement.....................302 cu in
Compression ratio...............10.6 to one
Carburetion...........1 x 4-bbl Holley
Power (SAE)...........290 hp @ 5800 rpm
Torque (SAE)..........290 lbs-ft @ 4300 rpm

DRIVE TRAIN
Final drive ratio...................3.91 to one

DIMENSIONS AND CAPACITIES
Wheelbase.......................108.0 in
Track............F: 59.5 in, R: 59.5 in
Length..........................187.4 in
Width.............................71.7 in
Height............................50.2 in
Curb weight.....................3415 lbs
Weight distribution, F/R.........55.9/44.1%

SUSPENSION
F: Ind., unequal-length control arms, coil springs, anti-sway bar
R: Rigid axle, semi-elliptic leaf springs, anti-sway bar

STEERING
Type....................Recirculating ball
Turns lock-to-lock.....................3.6
Turning circle...........................38 ft

BRAKES
F:.........11 3 in vented disc, power assist
R:..10.0 x 2.0-in cast iron drum, power assist

WHEELS AND TIRES
Wheel size........................15 x 7.0-in
Tire make and size.........Goodyear F60-15, Polyglass
Test inflation pressure....F: 28 psi, R: 28 psi

PERFORMANCE
Zero to	Seconds
40 mph	3.3
60 mph	6.5
80 mph	11.1
100 mph	17.0

Standing ¼-mile......14.93 sec @ 93.45 mph
80–0 mph panic stop..........296 ft (0.72 G)

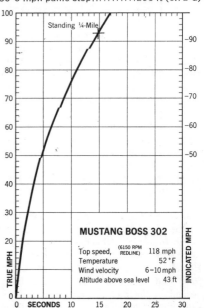

MUSTANG BOSS 302

Top speed, (6150 RPM REDLINE) 118 mph
Temperature 52°F
Wind velocity 6–10 mph
Altitude above sea level 43 ft

CHEVELLE SS454

Price as tested: $4470.05

Options on test car: Chevelle coupe, $2809.00; SS package $445.55; 450-hp engine, $263.30; automatic transmission, $290.40; power steering, $105.35; bucket seats, $121.15; deluxe belts, $12.15; floor mats, $11.60; door edge guards, $4.25; vinyl roof, $94.80, console, $53.75; visor vanity mirror, $3.20; cushioned rim steering wheel, $34.80; AM/FM radio, $133.80; rear speaker, $13.20; bumper guards, $15.80, clock, $15.80; limited-slip differential, $42.15.

ENGINE
Bore x stroke....................4.25 x 4.00 in
Displacement........................454 cu in
Compression ratio..............11.0 to one
Carburetion........1 x 4-bbl Holley, 780 cfm
Power (SAE)..........450 hp @ 5200 rpm
Torque (SAE)........500 lbs-ft @ 3600 rpm

DRIVE TRAIN
Final drive ratio.....................3.70 to one

DIMENSIONS AND CAPACITIES
Wheelbase...........................112.0 in
Track................F: 60.0 in, R: 59.8 in
Length...............................197.2 in
Width...................................75.4 in
Height..................................56.2 in
Curb weight........................3885 lbs
Weight distribution, F/R..........57.1/42.9%

SUSPENSION
F: Ind., unequal-length control arms, coil springs, anti-sway bar
R: Rigid axle, trailing arms, coil springs, anti-sway bar

STEERING
Type..........Recirculating ball, power assist
Turns lock-to-lock............................2.9
Turning circle.........................42.0 ft

BRAKES
F:............11.0-in vented disc, power assist
R:....9.5 x 2.2-in cast iron drum, power assist

WHEELS AND TIRES
Wheel size........................14 x 7.0-in
Tire make and size.........Goodyear F70-14, polyester
Test inflation pressure....F: 35 psi, R: 35 psi

PERFORMANCE
Zero to	Seconds
40 mph	2.9
60 mph	5.4
80 mph	8.7
100 mph	13.0

Standing ¼-mile....13.81 sec @ 103.80 mph
80–0 mph panic stop..........272 ft (0.79 G)

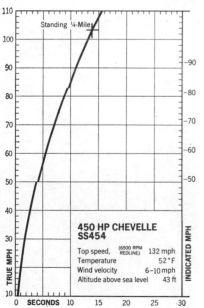

450 HP CHEVELLE SS454

Top speed, (6500 RPM REDLINE)	132 mph
Temperature	52°F
Wind velocity	6–10 mph
Altitude above sea level	43 ft

VALIANT DUSTER 340

Price as tested: $3455.70

Options on test car: Duster 340, $2547.00; bucket seats, $112.60; light package, $29.60; basic group, $82.60; decor group, $23.90; deluxe seat belts, $13.75; 4-speed transmission, $187.90; limited-slip differential, $42.35; special paint, $14.05; 50-amp alternator, $11.00; 59-amp battery, $12.95; tinted windshield, $20.40; day-night mirror, $7.10; dual horns, $5.15; pedal dress up, $5.45; undercoat, $16.60; door edge molding, $4.65; custom sill, $13.15; wheel lip molding, $7.60; belt molding, $13.60; bumper guards, $23.80; tach, $50.15; power steering, $85.15; vinyl roof, $83.95; vinyl side molding, $14.80; E70 tires, $26.45.

ENGINE
Bore x stroke....................4.04 x 3.31 in
Displacement........................340 cu in
Compression ratio..............10.5 to one
Carburetion...............1 x 4-bbl Carter AVS
Power (SAE)..........275 hp @ 5000 rpm
Torque (SAE)........340 lbs-ft @ 3200 rpm

DRIVE TRAIN
Final drive ratio.....................3.91 to one

DIMENSIONS AND CAPACITIES
Wheelbase...........................108.0 in
Track................F: 57.7 in, R: 55.6 in
Length...............................188.4 in
Width...................................71.6 in
Height..................................52.6 in
Curb weight........................3368 lbs
Weight distribution, F/R..........55.0/45.0%

SUSPENSION
F: Ind., unequal-length control arms, torsion bars, anti-sway bar
R: Rigid axle, semi-elliptic leaf springs

STEERING
Type..........Recirculating ball, power assist
Turns lock-to-lock............................3.6
Turning circle.........................41.0 ft

BRAKES
F:............10.8-in vented disc, power assist
R:....10.0 x 1.8-in cast iron drum, power assist

WHEELS AND TIRES
Wheel size........................14 x 5.5-in
Tire make and size.........Goodyear E70-14
Test inflation pressure....F: 35 psi, R: 35psi

PERFORMANCE
Zero to	Seconds
40 mph	3.0
60 mph	5.9
80 mph	9.9
100 mph	15.1

Standing ¼-mile........14.39 sec @ 97.2 mph
80–0 mph panic stop..........287 ft (0.74 G)

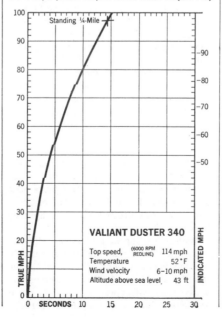

VALIANT DUSTER 340

Top speed, (6000 RPM REDLINE)	114 mph
Temperature	52°F
Wind velocity	6–10 mph
Altitude above sea level	43 ft

---

wide-open throttle and the curves abrupt changes of heading.

"The brakes are good for only about two laps and then they begin to fade. While they're working they are predictable, though. The biggest problem is the abrupt downshifts in the automatic transmission which breaks the tires loose and throws the rear end out. To get good control I have to shift manually at some point where I can stand a little twitch."

When it came to getting around corners the Chevelle proved to be quite agile in Posey's hands.

"The engineers who did this thing understand their problem—all that weight up front—and I think they've coped very well. The track is rough and the bumps are not throwing it off badly. It understeers but the understeer kind of cancels out the bumps. When the front tires are at the limit the rears aren't working so hard, just enough so they get some power to the ground and contend with the bumps too. Now, if we were teetering through these corners in an oversteer posture the car would be very sensitive to them."

From the lap times it was obvious that he was getting along well with the Chevelle. Already he was down to 1:10:4, which is a very good time for a street car. How would the other super car, the Duster, do? It was time to find out.

"For a gearshift here, hell, it looks like a stick for pole vaulting. And the funny little round knob. I don't know why they tried to make it look like wood. It is one of the most conspicuously fake things I've ever set my eyes on. Look at the little tach. It's tiny. I do like looking out over the orange hood though—gives me just a hint of being a McLaren driver. I'm a little apprehensive about all of this noise. We are going to have to shout."

After the smooth, quiet Chevelle the Duster was a vivid contrast. It rattled and buzzed at anything approaching speed and just generally broadcasted the same vibrance that made the Model A Ford seem so sophisticated in its day. As he started to work on faster lap times Posey wasn't optimistic.

"The power steering has nowhere near the road feel of the Chevelle and the car is not reacting well to the Gs. The suspension doesn't feel like the final solution. I don't detect the subtle hand of Colin Chapman in the geometry. What's happening is that as the body rolls in the turns it uses up all of the suspension travel and comes right in solid against the rubber bumpers. At that instant the weight transfer is complete on that wheel and the tire takes a terrible beating."

And, all the while the poor confused little Duster is being hurled around the track in a fashion it never dreamed possible. Through the Hook and into the Esses, tail out, tires howling and the lion-hearted 340 moaning spasmodically as Sam played the throttle for just the right amount of torque.

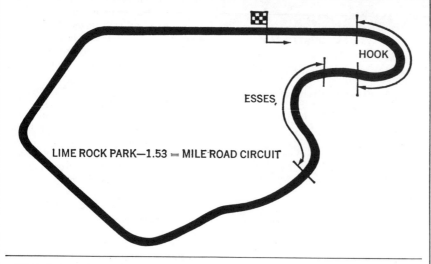

CORNERING CAPABILITY				
	Cobra	Chevelle	Mustang	Duster
Average speed through HOOK	67.5 mph	66.0 mph	64.6 mph	63.9 mph
Average speed through ESSES	63.8 mph	61.4 mph	61.1 mph	60.2 mph

HOOK

ESSES

LIME ROCK PARK—1.53 = MILE ROAD CIRCUIT

"It is both understeering and oversteering simultaneously, which is to say that it's sliding right off the road. The carburetor isn't helping either. It cuts out at the most inopportune times. Also, I'm having a lot of trouble with the shift, particularly into third."

The shifter problem is unfortunate. Chrysler buys the Hurst linkage, but because of confusion on the part of the executives as to which is most important, a solid, dependable shift or total absence of noise, the engineers are forced to rubber isolate the shifting mechanism to the point where its usefulness in changing gears is merely coincidental. And the tall lever contributes its share to the confusion by making the throw unreasonably long. Even though the Duster was having its problems Sam wasn't ready to give up.

"Notice that the tires are leaving black marks in the turns which suggests that they need more pressure."

With a best lap of 1:13:95 the Duster didn't appear to be much of a threat to the Cobra. Still, with more air in the tires it figured to improve. As the pressures were being raised from 30 to 35 psi we went on to the Mustang.

"The instruments may be at the end of the Holland Tunnel down there. They are big enough but still difficult to read because of the complex markings. The driving position is a bit peculiar. The steering wheel is plenty close but the floor is too far away to brace my left foot satisfactorily. A telescoping steering column would be a good idea. This car has far more lateral support than the others and it feels very solid and secure."

We had been impressed by the same sensation when driving the Mustang on the road. It is quiet and exudes quality, very much like an expensive European GT

car. The stiff suspension and high shock absorber control give it a very purposeful feel, and because the body doesn't quiver or rattle when you hit a bump the overall impression is most satisfying.

"With the manual steering it feels very heavy up front, particularly after the Duster which, although it didn't generate high lateral forces, was very easy to toss around. The steering effort is extremely high—certainly higher than any race car."

Within a few laps the Mustang's virtues and vices, which tend to be extreme, were laid out for inspection.

"The brakes are fabulous. I can go in way deeper before I have to brake with this car than I could with the other cars. And the pedal feel is excellent. Here, I can control the braking with pressure on the pedal where in the other cars the pressure stays about the same and the braking seems to depend on how far down I push the pedal. That is very tricky to do accurately, especially when you are going fast. But boy, does it understeer. Look, you'd think I was going into the pretzel business with my arms. I've got the wheel really cranked over and it just isn't getting the job done. The only way I can get the tail out is to trick it by hitting a bump at just the right time or setting it up with the brakes. Funny, I expect more of this car in handling than it's giving me. And it's busting my hands. Every time we hit a bump in the turns the wheel kicks back so hard that I can hardly hold on to it with my arms crossed up the way they have to be."

With a best lap of 1:12:35 the Mustang had been quicker than the Duster, but only with considerable effort. Once back in the pits the hardships of manual steering and extreme understeer were obvious for all to see. Sam's hands, in the crotch between

the thumb and first finger, were bruised and swollen from being battered by the steering wheel spokes. The front tires hadn't escaped either. The outer tread rib was badly shredded—so bad, in fact, that it looked like the tread might start to peel. This brings up an interesting point about wide tires like the Mustang's F60-15s. Chevrolet is reluctant to use them, particularly on cars like the Chevelle, because the front suspension camber pattern is such that it lifts the inside of the tread patch in hard cornering to the point where the front tires are operating at a disadvantage relative to the rears—which exaggerates understeer. Curiously, the Chevelle wasn't wearing bias-belted tires (which are standard equipment this year) but rather last year's Goodyear bias-ply, polyester cord Wide Tread GTs. As a point of interest, the Cobra and the Chevelle both had exactly the same type of tires.

With the preliminaries out of the way it was time to explore the limits of Detroit performance. The Chevelle was charging around the track, its ears laid back and its hood louver snapped open to battle position. In compliance with California noise laws the exhaust has been restricted to a benevolent rumble, but the air rushing into the carburetor to feed those 454 cubic inches sounded like it was trying to take half the landscape with it. The Chevelle is a big car, enormous on Lime Rock, a tight, twisty, 1.53-mile circuit normally inhabited by Formula Vees and other assorted fruit-cup racers, but it didn't matter. Across the start-finish line at 110 mph, hard on the brakes for the Hook, wheels cocked in for the turn and clipping the infield grass at the apex—it seemed right at home. And it was doing very well, too. With a best lap of 1:08:00 it was the fastest non-race car that Jim Haynes, the track manager, could remember. The cornering speeds were good too—

The "louver," more fun than functional.

COBRA VS. THE 1970'S

66.0 mph through the Hook and 61.4 mph through the Esses, a section with a left/right transition that is difficult for softly sprung passenger cars.

The Duster, now with 35 psi in its tires, began to show a new personality. At the end of the test Posey had revised his earlier opinion.

"Somehow, as the laps went by, this turned out to be the car that was a ball to drive. The steering is very, very light. Tremendous drift angles are possible, as are huge oversteers through the Esses with armloads of opposite lock. The car assumed nutty postures all the way around the course. It seemed to sort of get up on its tiptoes with the body rocking back and forth in a spectacular way and go really fast once I got used to it."

Of course, it still wasn't nearly as quick as the Chevelle, lapping at 1:11:7 and averaging 63.9 mph through the Hook and 60.2 through the Esses. But it was fun —a commodity that Posey didn't find much of in the Mustang.

"With the wide tires and stripes and louvers it looked so exciting in the pits. Perhaps because of my Trans-Am victory here in May with the Shelby car I had such high expectations for this one, but they just dwindled away as the laps went by. All I got out of it was sore hands. I'd rather just stand here and look at it."

At the beginning of the test we expected the Boss 302 to give the Cobra real chase, but with its 1:11:2 lap times it was only slightly quicker than the Duster. Of interest, however, was that its excellent transient handling made it only 0.3 mph slower through the Esses than the Chevelle.

With the Chevelle having established itself as the toughest of the Detroit representatives, the question now was how would it fare against the formidable Cobra. That confrontation could be put off no longer. Posey was already buckling himself into the cockpit.

"The most incredible feeling of immediacy exists in this car. Everything is up close to you. None of the remoteness found in the other cars. There was a feeling, in the others, that you had to penetrate the styling concepts to figure out which controls did what. Everything here is very obvious."

The Cobra is a shockingly single purpose car. No frills, no extra sound deadener, only the implements (tube frame, 4-wheel disc brakes, fully independent suspension) required for rapid transit. The flat instrument panel has simple, round, white-on-black gauges—one to monitor every factor you might need to check, including oil temperature. The external body sheetmetal extends right into the cockpit to form the top of the instrument panel and the windshield clamps down on the cowl, in traditional British sports car fashion, just inches in front of your nose. If there

is any doubt, at a skeletal 2322 pounds stuffed with a 271-hp Ford V-8, the Cobra is the archetypal high performance car.

"Oh, listen to the exhaust. If we were rating these cars on the basis of sound, this one would be the winner. The clutch is a heavy mutha. So is the steering, but it's very direct—much less lock required than in the other cars. And the suspension is very, very stiff. You feel *every* bump. Ah, see how nicely the tail comes out. This car has the feel of a racing car. The others didn't."

Because of its undisguised race car personality Posey adjusted to the Cobra in only a few laps. Partly because of its rearward weight bias—51.5% on the rear wheels—and partly because of its suspension rates, the Cobra was the only one of the cars that oversteered, and he used it to good advantage. In corners the Cobra adopted a curious posture. Because of its equal length arms, the independent suspension cambers the wheels in the same direction as body roll—which is exactly the wrong way. This, combined with the wide swinging tail, would have been humorous, except that the Cobra was ferociously eating up the circuit. Although the brakes began to fade after several laps the Cobra still made its point. With a best lap of 1:06:95 it was quicker than the Chevelle by slightly more than a full second. And, despite its suspension histrionics, the cornering speeds were faster too—by 2.5 mph in the Hook and 2.4 mph in the Esses.

Although lap times are a reliable indicator of a car's balance between handling and useful power, it doesn't tell the whole story about brakes, primarily because you never come to a complete stop on a road course. Fade and controllability of the braking process are measured but stopping ability is not. For that reason, the braking test had some interesting conclusions. The Cobra stopped quickest, requiring 256 feet (0.84G) from 80 mph. It was also the most controllable. The Chevelle was next at 272 feet (0.79G). Although it stopped in a straight line the braking was heavily biased toward the front wheels which meant that, to realize the full potential of the rears, the fronts had to be fully locked up, which will (and did) badly flat-spot the front tires. The Duster stopped in 287 feet (0.74G) with the rears tending to lock slightly before the fronts. The Mustang suffered from extreme rear wheel lock up—something that didn't show up significantly in the road course part of the test because a racing driver always avoids that situation if possible. Rear wheel lock up is a highly unstable situation which causes a car to skid sideways—which happened to the Mustang on one of its stops. Its best stop was 296 feet (0.72G)—an unseeming contrast to its stellar performance on the road course.

A point that Posey feels very strongly about, and so do we, is that controls, like brakes, should be sensitive to effort rather than travel. This problem shows up fre-

quently with the strong power assists that are necessary in Detroit's heavy cars. The Mustang's brakes are very good in this respect while the Chevelle's leave much room for improvement. And somewhat the same problem exists with power steering. The Duster's steering is so highly assisted that you sense the direction of the front wheels, not by feel, but by the position of the steering wheel.

After two solid days of testing we can see that improvement is required before Detroit can knock the Cobra off its "world's fastest car" pedestal—but not nearly as much as you may have thought. Those tweedy-capped purists who have been accusing Detroit's performance cars of being ill-handling hogs capable of little more than straight-line travel have had their legs kicked out from under them by the Chevelle. Naturally, the Chevelle was quicker in the straights, but it also made the fastest cornering speeds—significantly faster than the Boss 302, in fact, which has a reputation for good handling. After the test Posey commented on the Chevelle. "It's typically GM—wouldn't have offended anybody. It's quiet and well behaved—almost innocuous . . . I can't even remember what the dashboard looked like. But it has striking performance that you'd never suspect in traffic."

The Duster, although not the fastest, is certainly the most amusing. It's whimsical and has a kind of disposable air about it. Breaking it would not be a catastrophe— you just won't get your deposit back. For the price it delivers a full measure of performance but it has been badly compromised by confused priorities (the shift linkage) and inept stylists. Not only are the stylists responsible for many unnecessarily cheap looking details in the interior (fake wood knob, for example), but by their decree the Duster has been lowered on its suspension. This little trick for snuggling the Duster down against the ground has left the suspension jounce travel in an impoverished condition, detrimental to both ride and handling. Still, the Duster is a good start toward a compact super car— the basic mechanical parts definitely do the job—and with some work could be every bit as satisfying as the Chevelle.

Most of the Boss 302's problems could be cured by power steering (which is available) and less understeer. After driving the prototype Boss at Dearborn last spring we thought Ford had finally cured the understeer problem but, apparently, we were wrong. With its strong styling and quality feel the Mustang is an appealing road car, but that is quite apart from the implication of "Boss."

For now Perkins can continue along carefree paths, snuffing Corvettes in gymkhanas and autocrosses, confident in the knowledge that his aluminum-bodied Anglo-American hand grenade has got Detroit pretty well covered. But he is definitely not as anxious for the 1971 Chevelle as we are. ●

CHEVELLE SS 396

The best-selling Supercar isn't the quickest. But it looks tough.

And it's kind to women and children.

SEE THAT BRUISER over there, the one with the bulging shoulders, broken nose and HARD LUCK tattooed on his knuckles? He's a devoted family man, brings home puppies he finds abandoned in the road and has a glass jaw. But he looks so mean, when he talks, people listen.

As the politician-peddlers say, it isn't what you are, it's what projects.

The Chevelle SuperSport 396 projects. While Ford rules NASCAR and Plymouth concentrates on the drags, the Chevelle moves out of showrooms everywhere.

It always has, and it will in 1970. Chevelles have new outer body panels, only mildly changed from last year, and the SS396 has become almost a separate model. Distinct grille, stripes and bulging hood. While its rivals have trick heads, triple carbs or just huge engines, SuperSport greets the new model year with the good ol' 396. (The 454 will be along later, in one

of Chevrolet's confusing marketing tangles, but we'll hear about that in a while.)

The SS396 is a complete bill of fare. Chevrolet invented the cafeteria system, where the customer meandered down the line, picking an engine, a suspension option, brakes, trim, tires, etc. But it confuses the salesmen, or the computer or something, and the factory is edging away: Order the dinner and you get the salad and the vegetables whether you want them or not.

But eat, eat! It's all good. With the SS396 comes what used to be the F-41 suspension; stiffer springs, firmer shocks and a rear anti-roll bar. And power-assisted front disc brakes, 7-in. wheels, and F70 belted-bias tires. Transmissions are either the wide or close-ratio four-speed manual or Turbo Hydra-Matic.

The test car had some other good stuff. Variable-ratio power steering,

and the cold-air scoop, both in the enthusiast vein, and an AM/FM radio because we like music.

Listed on the test car's sticker as an option was the fume control for the gas tank and carburetor. For 1970, California requires that fuel evaporation be controlled. Basically, it's done with one-way air valves and a cannister of charcoal, where the fumes are stored until the engine inhales them. Worthwhile if it helps the smog problem, but next year, everybody pays the $37.

The cold-air scoop looks like the ones on last year's Corvettes and Camaros, but it's not. The emissions controls tightened, remember. When an engine is working, as in full-powered acceleration, it's cleaner than at idle, cruise or deceleration. So Chevrolet heats the air most of the time. The cold air only comes in when the accelerator is floored. The trap door is held shut by engine vacuum. When it drops, the door opens. It probably adds some power, and kids love it. (The Chevrolet people think the Plymouth equivalent, controlled from the dashboard, is too childish for words.)

There's the bulging shoulder and tattoos. The glass jaw is that the SS396 doesn't go very fast. Falls out of the Supercar class, in fact. It's picked up some weight, like it's a 3900-lb. Intermediate, but the SS396 never has been quick in street trim. We tested one in 1968, with performance gearing, four-speed and the 375-bhp version of the 396, and it barely made it into the class. We expressed disappointment then, and sales went up, so we have no qualms about expressing disappointment now.

The 396 is a good engine. The 350-bhp version isn't highly tuned, and it's smooth and all that. Compared to the average car, the test SuperSport is fast, indeed. But it won't keep up with the competition, and the ads say the competition has a hard time keeping up with the SuperSport.

Something of this problem showed up with the transmission. The ideal is stealthy creeps from one gear to the next under light throttle, and instant jolts under power. The test car bumped in town, leading one passenger to remark that it was no better than his Mercedes-Benz. (No comment. We pick on Mercedes-Benz enough as it is.) On the track, it took its own sweet time. Chevrolet pro-grams its transmissions to its engines. Behind the mild 350-cid V-8, the Turbo Hydra-Matics are smooth. Behind the L-88, they slam from gear to gear in sporting fashion. Possibly the transmission behind the SS396 isn't convinced it's supposed to be part of a Supercar.

One change this year, also part of the emissions laws, is a lock-out for the distributor's vacuum advance. It only advances in high gear. If we hadn't read the book, we'd never have known.

Where's the 454? It's out there somewhere, as we've been told by people who learned from Chevy's sales brochures that the engine will be offered later in the year. There was such a car on display at the magazine showings, but between that and our new-car issue, Chevrolet asked us to suppress any mention. You promise to keep the host's secrets or you don't get in the gate, so we kept quiet. So Chevrolet put the secret into the sales pamphlets. Last year the LT-1, this year the LS-5? (That's the option number, in case the salesman has lost his files.)

The handling has the aspect of falling into a time warp. Here you come, into the corner at speed. Crank the wheel, and the front end goes straight, carried away by the weight in front. Just like a 1964 Chevelle. Once enough positive lock is dialed in, the weight of the car transfers to the outside, at both ends. Then the rear bar goes to work. It stiffens the car's roll resistance, and puts more weight on the outside rear, in turn putting the rear into a greater slip angle. Clear? The rear tires are now slipping as much as the front tires, so the car is cornering in a neutral attitude. This is not the way toward quick lap times. The car can be fooled, by entering the turn too fast, and pitching the car into oversteer with wheel and brake. But when the driver wants some understeer so he can apply power, it's all been used up.

Nor is the F-41 as good on the Chevelle as it was on the Chevrolet Caprice. That was a larger, heavier car, with better balance, so it had less initial understeer to overcome. But it's worth having. In town, where the switch from straight to corner isn't so abrupt, there is no feeling of plow. And the ride was comfortable, which wasn't the case with the last SS396, where the handling package was limited to stiffer springs. A limited-slip differential would have been nice, too, for applying power coming out of turns. When you load the outside wheel, you unload the inside wheel, and it spins.

The brakes passed the test before they took it. As you might guess, the brakes were used on the handling circuit. All they got by way of rest was the speedometer calibrations, then they went through the usual sequence of one hard stop from 80, then six ½-G stops, then another full-power stop, measuring distance. The first time, the

UNDERSTEER predominates, even with rear anti-roll bar that comes with the engine.

SS 396
continued

car stopped in 259 feet, which is about 50 better than average. And the eighth stop was in half the distance we've seen in some other cars recently.

The dashboard is the only place Chevrolet hasn't concentrated on image. The standard SS396 doesn't have any gauges except fuel. Makes sense, in that the engine sounds wound up when it is, and warning lights are more apt to be noticed. It's just something we were surprised to see. More to the point, Chevrolet has been using people again when designing the con-

trols. There are makers who don't. Living, breathing people are subjective, and all they can say is, it doesn't feel right, or I can't reach it. And no two people say the same thing. The designers solve this by making dummies in the size and shape of the average person. Then they build the controls to suit that median non-person. Being a dummy, it can't say that the headlight switch is out of reach, or that human ankles don't bend in that dimension. Chevrolet engineers put enough people through the designing process that everything was in the right place.

One tester did wish that the people involved hadn't been quite so taken with lay-down racing seats. Too much backrest rake, he said. The other

testers like plenty of rake.

There was a control problem, created by something odd in the mechanisms supposed to satisfy the anti-theft requirements written into the safety laws. The car had the locking steering column, the buzzer to tell you the key's in the lock, and the requirement that the transmission be in park before key will come out. To be sure the steering doesn't lock while the car is in motion, there are various fail-safes and overrides built in. And one was too cautious. The engine wouldn't shut off with the transmission in park. Turn the key, and nothing happened. That is a helpless feeling, friends, sitting there wondering if theft is being prevented by making it impossible for the owner to leave his car. In desperation, we discovered that you could turn off the engine with the transmission in anything but park. Then the column would lock, and the key would come out. This and other infuriating devices had better be saving countless youths from lives of crime.

Adults can ride in the rear seat, as they should be able to in a car of this size. With the handling package, brakes, etc., the SS396 makes a fine family car. As long as nobody asks it to step outside, the tattoos will mean more than the glass jaw. ∎

1970 CHEVELLE SS396
CHEVROLET

CHASSIS/SUSPENSION
Frame type: Perimeter.
Front suspension type: Independent by s.l.a., coil springs, antiroll bar.
  antiroll bar dia., in.............1.2
Rear suspension type: Live axle, coil springs, control arms, antiroll bar.
Steering system: Integral power assisted recirculating ball.
  overall ratio...........18.6–12.4:1
  turns, lock to lock..............4.0
  turning circle, ft. curb-curb....n.a.
Curb weight, lb.................3990
Test weight.....................4310
Distribution (driver),
  % f/r.....................58/42

ENGINE
Type, no. of cyl.................V-8
Bore x stroke, in.......4.126 x 3.76
Displacement, cu. in............402
Compression ratio..........10.25:1
Fuel required.............premium
Rated bhp @ rpm.......350 @ 5200
  equivalent mph..............115
Rated torque @ rpm....415 @ 3400
  equivalent mph...............75
Carburetion: Rochester 1x4.
  throttle dia., pri./sec.....1.38/2.25
Valve train: Overhead rocker arms, pushrods and hydraulic lifters.
  cam timing
  deg., int./exh........28-78/75-31
  duration, int./exh........286/286
Exhaust system: Dual with resonators.
  pipe dia., exh./tail........2.5/2.0

BRAKES
Type: Power assisted disc/drum.
Front rotor, dia. x width, in....11 x 1
Rear drum, dia. x width....9.5 x 2.25
  total swept area, sq. in......332.4

DIMENSIONS
Wheelbase, in.................112
Track, f/r, in.................59/59
Overall length, in.............197.2
  width....................76
  height....................52.8
Front seat hip room, in.......2 x 24
  shoulder room...............58.3
  head room..................37.7
  pedal-seatback, max..........43
Rear seat hip room, in........57
  shoulder room...............57
  leg room...................32.6
  head room..................36.4
Door opening width, in........42
Trunk liftover height, in......29

PRICES
List, FOB factory............$2709
Equipped as tested..........$4926
Options included: SS396 option, $445; (includes: L34 350-bhp engine, F41 handling pkg., special wheels & tires, special trim); ZL2 hood, $147; power disc brakes; Turbo Hydra-Matic 400, $282; AM/FM; A/C; power steering; power windows.

CAPACITIES
No. of passengers.................5
Luggage space, cu. ft..........n.a.
Fuel tank, gal.................20
Crankcase, qt..................5
Transmission/dif, pt..........8/3.5
Radiator coolant, qt..........19

WHEELS/TIRES
Wheel rim size............14 x 7JK
  bolt no./circle dia. in......5/4.75
Tires: Firestone belted/bias wide oval.
  size....................F70-14

DRIVE TRAIN
Transmission type: 3-speed automatic Turbo Hydra-Matic 400.
Gear ratio 3rd (1.00:1) overall.3.31:1
  2nd (1.48:1).......4.90:1
  1st (2.48:1).......8.21:1
1st x t. c. stall (2.10:1)....17.24:1
  axle ratio.................3.31:1

PEOPLE designed this instrument panel, and everything has been put in the right place. Good for Chevrolet.

BULKY 396 engine is a tight fit. Soft rubber lip atop air cleaner seals against the cold-air trap door in hood.

COLD AIR is controlled by engine vacuum. Cruising, near right, closes the door. Floor the pedal, far right, and the spring-load door pops open.

CAR LIFE ROAD TEST

ACCELERATION (graph)

Vertical axis: MPH — 10, 20, 30, 40, 50, 60, 70, 80, 90, 100, 110, 120
Horizontal axis: ELAPSED TIME IN SECONDS — 5, 10, 15, 20, 25, 30, 35

Labels on curve: QUARTER MILE, 2nd-3rd, 1st-2nd

CALCULATED DATA

Lb./bhp (test weight).........12.3
Cu. ft./ton mile..............1436
Mph/1000 rpm (high gear).....22.2
Engine revs/mile (60 mph).....2700
Piston travel, ft./mile.........1692
CAR LIFE wear index..........45.7

SPEEDOMETER ERROR

Indicated	Actual
30 mph	29.5
40 mph	39.5
50 mph	49.3
60 mph	59.0
70 mph	68.3
80 mph	78.2
90 mph	87.2

MAINTENANCE

Engine oil, miles/days.....6000/240
 oil filter, miles/days....12,000/480
Chassis lubrication, miles...6000/240
Antismog servicing,
 type/miles..........check/12,000
Air cleaner, miles............24,000
Spark plugs: ACR 44T.
 gap, (in.).............0.033-0.038
Basic timing, deg./rpm.........TDC
 max.cent.adv., deg./rpm 21°@2000
 max.vac.adv., deg./in.Hg15°@15.5
Ignition point gap, in...........0.019
 cam dwell angle, deg.......28-30
 arm tension, oz............28-32
Tappet clearance, int./exh..hydraulic
Fuel pressure at idle, psi.........7
Radiator cap relief press., psi......15

PERFORMANCE

Top speed (5600), mph.........124
Test shift points (rpm) @ mph
 2nd to 3rd (5500).............82
 1st to 2nd (5200).............47

ACCELERATION

0-30 mph, sec...................3.3
0-40 mph.......................4.8
0-50 mph.......................6.3
0-60 mph.......................8.1
0-70 mph......................10.3
0-80 mph......................12.8
0-90 mph......................15.9
0-100 mph.....................20.2
Standing ¼-mile, sec..........15.5
 speed at end, mph.........90.42
Passing, 30-70 mph, sec.........7.0

BRAKING

Max. deceleration rate & stopping dist.
 from 80
 rate, ft./sec./sec..............26
 dist. ft.....................259
Rate & distance after 8—½ G stops
 from 80
 rate, ft./sec./sec..............25
 dist. ft.....................397
Overall brake performance...good

FUEL CONSUMPTION

Normal cond., mpg.........13.6

The Businessman'

454 Chevelle

Quite a few words have been written about "supercars" over the last few years, so let's back up a touch and analyze what it means. In 1964, when it all supposedly started (let's say with the GTO), Detroit decided to capitalize on the A/FX popularity by stuffing the largest engine available into an intermediate body and chassis. Add to this combination a four-speed transmission, heavy-duty suspension and miscellaneous cockpit gauges and presto — a production supercar. Frills and total car weight were kept to a minimum and, except for California-destined cars, there were no smog devices or lowered compression ratios to hinder what the car was intended to do — perform.

Where did these supercars come from? Many began life as compacts (you remember them) and grew from there. Today's new "supercars," generally speaking, boast bigger motors, less horsepower and a price comparable to a buck-a-pound and then some. Before you know it, the performance buyer is driving something that externally resembles a supercar but might as well be his folks' four-door freeway flyer. That's exactly what Mr. Businessman is into. On the other side of the fence, but not that far

away, is the pride of Metropolis and his "real" supercar, ready to prove that he can have his cake and beat Mr. Businessman, too.

Mr. Businessman's Chevelle is a great road vehicle, not a supercar, while Superman's Road Runner is something on the order of vice-versa. Originally, we asked Chevrolet for an LS-6 equipped, solid-lifter monster motor nestled in a Chevelle, but certain snafus (in conjunction with the GM autoworkers' strike) forced a change in our plans. What we did receive was a LS-5, 365 horsepower, hydraulic-cammed 454-incher. We also

CONTINUED ON PAGE 82

Rear opening scoop was to be deleted from '71's. Only a select few cars will display "SS 454" insignia as the GM strike will probably allow only a few to be constructed.

Supercar Versus Superman's Supercar

440-Six Pack Roadrunner

If supercars had a rebirth after their original inception with the GTO, it probably started with the Plymouth Road Runner. These automobiles were based on the "cheapo" Belvedere line and hit the 1968 youthful car-buying market like Thor's hammer. The base Road Runner had all the good stuff — a four-barrel carburetor, free flow heads and exhaust system, 383 cubic inch engine and a four-speed transmission, all as standard equipment. Sure, the inside of the thing looked like a taxi cab and the rear windows didn't roll down, but the car was quick and reliable and only cost three grand! For a few hundred dollars more you could even get a monster Hemi motor.

Like most other things, the car evolved. During this period it became more refined and more expensive. It became other things, too. Another engine choice was added; the body was stretched in all directions. It has become the epitome of the "now" supercar, just like the one Superman is brandishing. His has a 440 Six Pack engine, Torqueflite transmission and a 4.10 axle ratio housed in a Dana rearend. The tires on his Road Runner are Goodyear G60's, a full nine in-

ches wide and the largest production car tires in the business. (EDITOR'S NOTE: The fact that Plymouth offers the widest production tire available is yet another indication that this Detroit Division is still THE most tuned-in performance American auto-maker.) Power accessories have been kept to a minimum and include only power steering and power disc brakes.

With these necessary items the Road Runner becomes a very effective handler on the road. The heavy-duty suspension gives hint of the car's size and heaviness (4,020 pounds, gassed up). Our '71 Road Runner was red with

CONTINUED ON PAGE 83

Road Runner's "Air Grabber" added one mile per hour to its quarter mile speed. This is probably the last year to expect the "numbers game" to mean anything.

81

ABOVE — Typical of "smog motors," it's fun changing plugs.

RIGHT — Nice dash layout. Wheel feels good, tach is erratic.

BELOW — Cragar and Chevrolet. What else needs to be said?

CHEVELLE

CONTINUED FROM PAGE 80
ordered a Turbo transmission and 4.10:1 ring and pinion. The Turbo we got; the rearend ratio we didn't (the LS-5 comes only with the 3.31 cog). And, to make matters worse from the performance standpoint, we got all kinds of extra neat things like air conditioning, electric door locks and cruise control.

Our plan was to outfit or order the Chevelle and Road Runner with comparable equipment for the sake of equality. From the start, we knew the Road Runner would champion in the time department, but decided to help the Chevelle as much as possible. Before any hard drag testing began, we upped the seven odometer miles to somewhere around 900. We exchanged the engine's break-in lubricant with five fresh quarts of Valvoline 30W Racing Oil and ran it in Lion's Drag Strip's Sunday class and e.t.-bracket program. The Chevelle fell in AHRA's pure stock D/A and turned a 14.35/97.08, winning a class trophy and then going three rounds in brackets in the process.

From this baseline, we added a Schiefer Trans-Torque 4.10:1 ring and pinion and spacer kit to the 12-bolt differential. The gear installation was done by local Nugent Chevrolet mechanics who are well versed in high performance work. Cyclone Automotive Products helped tap the Chevelle's performance potential by fitting it with equal length headers and complimentary exhaust system. The primary pipes dumped into a 3.5-inch collector, 12 inches long. To complete the unrestricted exhaust network, 2.5-inch head pipes were mated with Cyclone mufflers. Although Cyclone makes headers that can be installed with air conditioning, the job is not a strict bolt-on and being patient helps considerably, to say the least.

Aesthetically, the car was aided by Cragar 7 x 15-inch wheels in front and 8.5 x 15-inchers in the rear. They were the famous "SS" type introduced years ago (but still very popular today) and utilized the new Firestone Wide Oval 60 series rubber. While in Parnelli Jones' Firestone chambers, we spied some 7.00/28.5x14-inch stocker drag tires and had them mounted on 6x14-inch Cragars.

For the remainder of the week the staff enjoyed the comfort of the Chevelle and loved it as a freeway mover and boulevard cruiser. It was unanimously received as about the most pleasant solution to the supercar premise we have encountered. The Cyclone set-up had a beautiful muffled ticking sound and we could immediately see, feel and experience the magical charisma of owning a big-cubic inch headed-equipped supercar. The torque of the great 454 engine even made the 4.10 gear bearable at highway speeds. We noticed above average engine noise (especially for hydraulic lifters) at speeds over sixty, even before the lower gear installation. Perhaps the 3.31:1 gear wasn't such a bad idea after all.

A super-cluttered engine compartment usually means extra pounds over the front wheels and a subsequent detriment to handling. The Chevelle was no exception in the weight department as it weighed in at an alarming 4,007 pounds with a full tank of gas. But handling is helped by front and rear sway bars and the heaviest springs available (because of the air

CONTINUED ON PAGE 84

ABOVE — The MoPar is not as cluttered. Note our neat wiring.

LEFT — Interior is roomy. Good instrumentation, lack of tach.

BELOW — Rocket wheels have 5¼-inch offset and look great.

ROAD RUNNER

CONTINUED FROM PAGE 81
the black strobe stripes that change color with indirect lighting (see October, '70 CC cover) and was outfitted with Rocket wheels at all four corners making it an instant hit with the hamburger clan. The mammoth wheel wells seemed to invite larger tires, but for street purposes the Goodyears were more than adequate. The car drove very nicely, the engine noise was at a minimum and the brakes worked exceptionally well. One thing we noticed was the absence of a tachometer. It probably was better that way since we undershifted the trans, not knowing our rpm.

Shifting. This is a point we ought to dwell on a bit. The Torqueflite in our car shifted as well as any we've seen. Getting it on in drive produced a neck-snapping "chirp" as the transmission shifted from first to second. Our beef is with the Slap Stick shifter. At first we thought it was an overzealous effort on our part when the shifter went from second to reverse at 50 mph during a drag strip time trial. Needless to say, the car stopped

promptly. Feeling not just a little foolish, we tried to find out the problem. The shifter was locked in drive and neutral, preventing any reverse action. A trip to the Plymouth dealer solved our dilemma. We did encounter additional shifting linkage problems, however, which made us wonder if the 2nd to reverse business was all driver error.

The initial outing at Lion's Drag Strip in Long Beach on a Wednesday night proved almost as discouraging as with the Chevelle. The car had unreal bottom end and boiled the hides on every pass. The best we could card was a 14.32/99.66, a good race for the Chevelle. We went home, disgruntled, and checked the car over. The timing was bumped ten degrees for a total of fifteen degrees at the crank. The next step was to make sure the triple carbs were opening correctly. The diaphragm housings on the end two-barrels were inspected for the correct yellow spring as well as venturi bind ("Six Pack for the Road," *Car Craft*, October, 1970). Once satisfied that everything was in order, we packed up and headed for "the Beach" for another session. The first run off

the freeway netted us a 14.19 at 101.01 mph. Things were looking better. A switch under the left side of the dash activated the Air Grabber and it turned out to be good for a full mile an hour. The only major change was in the way the car was being driven. Instead of allowing the Polyglas tires to spin, we would walk the car very slowly out of the gate (as you would when leaving a traffic light on the street), then jump on the throttle about 50 feet off the line. It seemed the slower the Road Runner came out, the quicker it would go. It was getting super-consistent in the low 14.20 range and we decided to call it a night after just a few more passes. Then it started to happen. On the very next run the big Road Runner clipped off an out of nowhere 14.02. We thought it was a bogus time so promptly got back in line in an effort to back it up. The run that followed was even more of a mind boggler as the car legged it to an unbelievable 13.71 at 101.23. Now we really thought we had someone else's time slip. A third back up attempt showed it was no fluke as the Road Runner ran a 13.78/101.46.

CONTINUED ON PAGE 84

conditioning), and considering the amount of weight concentrated over the front wheels the car handled amazingly well. The brakes and suspension were adequate for all but the most violent turns as long as a safe speed margin was retained. The front discs worked well for two or three panic stops, but had a marked propensity to fade after further high speed stops were attempted. What this actually means is that the brakes will give a lot more stopping power than most drivers will ever need.

In 1970, the LS-5 was rated at 360 horsepower with 10.25:1 compression. This year, the engine somehow picked up five ponies but dropped to a 8.5:1 ratio. We couldn't see the reasoning behind this because all other pieces in the '71 engine have been carried over from last year's

Chevelle came out of the gates quickly, fell on its face in high gear. Too bad you can't see the redlight in this photo.

motor. The camshaft specs are the same (also identical to the ones for the discontinued 396/350) and the Rochester Quadrajet carburetor and cast-iron intake manifold are the same. It may be interesting to note that a 1970, 396/350 Chevelle we spotted with exactly the same gear ratio, transmission and street tires as our '71 had before we swapped parts, ran in the low 14.80's. The only difference between the two seemed to be cubic inches. If 58 cubes gets you five-tenths of a second, then the engine can't be all bad.

Since we were testing two vehicles for one article, another strip evaluation was necessary. We headed into it on a pessimistic note, but came away feeling heartened. We discovered another 1970 Chevelle, this one with headers, eight-inch tires and a 3.31 rear axle ratio running consistent 13.60's uncorked. We tried ours with the headers corked-up and street tires, but the strong low end power annihilated the rubber. With a quick change to the Firestone slicks, the Chevelle plunged into the 14.0's. Opening the headers produced a best e.t. of 13.77 with the miles per hour

slightly over 100. The timing was checked and set to stock specifications, the plugs were original and the Quadrajet was left untouched. We wanted to play around with the motor, but all of the plumbing on top made tuning a nightmare. To compound the spark plug and lean carb condition, the 400 Series Turbo Hydro lagged terribly between gear changes, costing us an estimated two-tenths of a second. We were leaving the gate at 1500 rpm and shifting by the (erratic) factory tach at 5500 rpm. The car was capable of putting hole shots on practically every opponent, but died in third gear. This situation was probably caused by lack of jetting in the carb coupled with not being able to do some plain, old fashioned tuning. Here again, the gear change may possibly have worked against us.

Firestone seven-inch slicks worked fine for the automatic cars. They are 28½ inches tall and carried 12 pounds of air.

All the time we thrashed the car, we were trying to rationalize why the Chevelle's straight line performance was so marginal. We became happier people when we stopped our mental gymnastics and decided that the car just didn't make it as a weekend drag racer. However, it *does* come into its own as a personal performance car, if there is such a thing. Its creature comforts included AM/FM stereo, tilt steering wheel, power steering, power disc brakes, electric door locks, cruise control and air conditioning. These niceties make the driver forget all about running down the GTX, GTO or Road Runner and help him concentrate on how much pleasure driving can give. That's why Mr. Businessman digs it. He's still got the supercar image, the muscle "feel" with the Chevelle SS, but with all the comfort of a Monte Carlo. Mr. Businessman, you're smart; but stay in your own league. 🄲

Notice the difference in elapsed times as compared to the top end speeds. The speeds stay pretty much the same yet we managed to pick up over half a second. Once again, it was all in walking the Plymouth out of the gate. We even got to a point where the car would run 13.80's in drive. The only disappointment was in the top end. The Plymouth public relations man said the car should be going in the 102-104 range, but we couldn't figure out why ours didn't. As the car was carted off to Hedman for a set of pipes, we sat down to ponder our final assault on the quarter-mile.

Who needs water for smoky burnout. We boiled the hides with nothing more than Irwindale asphalt. Unreal low end torque.

Hedman returned the Road Runner with their new Hustler model having 1¾-inch primary tubes merging into a 3-inch collector 10½ inches long. An identical pair (to the Chevelle) of Firestone Drag 500's were shod on Rocket 14 X 6-inch wheels and positioned at the rear. A fresh change of plugs (Champion J-12Y) and five quarts of Pennzoil's new 20-40W Racing Oil completed our preparations. For the third time, we trekked to Lion's. The first run was with the headers closed to see how the Firestones would react to the Road Runner's advertised 490 pounds/foot of torque. Bringing the car out at 1800 rpm's and shifting at 5500 (via our newly installed Stewart Warner tach) resulted in a 13.53/103.09. Another run in the same fashion gave us a 13.46 at 103.44. Three-tenths with the slicks and closed headers, not bad. The pipes were uncorked and the tires

SS CHEVELLE

relieved of all but twelve pounds of air. The next three passes resulted in a 13.40, 13.42 and 13.35. The car was really freaky at speed and snaked its way all over the course. We thought it was from the low pressure, narrow rear tires. However, one of the local MoPar bunch told us of the same problem encountered on his Road Runner and explained that it could be cured by clamping the rear spring leaves.

Back in the pits, we tried to squeeze some more top end out of the car. The power steering unit was disconnected and the fuel line was re-routed to bypass the stock fuel filter. This is done because there is a pressure relief built into the filter which returns fuel to the tank. Use ⅜" i.d. tubing and install a high-capacity fuel filter above the fuel pump. The driving technique changed slightly as the car felt best when leaving at an idle and getting in it hard. We upped our shift points to 6000 rpm in second and 5800 in third. This move rewarded us with a 13.29 at 104.16 mph. The last run of the night was the best as we carded a 13.26/104.40. The miles per hour rose slightly, but we had hoped to dip into the twelves. The plugs were pulled and indicated a lean condition. A curved distributor and richer carburetor jetting might well pick up the needed two-tenths or so, but we felt things went pretty good, everything considered.

In summation, one of the really pleasant things that we have to report about the '71 'Bird is that in addition to radically improving the car's exterior styling, we were pleased to find that the design, execution and quality of the Road Runner's interior had improved about 1000%. No more Phillips head screws visually holding this dash together. In the styling and interior respect, the Road Runner seems to be closing on Mr. Businessman's mount.

Several days later, after a photo and burnout session at Irwindale Raceway, we had a chance to receive some impressions of the car as we drove home. In typical Los Angeles bumper-to-bumper traffic, some of our black brethren pulled alongside and came off with such euphemisms as "Outtasite!" "How fast will she go?" etc. etc. One guy in particular, obviously excited, yelled, "That sure is some kinda' bad machine, man." We asked him if he knew what it was and he replied, "Sure, that's a Dodge Road Runner." He may have been mistaken about who made the car, but he was right about the other. It *is* a bad machine!

CONTINUED FROM PAGE 49

was kept on some twisty L. A. County mountain roads. In the first serious encounter, an inordinate amount of tire squeal was produced by the "Tiger-Paws," so we beat it back to the nearest service station to check the air pressure, which turned out to be right on the suggested front specs. But wait—there is a hidden lie in the figures. Recommended settings are always values for cold tires, and as tire heat increases, do does air pressure. We didn't have time to adjust and readjust pressures so we settled on 28 psi (cold) all around.

As anticipated, the SS lived up to its advance billing and gave a good broken-field demonstration, limited only by tire adhesion. The car would charge into a turn, mild understeer would dissolve to neutral, and then shade to oversteer with the aid of the throttle. The "Tiger-Paws" are good, a measurable cut above the rest of the normal stuff, but there are several shoes, at least two from Europe, that would complement the Chevelle's road manners even more. That nice fellow, the average SS buyer, wouldn't find anything wrong with the Royal Red line because it was superior to his standard of comparison. But the fact of the matter is Pirelli, Michelin, Firestone and Goodyear have tires for a price that will, under near-impossible conditions, stick like glue.

Of all the things the SS 396 should be, it is competitive at the drags. We dyno tune some of our test vehicles and maybe slip on a set of slicks and/or headers. Just for a change, and because it didn't look too prosperous for a break in the weather, the Chevelle was left in pure condition except that the Holley 4-throat with its vacuum-operated secondaries was modified to open properly. For reasons of economy, the vacuum operation of the secondary is retarded by a small coil spring and, often as not, the tension keeps the back butterflies closed until quite late in the acceleration range, or until the vacuum overcomes the resistance of the spring. It was apparent while trying to get away from rest in best fashion without bogging that the engine had to be revved to about 3 grand. This induced much undesirable wheelspin. So the vacuum diaphragm housing was disassembled and two coils snipped from the spring. Presto! The low-speed power problem was corrected.

After a couple of wet weekends, the skies cleared and we went out to San Fernando Raceway for a half-dozen passes. The day was bright and sunny

but the temperature was down in the low 60's and a 30 mph head wind forecast not the most ideal racing conditions. Even using extreme caution, the first run produced some wheelspin, reflected in the e.t. of 16.30 seconds (86 mph). Since traction seemed the major problem, we thought a few of the match racer tricks might be of some help. So the tires were burned through puddles of bleach for super cleaning and some liquid traction compound painted on. This done, the machine recorded a better 15.70 e.t. at 92 mph. We realized that without the benefit of adequate dragging skins and a proper collector system, you can't expect miracles but the wind and cold track had something to do with it, too. Besides, there was a '65 Chevelle SS with 375 hp, NASCAR Holley, slicks, and who knows what else, that wasn't going more than a second quicker. His hydraulic lifters were adjusted a little tighter than ours and, therefore, permitted a rev limit about 200 rpm above our 5500 rpm. We also clipped off some 0 to 60's and 30's with the 3850-pound hardtop, which at 7.9 and 3.2 seconds respectively, along with the quarter-mile speed, indicates that the potential is there if plumbed properly.

All the time we drove the 396 SS it drew a great deal of attention from the younger set, who seemed to dig everything about it—especially the simulated hood scoops. Several who looked inside noted the luxurious maroon vinyl upholstery and gauges instead of idiot lights as something worth plunking down $3800 for. The bucket seats this year feel more straight-backed than previously and generally impart the idea that they provide better support on the sides. Appointments inside were almost all class "A" with a sensible dash layout whose only bad feature was that at night the illuminated tach face cast its reflection dimly into the windshield. We regard with mixed emotions that some of the trim on the dash is now chrome-plated plastic instead of metal, but at least in damp climates it will not rust, and this is some consolation for the cheapening effect.

As a synopsis of the random reflections that ran through our mind as we returned the car to the Chevrolet zone office, it could be said this 396 SS was the type of vehicle we hated to part with. It has just the right measures of ride-handling and acceleration that would make it the nuts for all kinds of driving, especially long trips. It's a fun car for today's dull traffic, and if it helps relieve the tedium of travel, you can't ask much more. ▪▪

A Date With Three Strippers

Come with us down to where the smoke and lights are

and meet a trio of tantalizing terpsichorean

— the Chevelle SS 454, Torino Cobra and the Road Runner 440 6-bb

Coming of age in America — 1970: tooling down to the local Big Boy in your shiny, new iron. Ergo, the SUPERCAR. But it's not just for kids. These gutsy intermediates are available with just enough velvet to capture the imagination of the briefcase gang as well. And that's their insurance; their ace in the hole. Even the establishment digs groovy cars ... for now, anyway. This year, they've continued to flourish and thrive, with ever-bigger engines, better handling, enough options to choke a memory bank and an abundance of gimmickry to amuse and delight this jaded old world.

IT WAS A GOOD PLAN, BUT . . .

As originally conceived, this was to be a no-holds-barred showdown between three comparably-equipped examples of the Supercar genre — a 360-hp SS 454 Chevelle, a 370-hp Drag Pack 429 Torino Cobra and a 390-hp 440 6-bbl. GTX, all with automatic transmissions, power steering and brakes, and gear ratios in the vicinity of 4:1. But logistics intervened and the grand design crumbled. We got our cars in mid-October, when new model demand was at a peak, with the result that we had to take what was available.

The Chevelle was fitted with a 450-hp 454-cubic-inch engine, alluded to by the computer as an LS-6 (that's LS as in Land Speed Record), Turbo Hydra-Matic transmission, 3.31:1 Positraction rear axle, F70x14 Firestone Wide Ovals and Cowl Induction hood. In addition, it had variable-ratio power steering and the SS 454 chassis and styling package, including power disc front/finned drum rear brakes, performance suspension with front and rear anti-sway bars, and 14 x 7 wheels. The engine breathes deeply through an 800 cfm Holley on an aluminum intake manifold, with valve action controlled by a .500-inch lift mechanical lifter camshaft. The heads are cast iron, but use large ZL-1 exhaust valves. This engine, as well as the 396 (which is actually a 402 this year), must be ordered with either a four-speed manual or Turbo Hydra-Matic transmission in the Chevelle. Our Turbo Hydro made full throttle upshifts at about 5200 rpm, but by shifting manually at 6000 we were able to improve our quarter-mile speeds and elapsed times. It's a very smooth shifting transmission, yet it's quite positive. The optional Cowl Induction hood is basically a rearward facing scoop, with vacuum-actuated internal flapper that picks up fresh air from the relatively high pressure area at the base of the windshield. There is an external trap door on the top of the scoop, but it's only for appearance sake (though it does tilt upward when the "real" one is working).

The Torino Cobra was the biggest
continued

of our trio of strip trippers, having gained a two-inch increase in tread width for '70 to allow shoehorning in the 429 CID canted valve head engine. Wheelbase was also increased by an inch (to 117) and overall length is 206.2 inches, up five (all in front) from last year. Our Cobra was equipped with the non-Drag Pack 370-hp Cobra Jet 429 with Shaker Scoop, SelectShift Cruise-O-Matic, 3.50:1 Traction-Lok rear axle, Competition Suspension, G78x14 fiberglass belted tires (though subsequent cars will have rayon belted tires), power steering, power front disc brakes and air conditioning, adding up to a test weight of just over 4000 pounds with our fifth wheel. The belt for the air conditioning compressor was removed for our tests to prevent damage. (Air conditioning is not available with anything higher numerically than a 3.25:1 rear axle, which our car originally had. The ratio was changed to 3.50:1 to give more representative performance.)

The various permutations of the 429 engine were discussed in the November issue, but there have been a few changes since then. To recapitulate briefly, the base engine is the 360-hp

429-4V, standard in the Torino Cobra. One step up is the 370-hp 429 Cobra, with hydraulic lifter camshaft, Rochester four barrel and big valves. The 429 Cobra Jet, also rated at 370-hp, is identical to the 429 Cobra, but has a functional ram air scoop. All of this has remained unchanged; however, the so-called "Super Cobra Jet," the beefed-up, top-of-the-line non-hemi 429 (also rated at 370 hp), is now referred to as the Drag Pack 429 Cobra Jet. It features a solid lifter cam, Holley carburetor, forged aluminum pistons, special connecting rods and an oil cooler. The Drag Pack option also includes a 3.91 or 4.30:1 gear ratio. Additionally, as of now, only Drag Pack Cobra Jets (i.e., ram air 429s) will be offered, whereas the Drag Pack was initially available with the non-ram Cobras as well. This may all sound very confusing, but it's infinitely easier to understand this way than it was previously.

At any rate, our test car had the "regular" 429 Cobra Jet, with hydraulic cam and Quadrajet carburetor. Its Select-Shift automatic, if placed in "D," will make full throttle upshifts at 5100 rpm. If the selector is placed in "2," the car will start in second gear, which

could save a few towing fees when the snow flies. The shifting, especially when the transmission kicks down into second, is smooth, yet firm. For manual shifting, best results are achieved by moving the selector as the tach reaches 5400 rpm, with the engine gaining only about 100 rpm more before the shift is completed. There's no point to pushing the engine any higher, due to the design of the camshaft and the airflow capacity of the carburetor. The Competition Suspension package is included on all Torinos with other than the base 429-4V engine. It includes high rate front and rear springs (500 pounds per inch on the front, 210 pounds per inch rear), 1 3/16" Gabriel shocks fore and aft, and a .95-inch diameter front stabilizer bar (compared to the .75-inch standard bar). On cars with four-speed transmissions, the rear shocks are staggered, one ahead of the axle, one behind, a drag racing trick.

Rounding out the field was the new Road Runner. *New,* because it's no longer just a stripped-down Belvedere with a big engine and heavy suspension. The window sticker on our hardtop started out at $3034 and totalled out at $4417 delivered. Included in the

"... they were loaded with the creature comforts you usually don't associate with

450 horsepower from 454 cubic inches! That goes back to the old magical, mystery one-pound-per-cubic-inch barrier. Of course, Chevrolet would have to have it. Like the way their engine compartments seem to be uncluttered, too.

While Ford mills are less mighty, they also seem to be rammed into the car and randomly covered with wires and hoses. Things like spark plugs accessibility is too grim to be part of a high performance car. Shaker hood is great.

list of equipment; 440 6-bbl. engine, four-speed manual transmission, Super Track Pak, Air Grabber, F60x15 Polyglas GT tires and vinyl buckets. (Normally we wouldn't mention that last item, but these are worthy of note, as they are exceptionally well-designed.) A Track Pak or Super Track Pak is mandatory with 440s and Hemis ordered with four-speed manual transmissions. The Super Track Pak includes a Hurst shifter with pistol grip handle, 4.10:1 Sure Grip rear axle, power disc brakes, dual point distributor, seven-blade Torque Drive fan and high performance radiator.

The engine is rated at 390 hp at 4700 rpm and carries three Holley two-barrel carbs. These carburetors were designed specifically for this setup and shouldn't be confused with the new Holley 500 cfm two barrel. Actually, their combined air flow capacity is about 1100 cfm, with the center carburetor being smaller than the outboard two. Idling and normal cruising is handled by the center jug, simplifying the emissions situation, with the auxiliary carburetors coming in "when needed," determined by engine vacuum. Vacuum actuation results in a smoother application of power and works out better than a mechanical linkage the vast majority of the time. The Road Runner's particular brand of fresh air delivery system is the Air Grabber, a flip-up trap door/scoop which is controlled by an under-dashboard switch. The sides of the Grabber, which is timed to come up within the interval of a stop light, is illuminated with the same eyes and teeth that distinguished the Flying Tigers' P-40's back in WW II. When not in use, it lies flush with the top of the domed hood, away from prying eyes and fingers.

PERFORMANCE

The massive 450-hp engine in the Chevelle *had* to come out as top dog in our forays on the quarter-mile. Even with the 3.31 rear axle it proved strong enough to produce a best elapsed time of 13.8 seconds (this, as in all of our tests, was with two people aboard and a fifth wheel on the back). The key to getting good times was the start, as it was easy to lose over a second due to excessive wheelspin. Best results were obtained by rolling out at idle and smoothly applying more throttle as the car moved out, shifting the transmission manually at 6000 rpm. Running the quarter in "Drive" resulted in times in the 14.5-second area. All runs were 15.0 seconds or better and speeds ran between 96.0 and 97.5 mph, a little lower than expected. The engine runs clean and strong all through the rpm range and gives no evidence of any strain even at 6000. It's a runner.

The engine in the Torino was the mildest of the three tested, yet the car had the quickest 0-30, 0-45 and 0-75 times, and matched the Chevelle's six seconds to 60 mph. It also ran the highest quarter-mile speed, 100.2, a fact which is even stranger in view of its weight. The weight obviously helped traction, as it was fairly easy to accelerate away from a standing start with only a modicum of wheelspin, but that same weight should have cut down the top end speed. Maybe this "shaped by the wind" thing is for real. Again, manually shifting the automatic gave the best results, with the slowest drag strip run being at 14.8 and the best a 14.5. Speeds ranged between 95.4 and 100.2, the majority being in the 99.5 mph bracket through the traps on top end.

continued

ed. Could be were getting into a new bag — the mature Supercar."

In the meantime, Chrysler is learning. The Road Runner compartment is a good backdrop for the engine and only a couple of the plugs are hard to get at. Progressive carburetor linkage saves gas mileage from total disaster.

Nurtured by the evolution of the Z-28, the Chevelles, even the big ones, dart like whippets through the tightest turns.

Unlike the other two, the Torino came around the bends in what amounted to a "confidence inspiring power slide."

On the other hand, the Road Runner tended to understeer at low speeds. Lack of power steering builds strong arms.

THREE STRIPPERS
continued

The combination of four-speed transmission and 4.10 rear axle should have given the Road Runner an edge on the drag strip, but traction and difficulty in shifting cancelled out any potential advantage. On the day we took the car to Irwindale Raceway, the wind had blown a light coating of sand onto the track surface. Even with those giant 8½-inch-wide Polyglas GTs, it was possible to take off from an idle and spin the tires all the way through first and most of second gear. The shifter, which has a familiar feel to anyone who's ever flown a fighter, is virtually indestructible, but proved hard to shift. Shifting effort is moderate for normal gear changes, but it increases abruptly with any attempt to speed-shift. This seemed unusual in view of Plymouth's efforts to improve shifting

Hair, Teeth and Eyes

Good Vibrations

Cowl Bonga

SPECIFICATIONS

	CHEVELLE	TORINO	ROAD RUNNER
Engine	90° OHV V8	90° OHV V8	90° OHV V8
Bore & Stroke — ins. **Displacement — cu. in.** **HP @ RPM** **Torque: lbs.-ft. @ rpm** **Compression Ratio**	4.25 x 4.00 454 450 @ 5600 500 @ 3600 11:1	4.36 x 3.59 429 370 @ 5400 450 @ 3400 11.3:1	4.32 x 3.75 440 390 @ 4700 490 @ 3200 10.5:1
Carburetion **Transmission** **Final Drive Ratio**	1 4-bbl. Automatic 3.31:1	1 4-bbl. Automatic 3.50:1	3 2-bbl. 4-speed manual 4.10:1
Steering Type	Power, Variable-Ratio	Power	Power
Steering Ratio **Turning Diameter** (Curb-to-curb-ft.) **Wheel Turns** (lock-to-lock)	18.7:1-12.4:1 42.0 2.9	20.6:1 42.8 3.5	28.8:1 40.6 5.3
Tire Size	F70x14	G78x14	F60x15
Brakes	Power front disc, drum rear	Power front disc, drum rear	Power front disc, drum rear
Front Suspension	Independent, coil springs	Independent, coil springs, strut stabilized lower arms	Torsion bars
Rear Suspension	Linked; Salisbury axle fixed by control arms	Hotchkiss, semi-elliptic spring	Parallel, semi-elliptic spring
Body/Frame Construction	Welded perimeter with crossmembers	Unitized Frame	Unitized
Wheelbase — ins. **Overall Length — ins.** **Width — ins.** **Height — ins.** **Front Track — ins.** **Rear Track — ins.**	112.0 197.2 75.4 52.8 61.3 60.3	117.0 206.2 76.8 51.0 60.5 60.0	116.0 203.8 76.4 53.0 59.9 59.2
Test Weight — lbs. **Fuel Capacity — gals.** **Oil Capacity — qts.**	N.A. 20.0 5	4002 22.0 (20.0-Calif.) 5	3935 19.0 5

PERFORMANCE

	CHEVELLE	TORINO	ROAD RUNNER
Acceleration 0-30 mph 0-45 mph 0-60 mph 0-75 mph	 2.8 secs. 4.3 secs. 6.0 secs. 9.0 secs.	 2.6 secs. 4.2 secs. 6.0 secs. 8.8 secs.	 2.8 secs. 4.7 secs. 6.6 secs. 9.2 secs.
Standing Start ¼-Mile	13.8 secs. 97.5 mph	14.5 secs. 100.2 mph	*14.4 secs. 99.0 mph
Passing Speeds 40-60 mph 50-70 mph	 3.0 secs. 3.7 secs.	 3.2 secs. 3.5 secs.	 2.8 secs. 3.2 secs.
Speeds in Gears 1st ...mph @ rpm 2nd ...mph @ rpm 3rd ...mph @ rpm 4th ...mph @ rpm	 55 @ 6000 91.5 @ 6000 100 @ 4400	 48 @ 5400 82 @ 5400 100 @ 4500	 31 @ 4700 43 @ 4700 60 @ 4700 85 @ 4700
MPH Per 1000 rpm (in top gear)	22.7	22.2	18.1
Stopping Distances From 30 mph From 60 mph	 23.4 ft. 118.6 ft.	 26.0 ft. 128.0 ft.	 26.1 ft. 125.5 ft.

*14.06/101.69 after tune

THREE STRIPPERS
continued

in their '70 cars, including internal changes to the transmissions. Of course, our Road Runner was just barely broken-in and perhaps the shifting will become freer with time. Owner reports say that shifting is usually no problem.

The optional factory tachometer is red-lined at 5000 rpm, but we stretched the shift points to 5400 rpm with no apparent adverse effects. At any rate, the car was going through the traps at the end of the quarter at close to 5500 in top gear, turning 99 mph. This gearing is obviously not very practical for the street, as the engine is turning over 3800 rpm at 70 mph. A better choice for all-around use would be the 3.54 option. Despite the traction and shifting problems, the Tor-Red Road Runner ran consistent mid-14 second quarters, with a best of 14.4 and a worst of 15.1. The speeds ranged between 94 and 99 mph. The car did have the best passing speeds, taking only 2.8 seconds to get from 40 to 60 mph and 3.2 to make it from 50 to 70, both in third gear. (For comparison, 50-70 in fourth gear was 3.9 seconds.) We made comparison runs with and without the Air Grabber deployed and found it cut 0-30 and 0-45 times significantly, but we couldn't detect any difference in the quarter.

HANDLING AND BRAKING

The Chevelle has the type of handling (and the performance to go with it) that makes you want to go flat-out into hard corners. It really sticks to the road, though there is a tendency to over-correct if you're not used to the variable-ratio power steering. The Road Runner, on the other hand, tends to understeer at low speeds, but you can put it into a turn, set the attitude and just hang in there, being quite comfortable at relatively high speeds. The Torino is completely different: The car goes through tight turns in a confidence-inspiring controlled slide. It's all very smooth ... and unusual. The lack of power steering on our Road Runner, combined with the wide tires, made parking a chore to say the least. Power steering with any of these big-engined cars would be a good thing.

The same forward weight bias that makes power steering a necessity also contributes to a tendency for the rear end to come around on hard braking, most noticeably in panic stops from 60 mph and above. All three cars exhibited this trait, but it was most pronounced on the Road Runner, though its stopping distances were good.

OBSERVATIONS

The Chevelle we tested was a prototype, basically an SS 396 with a bigger engine. Regular SS 454 production may have already started as you read this, but, as of now, the beginning date for LS-6 Chevelles is uncertain. Our guess is the first of the year. The car was a ball to drive because of the engine response and improved (over last year) suspension. Even

though it was equipped with a mechanical lifter cam, engine noise at cruising speeds was low, due to the 3.31 rear axle. The Torino was even quieter, though a Drag Pack version (with mechanical cam and 3.91 gears) which we drove, was very noisy, giving the impression that you were somehow still in second gear instead of high at anything over 50 mph. The Road Runner was just plain turning a lot of "r's" at turnpike speeds, but the noise level really wasn't excessive. One thing — you didn't have to boot it to get it to jump at speeds of 60 mph and above; a little tickle with the toe was all that was needed.

As mentioned before, the Road Runner's bucket seats are tops, giving good lateral support, and are certainly preferable to the bench seat. The Ford seemed to have the best quality control in regards to interior and exterior finish overall, though it is difficult to generalize from such a limited sampling. Likewise, it isn't fair to pick any one of these cars as being better than the other two, because of the wide variance in engines and options, but we couldn't help but be impressed by the Chevelle. It was certainly the strongest — the most super — of the three, but we didn't have it long enough to determine how much work it would take to maintain its tune. Neither did we get a chance to drive it in heavy traffic, or even establish representative gas mileage figures. The Torino seemed to be the easiest to live with, though its hugesque dimensions made it difficult to park. Not that it requires a tugboat to get you into a berth, it's just a big car. The Road Runner was the closest thing to a strictly drag strip machine. The addition of power steering and a switch to a more realistic gear ratio would do wonders for its day-to-day driveability.

We were a bit concerned over our particular test car's performance compared to what other similarly-equipped Road Runners are doing, so we had the engine checked-out after our bout on the drag strip. Mopar expert Norm Thatcher diagnosed the problem as sticky valves and lifters, which he cured. He also richened the center carburetor and reset the ignition timing.

Going back out to the strip, we decided to employ a few of the drag racer's tricks: we pumped up the rear tire pressure to 35 psi (Polyglas tires give better traction with higher pressure) and loosened the fan belt. These are things the average owner could and would do. The cumulative effect was evident, with the car running a best elapsed time of 14.06 and a best speed of 101.6 in the quarter. There was a noticeable improvement in performance in the higher rpm range, thanks to Thatcher's tuning.

All three of the vehicles tested had, to varying degrees, the performance, handling and braking that you'd expect from a *Supercar*, but they were also loaded with the creature comforts you don't usually associate with the breed. Could be we're getting into a new bag — the mature Supercar. **/MT**

CONTINUED FROM PAGE 65

had ever been our mispleasure to encounter. Not only that it was all tied to the *crossmember*, not to the trans itself. It didn't take much figuring from there to determine that when the engine torques under power, the linkage arms are strained at all kinds of angles from their mounting positions on the crossmember, binding against the member and effectively closing the normal shift gates. The gate can only open again when you release pressure on the gas pedal, relieving the twist against the shift arms. What's it all mean? From here, it looks as if your first purchase after buying your new Chevelle should be a positive shifter that mounts *on the trans* — Hurst or otherwise.

While we're talking transmission, here's another tip that may help you toward record performance: stick with the 2.20 low gear four-speed option, at least on this model. Our car was thus equipped, and even though the 3.08 rear hurt us in winding up the engine, we're sure matters would have been even worse with the 2.54 low option because of the "long haul" between changes.

In the rear, there are no less than 11 ring and pinion sets available from Chevrolet for the SS 396. They range from 2.73 to 4.88, with the latter probably the best choice for strictly dragging and the 4.10 as probably the best street-strip compromise ratio.

What else can you do to edge your way towards the record marks? Make sure you've got a good set of headers. We had a set installed for us by Hooker Headers that fit with an absolute minimum of cutting — just a couple of notches in the inner fender wells that can be rewelded right back to stock appearance should you ever want to go back to the stock system.

Then, of course, an engine blueprinting is in order, and you can go to work on the suspension, although we found that the factory installed heavy-duty suspension did an excellent job of handling all the gobs of torque the 396 puts out. After that, head for the strip and start looking for a new place to store all the "gold" you're about to win with your '68 Chevelle. **©**

"Don't let the appearance fool you Jack."

By Steve Kelly ■ That first supercar Chevelle, back in 1965, was some kind of a strong machine. It had a 375-horse 396, and while it lacked a few of the refinements that occur with aging, it began life as the hottest Chevrolet, except for Corvettes, ever to run off the end of an assembly line. The 350-horsepower 327 V8 Chevy II was a fair equal, but the lengths to which it could be taken weren't as far-reaching as the inaugural issue of the SS396. The first model was a brute, and the last model of the Chevelle muscle car is the epitome of parts-gathering from existing bins for adaptability to something that can and will perform. And last in the line of supercar products by Chevrolet may well be this one: a 454-cubic-inch, 460-horsepower, V8-driven SS Malibu. It could be the last because, even though buyers might still be available after 1971, strict legislation concerning emission outputs, coupled with ascending insurance rates, will render this car — or this type of car — worthless. Non-leaded gasoline will be mandatory in California late in 1971, and one year later, the entire U.S. will follow. Unless some other way of using this kind of fuel is found, compression ratios of 8.5 to 9.0:1 will be the order of engine op-

eration. When insurance rates reach one-third of a car's value, and that's the direction in which they're headed, it is usually not economically feasible to own this kind of thrasher. We savored every moment of this car, for the memory may have to last a long time. I hope this experience can be related well enough for all of us to enjoy.

This particular Malibu is a hard one to trace through normal specification sheets and pricing literature. In a sense, it doesn't exist. Chevrolet doesn't emphasize that an LS6 454-cubic-inch V8 option is available in anything other than a Corvette. But Chevelles can have it too, along with a cowl induction hood ($147.75), M-22 Muncie four-speed close-ratio gearbox ($221.90), and a limited-slip-equipped 4.10:1 rear axle ($25.30, special order). That's just some of the equipment our earth mover came with, plus the SS package that retails for $503. The LS6 is an additional $263.00, and although it shows as 450-horse when applied to Chevelle models, everything about it is identical to the 460. Chevrolet offers another

454-inch option, the LS5 engine (or Z15 option), and it is rated at 360 horsepower; but here again is an identical powerplant to the 390-horse variety fitted to big Chevys. The LS5 has a hydraulic lifter valve train, one point lower compression (10.25:1), Quadrajet carburetor, lower price and less startling performance. The $263 price difference is less than building up a 360/390- to a 450/460-horse version.

The M-22 Muncie transmission is perfectly suited to this engine, but its linkage isn't. This one was probably the smoothest we've had, but the stick angle is such that it is easier to go from third to second than from third to fourth. All of us were leary of pulling the stick hard, because the top mast is angled toward the driver, and unless he consciously pulls straight rearward, chances are good of the shifter catching on the neutral gate. It never went to second, except during low-speed tryouts to get the knack. The close-ratio box is noisy, and it has finer clutch drive gear splines than the regular production option M-22, as well as larger

The past is gone. The future may never see a car like this. It is one of the brutes, and all it needs is a way of staying in contact with terra firma

Earth Mover

photography: Eric Rickman and Henry Thomas

and heavier mainshaft rear splines and a pressed-on speedo drive gear. It is not *directly* interchangeable with the RPO M-22. Its heavier construction ensures a greater amount of reliability.

The best quarter-mile time was accomplished at Irwindale Raceway by John Dianna, who has a definite knack for this sort of thing. His low time of 13.44 seconds was followed by two other runs of 13.48 and 13.52, showing a consistent pattern. Shift points proved best at 6100-6200 rpm, and the maximum engine speed for coming off the line was 900 rpm. After some shock changes, the initial engine speed still couldn't be higher than 900, which is idle speed. There is so much bottom end on this car that it is impossible to use all of it effectively with street tires. These happened to be F70-14 Firestone Wide Ovals, with best pressure settings at 30 psi on the left rear and 28 psi on the right. Any throttle stabbing off the line would cause the tires to go up in

smoke, and the car generally wanted to get sideways as a result. A decent set of drag slicks would naturally get more bite to the ground, but the immense amount of torque going through the drive line would just as naturally start breaking parts. Better to cool it and not have to walk home. If this were our car, we'd invest in a big 9¾-inch ring gear carrier and housing, with a good traction bar setup. Traction bars are a good recommendation for stock rear setups. The 10.5-inch-diameter, bent-finger, single-disc clutch didn't even hint at giving up, even after thirty runs. We did get rid of some of the disc facing, increasing freeboard length, but that's merely an adjustment job. The pilot bearing got a little noisy after many back-to-back runs, and while an owner of such a car as this has the gearbox out to install a formidable scattershield, it will pay him to replace the throwout if the car has already logged a few thousand

miles. The installation of a blast shield is mandatory for this car. Don't even think about not doing it. Chevrolet would've been smart in doing it on the line. Ours received a Lakewood shield.

CHEVELLE 454

VEHICLE ... Chevelle Malibu Sport Coupe SS 454

PRICE ... Base, $2809.00; as tested, $4852.30

ENGINE ... 454-cubic-inch OHC V8, 4.251-in. bore x 4.00-in. stroke. 450 hp @ 5600 rpm; 500 lbs.-ft. torque @ 3600 rpm. 11.25:1 compression ratio. Bore spacing, 4.84-in.

CARBURETION ... Single Holley 4-bbl, 1.689-in. primary & secondary bores.

VALVE TRAIN ... Solid lifters, .020-in. clearance intake & exhaust. 1.70:1 rocker ratio. Intake valve diameter, 2.190-in.; exhaust, 1.880-in. Intake opens 62° BTC, closes 105° ABC, 347° duration. Exhaust opens 106° BBC, closes 73° ATC, 359° duration. Overlap: 135°. Alloy steel valves, aluminized face & head

DRIVE TRAIN ... Muncie M-22 4-speed. Ratios: 1st, 2.20:1; 2nd, 1.64:1; 3rd, 1.27:1; 4th, 1.0:1. 4.11:1 rear axle gear with limited-slip. 8.875-in.-dia. ring gear

BRAKES .. Front floating caliper disc/rear drum with integral vacuum assist. 11.0-in.-dia. disc, 9.5-in.-dia. drum. 106.1-sq.-in. effective lining area

WHEELS & TIRES ... 14-in. x 7-in. steel wheels. F70-14 Firestone fiberglass bias-belted tires.

SUSPENSION ... Front: Independent, short-long-arm type with coil spring & spherically jointed steering knuckle for each wheel. Double-acting tube shocks, 1.00-in. piston dia. Link-type stabilizer, .812-in.-dia. Rear: Salisbury axle with location by upper and lower control arms. Coil springs and 1.00-in.-piston-dia. tube shocks

STEERING . . . Power-assisted variable ratio. Semi-reversible, recirculating ball nut. Gear ratio: 16.1-12.4:1; overall ratio 18.7-12.4:1. 2.9 turns lock to lock, 16.25 x 15.50-in. wheel. 42.5 ft. curb to curb turning dia.

PERFORMANCE . . . Quarter-mile (best): 13.44 sec., 108.17 mph

DIMENSIONS . . . Wheelbase: 112.0-in.; front track: 60.0-in.; rear track: 59.8-in.; overall height: 52.6-in.; overall width: 75.4-in.; overall length: 197.2-in.; shipping weight: 3759 lb.; body/frame construction: separate perimeter frame; fuel tank capacity: 20 gal.

LEFT — Underhood is filled with plumbing and horsepower. The 454 wants to run warm, but that doesn't hurt performance when below the 200° mark.
BELOW LEFT— There's been some good planning on the inside. It's comfortable, and the panel arrangement is the best Chevy has ever done in this series. Thicker wheel rim and straighter shift lever are needed. Add an oil gauge and the system would be great.
RIGHT — Back view kind of reminds us of a GTO, and that's a compliment. Dark section in rear bumper is a shock-absorbing, synthetic-material filler. Rear fender clearance is adequate for stock-class slicks and wide wheels.

Earth Mover

Our better quarter-mile times were made when the air-filter element was removed and the engine·was fairly warm, just a shade under the 195° mark. The warm motor killed a bit of the bottom end, making it easier to get the car moving. After a full cool-down, low-end torque was so tremendous that there was no way the car would leave smoothly. It either bogged or it cranked the rear wheels into the outer limits. Torque isn't a passing phase in this 454. No matter what the shift point, the rear tires *always* spun off a bit of elapsed time with each upshift.

We can't vouch for the effectiveness of the cowl induction air inlet, but it seems that it would work better if it were both wider and farther to the rear. A plenum chamber using the domed section of the hood and fed from an opening very near to the windshield offers more force-feeding action. The opening and closing action of the present door is actuated by manifold vacuum.

If you can afford this car, you also have to feed its appetite, and this might result in a cost equal to monthly payments. An 11:25:1 compression ratio demands the best of leaded gasoline. Our poorest mileage figure was 7.30 miles per gallon, and the best was 10.006. The average consumption turned out at 8.414. A full tank of fuel won't last 200 miles at this rate. And this 4150 series Holley was lean on the primary side, which has to be done to make engines like this pass emission tests. The lean condition causes minor surging in 60-70-mph traffic.

Driving for the fun of it is a pleasant pastime. The 454 operates smoothly in congested traffic, and its handling is as good as other GM intermediates. We changed shock absorbers, adding Hurst/Gabriel Dual-Duty units — which, incidentally, will be the subject of a technical feature in next month's *Hot Rod* as a result of our testing them on this car. The stock Delco shocks have a 1.00-inch-diameter piston, and they really don't offer any drawbacks. The Hurst/Gabriels, with their $1\frac{3}{16}$-inch piston, combined with other refinements, simply made handling better. Power front disc/rear drum brakes are a part of the SS option, and so are seven-inch-wide wheels. The variable ratio power steering and front and rear stabilizer bars, worked in with everything else, contributed to an overall good handler and a pleasant and very predictable road and highway car.

It's a quiet car too, even with the windows rolled down. Road and operational noise is well isolated. The interior treatment shows signs of approaching GTO and Olds 4-4-2 in both sophistication and quality. The optional instruments require $84.30 extra investment, but you can see them all and they all work. An oil pressure light is used, and there should be a pressure gauge available, working in conjunction with the warning light.

There were a lot more things we liked about this car than we found not to our liking. It's obvious the SS Malibu 454/450 isn't meant for paper routes, or drivers who don't like being able to go quick and corner flat. An expensive proposition is what it is, and speed costs money, so it's a matter of how fast you care to go. It isn't charitable to throw stones at a dying breed; and while we all hope this isn't going to be the case, we'll just keep our five smooth stones waiting for some Goliath that says it can do as well, then doesn't. ■ ■

LEFT — Short-stack atop Holley 4150 gets filter pan against cowl induction hood (above) and air stream from flapper scoop. BELOW — Front end isn't very aerodynamic, but it makes the grade on looks. High view is splendid for today's muscle cars, but tomorrow will be different.

CHEVY 396 SS

SS Super Sports or Strip Screamer

In spite of what the automakers say about a given model being 'all new,' a favorite phrase even when changes are minimal, there is merit in carrying over basic components; the engineers get a fighting chance to refine the design. The result is that each model year the product gets a little better provided that each model year's new features are limited to cosmetic changes, and engineering revolution is shunted aside in favor of evolution.

With that bit of philosophy, which Volkswagen owners will recognize, we bring to center stage the 1970 Chevelle Malibu SS 396 sport coupe. There are sheetmetal changes which give it a fresh appearance over the 1969 model, but underneath it is very much like the 1969 SS 396. In fact, there was a 1966 SS 396 Chevelle which, although different, had a distinct family resemblance to the '70 under the sheetmetal.

What Chevrolet has done with the '70 is produce a Chevelle which handles exceedingly well — better, in fact, than many of the GT types which are supposed to handle. That's pretty strong talk, but we base it on several observations. The test car turned out to be more than a fire-engine red hardtop with black stripes, cowl induction hood, racing-style hood lock pins and fancy wheels. It attracted attention wherever we took it . . . and it performed just as it looked it should.

Drive train

Chevrolet did a couple of curious things to their 396 engine this year. For one thing it's not a 396 anymore, even though the fender plate insists that it is. At the very beginning of the model year no one at Chevrolet mentioned that the displacement had changed slightly but then a handful of sharp-eyed types spotted an increased cylinder bore in the specification sheets. "Yes," said a spokesman for Chevrolet's engineering department, "the engine is now 402 cubic inches and new spec sheets will so indicate."

The engine is rated (conservatively, we believe) at 350 hp at 5200 rpm. Last year's powerplant for the SS 396 was only 325 hp, with options for 350 and

375 horses. This year 350 is the limit when a customer orders an SS 396. However, he can stay with the SS package, move up to the new 454-cubic-inch V8 and opt for either 360 or 450 hp. The extra 10 horses (350 to 360) will cost $58 above normal SS suggested list, while the biggest ground-thumper available will run our potential street rodder an extra $321.

We should point out that the SS option package is more than an impressive nameplate. It makes the car worthy of notice by any serious motorist. We don't say it gives the roadworthiness of a Corvette or the latest Ferrari, but it permits the available power to be utilized with safe handling and braking — and that is why you cannot buy the hottest engines without also buying the suspension, tires and brakes that Chevrolet engineers have learned work best. Some manufacturers sell supercars with minimal suspension and brakes, assuming that customers plan to go drag racing where such items matter little or will be altered. It's not such a hot idea to trust a customer that far. At Chevrolet they assume that the customer can *remove* what he doesn't want for racing.

According to Chevrolet's official dealer specs the SS package includes the following pieces and rules of use: "V8 Sport Coupe or Convertible models

Sheetmetal has been altered (but not severely) for 1970 giving the car a larger look although its overall size is essentially the same as '69. Important mechanical details are virtually unchanged.

Sport striping, which is standard with cowl induction hood and optional on other SS 396s, is carried over the rear deck, identifies the car as something special.

with 4-speed or Turbo Hydramatic transmissions only. Includes bright engine accents; power front disc brakes; dual exhausts with bright tips; black painted grille; wheel opening moldings; special rear bumper with black insert; special domed hood and suspension; SS emblem on grille, fenders, rear bumper, steering wheel and door trim panels; 14×7 sport wheels and F70-14 bias belted ply white lettered blackwall tires. Body sill and belt line moldings deleted."

A quick reading should enable one to sort out the significant items including discs, special suspension (which includes rear stabilizer bar and heavy duty equipment all around), the wheels and tires. Everything else is more or less window trimming on a pretty package.

We got the Turbo Hydramatic transmission with Positraction rear axle and the standard ratio of 3.31-to-1. The other two optional transmissions are four-speed: one with 2.52-to-1 low gear, the other a close-ratio gearbox with 2.20 low. The four-speed trans works just fine but somehow this sort of car — a luxury supercar if you like — seems better with the three-speed automatic. The fact that the control is mounted on a center console makes it neither more nor less sporting.

Power and performance

At maximum throttle the 396 SS upshifts into second gear at 46 mph and into third at 74, speeds which never strain the engine and explain why it is possible to pull slightly better acceleration times out of the engine by shifting manually, running the engine just past the 5500 rpm redline before shifting. Without doubt the engine will turn several hundred revs past the limit we used, but we hate to abuse an engine without cause.

A few words about the cowl induction hood are in order. It seems to be the 'in' thing this year to power-actuate visual gimmicks to induct cold air for maximum performance. There's no question that they work; the driver and his passengers can see them operate. Do they do any good? Not that we could see, at least in normal driving. Possibly the cold air inducted at the base of the windshield would be helpful at very high speed, but a similar Chevelle SS 396 without cowl induction ran essentially the same speeds. Cowl induction is vacuum operated; the only time the valve is open is when the engine is off or when it is being operated at full throttle. It's a gimmick, but sometimes people need fun little gimmicks. Under the hood the top of the air cleaner is open and seals itself via a soft rubber ring to the inside of the domed hood which leads to the flip-top air induction valve. For ordinary motoring the carburetor draws in relatively warm underhood air through a conventional air cleaner snorkel but when the pressure is on it can gulp great quantities of ambient air through the extra valve.

The 396/402 engine in its 350 hp stage of tune provides plenty of power.

But is it a supercar? Not in the sense that if one compares it to the competition turning better than 100 mph in the quarter-mile with elapsed times down in the 14s, the SS 396 comes off second-best. There are several reasons. One (correctable) is street tires. The most significant is the fact that the Chevelle is somewhat heavy. Curb weight is rated at 3757 pounds; test weight was about 400 pounds more. Anyone who needs a real supercar can go to the 454/450 version. Our best et at Orange County Raceway was 15.27 with a trap speed of 92.98 mph.

Roadability and handling

Rather than a supercar we consider it more closely allied with a luxury GT.

Most of the supercars are straight-line terrors, but turn them loose on a twisting mountain road and look out. The Chevelle is a different story. It's quiet inside. Wind and engine noise are at a minimum. The only significant sound which we didn't like was the fan noise. Push the SS through a corner and it behaves like a GT car should. The variable ratio power steering makes the act of steering pleasurable, even though there isn't as much road feel as some of the purists seem to prefer. Tires are F70×14 mounted on seven-inch-wide rims, quite wide and definitely contributing to the car's ability to stick to the road.

In a moderately hard turn the car exhibits the expected amount of under-

steer, then can be powered around pretty much neutral. In very hard corners there is plow. It would not be impossible to make it swap ends, but a driver would have to work at it.

Brakes and safety

Braking combination — front discs, rear drums — is so good as to merit real praise. Fade is virtually nonexistent; repeated panic stops required very little additional pedal pressure. Stopping is in a straight line with no tendency to swerve or pull, which is most reassuring. Deceleration now matches anything of its weight and size at a best stop from 60 mph of 24-26 ft. per sec.² or about 150 ft.

The seat belt system is still something of a forest of black straps. Basic lap strap is self-adjusting, quick and easy to use. The shoulder restraint is something else, and because the upper belt tends to get in the way we (and a lot of other drivers) ignore it. Until GM gets a system as advanced as, for example, Volvo's, we predict that large numbers of customers will continue to ignore it.

Comfort and convenience

After an examination of the interior package, along with considerable driv-

Seating in the two buckets was judged to be very good although a trifle low. Rearward rake of the backrests is more than most cars of its type.

Handling is one of the SS 396's strong points. It corners with minimum body lean and remains controllable in tight bends at high speeds.

ing of the Chevelle, we decided that the design and layout was quite satisfactory. It is possible to order the car with bench seats but we had buckets. Compared to last year's buckets they seem to position driver and passenger lower with more rearward rake of the backrest. Ordinarily for a full arms-out driving position we require the seat at the maximum rear adjustment; it wasn't necessary on this car. The seats cradle their occupants and offer very good support. (A backrest adjustable for rake would be a welcome option.) We had the optional tilt wheel ($45.30) and recommend it as most useful, especially for drivers who are at the extreme ends of the size scale. American cars are made to fit the size range of *most* of the population but some of us are larger or smaller than the averages, and cars do not fit well; the tilt wheel helps, but not as much as the sliding spline wheel on the Corvette.

On the standard SS, instrumentation is quite basic. For $84.30 we got special instrumentation which includes clock, tachometer, ammeter and temperature gauges mounted in the panel where they are visible. In previous years they were mounted in a cluster out of sight on the console.

Rear seat room is adequate. What more can one say about a car of this size? There is sufficient headroom and

three can ride, although the center passenger is never going to be comfortable on a long trip. There is plenty of knee room and if driver/passenger seats are adjusted forward to a medium position any size rear seat passenger has all the leg stretch he'll need.

Chevelle's heat/vent system is a good one. Gone are the vent windows, and many people miss them although we suspect that their greatest value was for tossing out cigarette butts and gum wrappers. With the flow-through ventilation system of the Chevelle it is quite practical to ride with windows closed and get full circulation of outside air by pulling a pair of vent knobs on each side below the dash. Need to cut the chill? Push the slide levers for air and heat and turn on the fan to the desired level.

The few controls needed on the Chevelle are well placed. Shifting on the console does not even require a glance to determine correct gear after the first couple of times. It is a sporty (not to be confused with sports car) option but we could have shifted just as well with the old-fashioned stick on the column. Ignition key is in the column and cannot be removed unless the transmission is in park, at which point the wheel is locked and the transmission is locked in park. It is another of GM's anti-theft devices and it should work because about the

Drag performance of the SS 396 is good but not outstanding compared to other makes of supercars which tend to be lighter in weight. However, there is another SS option with 100 more horses which should perform brilliantly.

Cowl induction hood is vacuum operated, opens only at full throttle or when engine is off. It permits cold air from atmosphere to feed carburetor at points of maximum demand.

Dash panel layout is well executed, clearly visible. Instrument assortment includes optional special instrument package which displaces most of the indicator lights, tells the driver what is happening.

only way to steal a car locked in park is to tow it away with the rear lifted up. Even so it wouldn't trail well because the front wheels are locked in a slightly off-straight-ahead position.

Trunk space in a car of the Chevelle's class is not ample. The spare tire takes up more than its share of room, but that's how things are. Luggage capacity is rated at 14.6 cubic feet. A traveler will find it difficult to stuff more than a couple of two-suiters and some miscellaneous small pieces aboard.

Economy

Chevrolet suggests that its dealers sell the Malibu coupe for $2809 base. Our test car totaled out on the sticker at $4433.80 including $159 destination charge. Of some $1465 in extras, those which brought the price up in great amounts at a time included: strato-bucket front seats $121.15; center console $53.75; Turbo Hydramatic $221.80; power steering $105.35; AM radio $61.10; cowl induction hood

Engine compartment of SS 396 is distinguished by special air cleaner with rubber seal at top which mates with inside hood opening for the cowl induction. Under normal driving air is taken in through air cleaner snorkel.

Chevelle trunk is barely adequate and not one of the roomiest in the industry. A couple of two-suiters and loose packages will fill it.

$147.45; and SS 396 equipment $445.55. The balance of the money came from deluxe belts, tinted glass, remote control mirror, positraction, evaporative emission control, front bumper guards and auxiliary lighting.

A customer looking for a lighter-in-equipment SS 396 might leave off some of the items and have a perfectly satisfactory car but we felt that we could justify everything it had for one reason or another.

As for operating economy, normal driving will range from 10.5 to 13.5 miles per gallon. That's not much economy but people don't buy an SS 396 for outstanding fuel mileage. In fact, we'll bet most SS 396 owners (and those who drive other supercars) rarely bother to check their gas mileage. After all, it is

not an aspect of the car's performance that would make for prideful conversation.

Summary

The Chevelle SS 396 has been a very fine seller with Chevrolet and it is not difficult to see why. It has strong youth appeal but Chevrolet management feels that it is beginning to be noticed by a much older segment of the buying public. It is a car that can put a little excitement into the life of a jaded motorist without making him look a total hot rodder. (The sports stripes on the hood are included with cowl induction, and they are a mite gaudy.)

Overall we were very pleased with the car; its performance, handling and comfort we found quite satisfying. It's not a perfect car but it's a good one and the engineers have had several years to refine the design. As mentioned, that extra time can make a lot of difference in the finished product. ♠

Chevelle SS 396

Data in Brief

DIMENSIONS

Overall length (in.)	197.2
Wheelbase (in.)	112.0
Height (in.)	52.6
Width (in.)	75.4
Tread (front, in.)	60.0
Tread (rear, in.)	59.8
Fuel tank capacity (gal.)	18.0
Luggage capacity (cu. ft.)	14.6
Turning diameter (ft.)	42.0

ENGINE

Type	V8 OHV
Displacement (cu. in.)	402
Horsepower (at 5200 rpm)	350
Torque (lb./ft. at 3400 rpm)	415

WEIGHT, TIRES, BRAKES

Weight (lb.)	3757
Tires	General bia/belt F70×14
Brakes, front	disc
Brakes, rear	drum

SUSPENSION

Front . . . . . independent, single leading arm type with coil springs and concentric shock absorbers; stabilizer bar

Rear . . . . Salisbury axle with control arms, coil springs, hydraulic shock absorbers, stabilizer bar

PERFORMANCE

Standing ¼ mile (sec.)	15.27
Speed at end of ¼ mile (mph)	92.98
Braking (from 60 mph, ft.)	150

The Invisible Cars

350 Chevelle — 351 Torino — 318 Satellite: unexciting, unloved, and more often than not — unwashed. Mobility for the masses — transportation for the silent majority / By Jim Brokaw

Much like the *Purloined Letter* in the Sherlock Holmes classic, the American intermediate sedans are seldom seen, commonplace, indistinguishable one from the other, and yet very much in plain sight. One usually sees a lawn, but not the blades of grass; a crowd, but not the people; the absence of an available parking space, but not the line of invisible cars tethered to the parking meters on Main Street. These are the Detroit draft horses, the darlings of the transportation purists who Naderize styling and elegance. Scorned by the body-shirted, tight-trousered aficionados, they are the beasts of burden which sell by the million year after year.

Having already tested the big family sedans and low priced compacts, and a sprinkling of specialty vehicles in between, one of the few items remaining on our domestic evaluation list is the middle-buck transportation car. By a stroke of good fortune, modified by the vagaries of low public relations budgets, our samplings represent the high, low and middle price classes of the available configurations of the cars most of you buy. The Plymouth Satellite four-door sedan, a bare bones, Plain Jane version; Ford's Torino four-door hardtop, the high buck, super luxury offering; and finally, the mini-BMW Chevrolet slipped us, a two-door semi-performance model, equipped with, seemingly every option known to man.

The intended comparison was a straight across match-up of unadorned four-door sedans with 2V medium powered engines, radio, heater, power steering, power brakes, good tires, and very little else. What we wound up with provided a much more graphic comparison of what may be desirable, as well as what is downright necessary.

The primary function of these vehicles is to transport four adults in reasonable comfort at a reasonable cost. They are also employed to transport salesmen and their sales items; construction supervisors with their charts, instruments and lunch pails; city, county and state employees, as well as an innumerable variety of lesser corporate employees whose duties require mobil-

ABOVE: Chevelle Malibu was the only two-door model tested. Rear seat leg room was insufficient to comfortably transport adults for any length of time. Rear sway bar provided excellent stability. Below: Sport interior in Chevelle had best dash layout of all three vehicles. Bucket seats were very comfortable, but robbed front seat of extra space desired for the intended use of the vehicle.

ity. A few low budgeted municipalities are using these models for police work. In essence, comfort without luxury; economy without spartanism.

Before we even start through the checklist of goods, bads, and nice-to-have-but-too-expensive items, I would like to state unequivocally that two-door models are out. In spite of advertising to the contrary, if you plan to carry an adult or two in the back seat — even a relatively small female adult — there will be gripes and groans about the availability — or lack of it — of rear seat leg room.

SEATING COMFORT and INTERIOR SPACE: Having dispatched the two-door version to the racier set, let us get on to the people-packaging. Picking your seat is a very critical operation, since that's where you spend most of your in-car time. The basic economy bench seat was in the Satellite. It was terrible. Lumbar support was non-existent; post-bump vibration dampening was an abject failure; there was a strange harmonic in the seat-back springs which set to humming on

roughly paved roads; and, to complete the picture, the genuine plastic vinyl seat covering had wrinkles in it.

Chevelle had the pseudo-leather bucket seats with spine straightener seat backs. These were well padded, gave excellent support on long or short trips, and somewhat defeated the purpose of the low-buck intermediate; that of maximum utilization of space. Buckets are out.

Torino, with the brougham interior, had a full bench seat which could hold two adults and a child for distance traveling, or three adults on a short trip. The cushioning and support was excellent with the exception of the seat back rake angle, which was more suited to a Can-Am car than a sedan. The angle can be adjusted to taste, however, with a little help from your local Ford mechanic. The upholstery was magnificent green brocade tricot — just a little bit up-town for the image we're trying to set. The ideal setup would be the next higher option bench seat above the super cheapy. This is not intended to imply that Chrysler makes bad seats

nor that Ford makes only good seats. Or, maybe it is just Plymouth who makes bad seats? Right now you're saying that everybody's standard seat is bad. The point is that the bottom-of-the-line, standard seat made by anyone is inspired by minimal cost of manufacture and little else. The top of the line fancy brougham interior is very expensive. So shoot for something in between.

Interior space was quite adequate in both four-doors, and not quite enough in the rear for the two-door. All models have from 2 to 3 more inches of back seat living space in the four-door version. Chevy and Plymouth have longer wheelbases on the four-door machines, but Ford managed to ace the passengers out of some space while retaining the same wheelbase on the two-doors.

The Satellite did have one annoying characteristic not shared by the other two: the "B" pillar, or center post, is flared below the belt line. This necessitates angling the side window track forward. When you crank the side window down a few inches to change the smog inside the car, a chilling blast of muscle-stiffening air blows directly across the back of your neck. Apparently, when Chrysler puts in flow-through ventilation, they intend for you to use it. You will *not* be old fashioned and wind down the window.

DASH PANEL LAYOUT: Chevelle took top honors in this category with their sport dash, which has a full bag of instruments, well laid out and backed up by idiot lights. It costs a bit more money, but the included tachometer, water temp, oil pressure and ammeter gauges are well worth it. Neither the Satellite dash nor the fancy Torino dash was bad; they just didn't have enough monitor gauges. I have this weird fetish for wanting to know what my engine is doing instead of what it just ceased doing. All three had good control knob accessibility. For you smokers, the addition of the courtesy light group includes a bulb for the ash

Above: Plymouth Satellite represents new Chrysler concept of designing four-door sedans with consideration for people packaging first, styling second. Result is a tastefully executed compromise with flared fender wells and upswept rear beltline to break the monotony of unadorned sheet metal. Horizontal taillights are placed, well proteced, within bumper loops.

Invisible Cars

tray, saving a lot of fumbling and near misses during night smoking operations. Chevelle also had the best steering wheel, their small diameter, vinyl covered sport model. This is strictly a matter of taste, however, and the ultimate choice is in the hands of the driver.

RIDE and HANDLING: Torino had the best ride until one encountered a large bump. The bump itself was taken in good fashion, but the front end tended to oscillate two or three times too often after level ground was reached. Chevelle's sport suspension, with 7-inch wheels and F60-15 Polyglas tires, predictably afforded the best handling of all three. Here again, the object is not to compare apples and prunes, since the standard passenger suspensions offered by the three manufacturers are quite similar in performance, as are their heavier duty options. In the case of all three, the next firmer suspension above normal will give the best compromise between ride and handling, and the plain truth is that it should be standard. If the government has its way after 1973, it will be. The trailer towing package is generally the most economical way to achieve this, usually for under $25. Satellite gave a comfortable, but noisy, ride with satisfactory handling. The suspension tended to take a rather exaggerated set going into a highway turn, but the roll moment was most stable once the suspension was set. Chevelle sacrificed a portion of ride comfort on some of the rougher roads in deference to superior handling. It is really driver's choice in this area; however, the handling options should at least be experienced in the dealer's demo.

BRAKING: At 60 mph, Chevelle came in with the best stopping distance. There was a slight tendency to turn out at the end of the full-lock stop, but not enough to leave your assigned lane. Torino came in second with no adverse

Above: Satellite's bottom of the line, economy seat was uncomfortable and poorly assembled. Next higher option would be a wiser purchase in terms of comfort and durability.

Satellite

GOOD POINTS

Excellent engine response

Transmission operation

Visibility

Rear seat leg room

BAD POINTS

Brakes

Front seat

Front side window function

Outside mirror

Power steering

reactions. Satellite was a decided third, but this was expected inasmuch as the Satellite had manual brakes and the other two had power disc/drum brakes — all of which pointedly reaffirms that it just isn't worth the money you may save, to stick with manual brakes on anything but a sub-compact. Pedal pressure on the Satellite's non-power brakes was excessive; application resulted in uneven locking of the wheels; and, until the brakes heated up, the runout was a bit squirrelly. Any intermediate sedan needs power disc/drums for maximum safety. Insurance companies should give a discount for them. Having tested Ford's manual brakes on previous models, we'd place them in the same performance category as those on the Satellite; one may assume that Chevrolet would do no better.

POWER and RESPONSE: On paper the 2V versions of the 350 (Chevy), 351 (Ford) and 318 (Plymouth) don't sound very perky, and you'll never see one of them pulling a NASCAR stocker around the high banks at Daytona; however, the astute engineers in the

Torino

GOOD POINTS

Engine response

Power steering

Interior quality

Paint

BAD POINTS

Door latches improperly adjusted

Seat back rake angle

Ride control on bumps

Below: Torino's well-balanced styling lends itself quite handily to the four-door configuration. Bumper is a bit skimpy, chrome strip is set too low for avoiding parking dings.

hidden laboratories of the big three have slide-ruled a surprising bit of performance into these mundane little clean-air engines. By selecting the proper rear end gear ratio, installing the correct cam, and jacking the timing around to bring out the right numbers on the dyno digital indicators, the point of maximum torque has been put right down where you'll do most of your driving. On the acceleration tests, all three machines consistently chirped the tires coming off the line, while Torino actually did some smokey wheel spinning. All three were responsive in traffic and presented no problem in attaining freeway on-ramp speeds. They do get a bit tired at the top end, but there is still plenty of energy to do any prudent passing which may be required. Of the three engines, the Ford 351 showed just a bit more spirit, but not enough to induce anyone to cross long term loyalty lines. If you're a Chevy nut, the 350 will satisfy; if Chrysler is your bag,

the 318 will give no cause to hide your head. Fuel economy was not up where I expected it to be, ranging from 13.45 to 14.47 mpg, but the machines were run exclusively on low lead regular fuel. It is a conceded fact that mileage is one of the sacrifices we must make in the battle for clean air.

Before any Plymouth fans get irate over the apparent mismatch of the 318 against the two larger opponents, remember the 318 is the only engine that competes in this category. The 340 is a high performance engine and, at this writing, the low emission 360 is not available in the Satellite model. Besides, it held its own on performance and came in with 14.47 mpg, the best mileage of the three. The reason for selecting these engines over the 5-liter models was to permit an assessment of power options as well as air conditioning if it happened to be installed, as it was on the Torino. The 5-liter engines can't really cut the mustard with a full

Below: Torino interior was most elegant of the lot, but a bit too expensive for the intended market. Pile carpeting is a worthwhile consideration as it is definitely more durable than standard floor covering. Solid seat back should accommodate over the shoulder restraint harnesses if they ever become fashionable with the safety set. Bench seat was most comfortable.

power bag and air conditioner on board.

QUALITY OF MATERIALS: Naturally, the brougham interior of the Torino put down the other two in every respect except cost. The rough grain vinyl in the Chevelle was just acceptable, and appeared to be a bit more durable. Paint, fit and finish awards were equally divided between the Chevelle and Torino. Since this is not a function of cost, Satellite should have been right in there swinging, but it wasn't. Chrysler realizes they suffer an acute quality control problem and have put former Dodge Division General Manager Byron Nichols in charge of a special program to translate customer complaints into remedies. Ford's exterior finish was the best, but the rear doors failed to close properly without a resounding slam. You can lay this off to improper door latch adjustment, but you get irritated at having to stop and reclose the door. So, a penalty point on Ford. The remainder of the various latches and fixtures on all three func-

Invisible Cars

tioned as were originally intended.

The eternal question looms heavily in the final pages of any multi-car comparison: which is the "best" car? In view of the diverse configurations of the machines in question, I'm going to mealy-mouth it and not pick a best car. The primary reason for evading the issue is the vast difference in quality between the bottom end super cheapy version of these intermediates and the next higher model. The quality of assembly and materials on the Satellite was so far below other Plymouth products we've tested that it would be grossly unfair to the potential consumer to "pick a winner."

The conclusion you may draw from all of this is: don't buy the car until you have personally witnessed the difference between the interior finish and appointments on the low-buck offering as compared to the next higher quality model. It may save you a lot of disappointment in the long run.

Regardless of the model selected, minimum additional equipment should include automatic transmission, power steering, power disc/drum brakes, tinted windshield, *dual* outside mirrors, and trailer towing package or sport suspension, whichever is offered as the next firmer suspension above standard. The trailer towing package is usually one of the best bargains offered, as it includes a large radiator and HD alternator.

Comfort options should include a radio; and if you do not go for air conditioning, consider power windows as an alternate means of driver-controlled ventilation. Flow-through works fine, but some like a bit more air movement.

The best combination of all would be to put the Ford power steering and interior into a Chevelle body with SS suspension and use the Plymouth 318 and torqueflite trans to move it. You will not find these options available at your local dealership.

Four-door intermediate sedans may leave you cold, but turn-on is not their bag. They are specifically designed as a means of getting the occupants from one point to the next in reasonable comfort. This they do very nicely. So leap into your Plain Jane four-door, crank up that 2V engine, glide carefully out into the traffic and disappear from sight. /MT

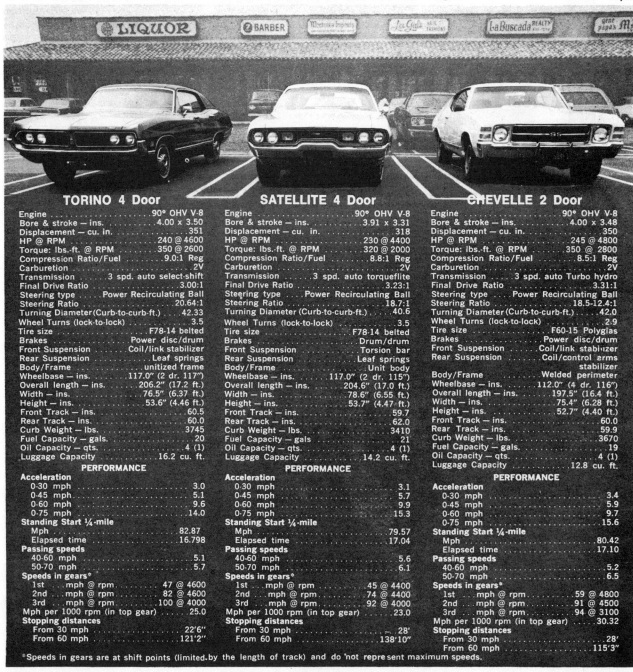

	TORINO 4 Door	SATELLITE 4 Door	CHEVELLE 2 Door
Engine	90° OHV V-8	90° OHV V-8	90° OHV V-8
Bore & stroke — ins.	4.00 x 3.50	3.91 x 3.31	4.00 x 3.48
Displacement — cu. in.	351	318	350
HP @ RPM	240 @ 4600	230 @ 4400	245 @ 4800
Torque: lbs.-ft. @ RPM	350 @ 2600	320 @ 2000	350 @ 2800
Compression Ratio/Fuel	9.0:1 Reg	8.8:1 Reg	8.5:1 Reg
Carburetion	2V	2V	2V
Transmission	3 spd. auto select-shift	3 spd. auto torqueflite	3 spd. auto Turbo hydro
Final Drive Ratio	3.00:1	3.23:1	3.31:1
Steering type	Power Recirculating Ball	Power Recirculating Ball	Power Recirculating Ball
Steering Ratio	20.64:1	18.7:1	18.5-12.4:1
Turning Diameter (Curb-to-curb ft.)	42.33	40.6	42.0
Wheel Turns (lock-to-lock)	3.5	3.5	2.9
Tire size	F78-14 belted	F78-14 belted	F60-15 Polyglas
Brakes	Power disc/drum	Drum/drum	Power disc/drum
Front Suspension	Coil/link stabilizer	Torsion bar	Coil/control arms stabilizer
Rear Suspension	Leaf springs	Leaf springs	Coil/control arms stabilizer
Body/Frame	unitized frame	Unit body	Welded perimeter
Wheelbase — ins.	117.0" (2 dr. 117")	117.0" (2 dr. 115")	112.0" (4 dr. 116")
Overall length — ins.	206.2" (17.2 ft.)	204.6" (17.0 ft.)	197.5" (16.4 ft.)
Width — ins.	76.5" (6.37 ft.)	78.6" (6.55 ft.)	75.4" (6.28 ft.)
Height — ins.	53.6" (4.46 ft.)	53.7" (4.47 ft.)	52.7" (4.40 ft.)
Front Track — ins.	60.5	59.7	60.0
Rear Track — ins.	60.0	62.0	59.9
Curb Weight — lbs.	3745	3410	3670
Fuel Capacity — gals.	20	21	19
Oil Capacity — qts.	4 (1)	4 (1)	4 (1)
Luggage Capacity	16.2 cu. ft.	14.2 cu. ft.	12.8 cu. ft.
PERFORMANCE			
Acceleration			
0-30 mph	3.0	3.1	3.4
0-45 mph	5.1	5.7	5.9
0-60 mph	9.6	9.9	9.7
0-75 mph	14.0	15.3	15.6
Standing Start ¼-mile			
Mph	82.87	79.57	80.42
Elapsed time	16.798	17.04	17.10
Passing speeds			
40-60 mph	5.1	5.6	5.2
50-70 mph	5.7	6.1	6.5
Speeds in gears*			
1st mph @ rpm	47 @ 4600	45 @ 4400	59 @ 4800
2nd mph @ rpm	82 @ 4600	74 @ 4400	91 @ 4500
3rd mph @ rpm	100 @ 4000	92 @ 4000	94 @ 3100
Mph per 1000 rpm (in top gear)	25.0	23.0	30.32
Stopping distances			
From 30 mph	22'6"	28'	28'
From 60 mph	121'2"	138'10"	115'3"

*Speeds in gears are at shift points (limited by the length of track) and do not represent maximum speeds.

104

TORINO BROUGHAM 4-DOOR HARDTOP 8-CYLINDER	
Base price	$3,248.00
Wheel covers	NC
Foam-padded seats	NC
Color-keyed nylon carpeting	NC
Flow-thru ventilation	NC
Dual headlights	NC
Belted tires	NC
351 cid 2v 8-cylinder engine	45.00
Vinyl roof	95.00
NOX emission control system	NC
Select-shift Cruise-O-Matic	217.00
F78 x 14 belted WSW tires (five)	30.00
Visibility group	38.00
Power steering	110.00
Power front disc brakes	70.00
Air conditioner — Selectaire	407.00
AM/FM stereo radio	214.00
Tinted glass — complete	43.00
Power side windows	122.00
Deluxe wheel covers	52.00
Total	$4,691.00

CHEVELLE MALIBU SPORTS COUPE	
Base V8*	$2,980.00
245-hp 350 2v	26.35
SS Equipment Group: Power disc/drum brakes; L.H. mirror — remote; Sport suspension; 15 x 7 wheels; F60 x 15 W.L.; Function symbols — knobs	357.05
Appearance guard group	31.60
TurboHydramatic	216.50
Trailer rear end ratio — 3.31	12.65
Power steering	115.90
Deluxe safety belts	15.30
Tinted glass	43.20
Special instruments	84.30
Aux. lighting	21.10
Heavy-duty radiator	21.10
AM radio	66.40
Rear speaker	15.80
Sport steering wheel	15.80
Bucket seats	136.95
Total	$4,160.00
*4-Door V8 base price	$2,773.00

PLYMOUTH SATELLITE 8-CYLINDER 4-DOOR SEDAN	
Base price	$2,829.00
318 cid engine 8-cylinder	NC
Bench seat — vinyl	NC
TorqueFlite Transmission	216.40
Tinted windshield	29.80
NOX exhaust emission control	12.95
AM radio — solid state	66.40
Power steering	116.75
Deluxe wheel covers	27.35
Tires — F78 x 14 WSW	31.95
Total	$3,330.60

HOW TO BUY

TORINO ECONOMY VERSION

Even if we're interested in saving the most bucks we can, we'd still choose a V8 over a six. Why? Because this car holds six people, and, if you include luggage, that's going to be straining a six. So our minimum choice would be the 302, followed by the two-barrel 351; the first mated to the manual 3-speed and the latter to Ford's fine 3-speed Cruise-O-Matic.

MODERATE VERSION

Let's face it — if the whole car's economical, you can afford to splurge a *little* money on extras; so, order the 351-2v with automatic, power steering and an AM radio. If you care about handling at all, order F70 x 14 tires instead of the standard E78s. For extra stopping protection, order front disc brakes.

CHEVELLE ECONOMY VERSION

As with the Torino, we would have to choose a V8 as a minimum in a car that conceivably might be called upon to haul a family and its gear on vacation. In this case, the 307 two-barrel would be adequate, mated to the optional three-speed TurboHydramatic.

MODERATE VERSION

Two-barrels are lean on gas but the 350-cu.-in. two-barrel has more torque than the 307; so, if you can come up with a few extra bucks, it's worth it. We'd mate this to an automatic for city driving and order power steering.

SATELLITE ECONOMY VERSION

For the same reason as the other two brands, we'd order the base 318 V8 as a minimum in a family car. You really should order an automatic if you can afford it. Plymouth has a good one, the TorqueFlite. Order power steering too.

MODERATE VERSION

With the Satellite's engine offerings, there's a big jump between the 318 and the next larger engine, the 383. But don't let the big increase in cubic inches scare you, because there's an economical two-barrel version rated at 275 hp. You have to order it with an automatic, and we'd specify power steering and wider tires if you can see the benefits vs. the extra cost. We think these two should be mandatory options with the big American sedans.

1971 TORINO 4-DOOR SEDAN ECONOMY POWER TEAMS

Engine	Transmission Available	Torque	Car-buretion	Comp. Ratio Fuel	Rear Axle Ratio
145-hp 250 Six	Manual 3-speed Cruise-O-Matic	232 @ 1600	One-barrel	9.0/R	2.79*, 3.00
210-hp 302 V8	Manual 3-speed Cruise-O-Matic	296 @ 2600	Two-barrel	9.0/R	3.00*, 3.25
240-hp 351 V8	Cruise-O-Matic only	350 @ 2600	Two-barrel	9.0/R	2.75*, 3.25*
285-hp 351 V8	Man. 3- or 4-Spd Cruise-O-Matic	370 @ 3400	Four-barrel	10.7/P	2.75*, 3.00* 3.25, 3.50

1971 CHEVELLE 4-DOOR SEDAN BASE POWER TEAMS

Engine	Transmission Available	Torque	Car-buretion	Comp. Ratio Fuel	Rear Axle Ratio
145-hp 250 Six	Manual 3-speed or Powerglide	230 @ 1600	One-barrel	8.5/R	3.8
200-hp 307 V8	Manual 3-speed Powerglide	300 @ 2400	Two-barrel	8.5/R	2.73*, 3.08 3.31°
245-hp 350 V8	Manual 4-speed TurboHydramatic	350 @ 2800	Two-barrel	8.5/R	2.56*, 3.36 3.31°
270-hp 350 V8	Man. 3- or 4-Spd TurboHydramatic	360 @ 3200	Four-barrel	8.5/R	2.73*, 3.86 3.31°

1971 PLYMOUTH SATELLITE 4-DOOR SEDAN ECONOMY POWER TEAMS

Engine	Transmission Available	Torque	Car-buretion	Comp. Ratio Fuel	Rear Axle Ratio
145-hp 225 Six	Manual 3-speed or TorqueFlite	215 @ 2400	One-barrel	8.4/R	2.93*, 2.94* 3.23, 3.55
230-hp 318 V8	Manual 3-speed or TorqueFlite	320 @ 2000	Two-barrel	8.8/R	2.71*, 2.94 3.23, 3.55
275-hp 383 V8	TorqueFlite only	375 @ 2800	Two-barrel	8.7/R	2.45*, 2.76* 2.94*, 3.23*
300-hp 383 V8	Man. 3- or 4-Spd TorqueFlite	410 @ 3400	Four-barrel	8.7/R	2.76*, 3.23 3.55

*Available with automatic only

NOTE: Higher-performance engines are available, but are not shown due to economy nature of test

°Avaliable only with TurboHydramatic and special suspension as Trailering Option

CHEVELLE 350ss

Biggest selling image car of them all, the SS in basic form combines family usefulness and above average performance.

Black matte grille, hood pins and power bulge are part of the $357 SS package. Single lights, adapted from '70 Monte Carlo, are more powerful than standard.

Any buyer seeks a car which will provide the best combination of style, size, performance and price. The possible combinations of these factors are virtually without number. For the typical young buyer the first three often resolve to seating for two adults and two children, at least a stand-off in the stop-light grand prix eight or nine times of each ten out of the gate, and styling that will rate at least a second look at the local drive-in. Budget considerations usually dictate that these three goals be met with a minimum capital outlay.

Any car fulfilling these requirements will command a substantial portion of the market, and the industry offers a virtual proliferation of choices. They follow a similar format — intermediate size averaging a 112-inch wheelbase, two-door sports coupe body, a list of

trim options as long as your arm and a wide variety of power alternatives.

The shopping list includes Road Runner, Barracuda, Charger, Cobra, GTO, Firebird and for the Chevrolet minded, Camaro and Chevelle SS. We recently spent a week with a Chevelle SS to refresh our opinion of how well it fits into this market group. The Chevelle was introduced into the Chevrolet line in 1964, and last year accounted for 21.5% of Chevrolet passenger vehicle sales. The high-style, added-trim SS (for Super Sports) version, which made its debut in 1965, commanded 14% of all Chevelle sales in 1970. The Chevelle SS is available this year as either a sports coupe or convertible and there is also an SS version of the popular El Camino sports pickup truck. The 145 hp 6-cylinder engine is standard, although

almost never purchased. The choice of V-8s runs from a 200 hp, 307 cu. in. base engine to the top line 365 hp, 454 cu. in. high performance special engine which is available only in the SS.

There are no major styling changes in the 1971 Chevelles, which last received an all-new body in 1968. This year's changes are directed toward safety, comfort, convenience, dependability and keeping the air clean. New features for '71 include brighter Power-Beam single unit headlights, a restyling of the front grille and bumper, front fender lights that serve as parking, turn signal and side marker lights, wheel opening moldings, wide body sill moldings, and a new rear bumper with circular openings for built-in tail lights.

Our test car was a sport coupe finished in a rich burnished brown color

Styled wheels of this type are one of several factory options. Major rear styling change involves the round tail lights imbedded in the bumper.

Instrumentation and steering wheel pictured here is part of a $100 accessory package but it's complete and thoughtfully laid out.

described in sales brochures as "Rosewood Metallic," with the interior in beige vinyl except for fabric inserts in the seat areas. The optional SS equipment group includes such items as power disc brakes, domed hood with lock pins, left hand remote mirror, 15×7 styled wheels mounted with F60-15 raised letter wide oval tires and some additional minor trim options. The style accessories also included an appearance guard group and an auxiliary lighting group. Although they are not in the SS equipment group the special instrumentation package and the 14-inch diameter padded sport steering wheel are definitely a part of the SS concept. The power train consisted of the 350 cu. in. L48 V-8 engine, 3-speed Turbo Hydramatic automatic transmission, and limited-slip differential with the optional 3.31 ratio instead of the standard 2.73 ratio.

Comfort and convenience options included deluxe seat belts, AM radio with rear seat speaker, variable ratio power steering, air-conditioning and tinted glass. The entire combination priced out at a total of $4,522.10, to which of course must be added destination charges, dealer preparation, tax and license.

That is a pretty healthy price tag, to be sure, but the set-up on our test car would pretty well match the average requirements of the Chevelle SS owners who responded to our *Road Test* Owner's Survey. The favorite reason listed for purchasing the car was to get a "good looking high-performance car," closely followed by price and straight performance considerations.

Notwithstanding the fact that performance is uppermost in the mind of many, we selected what would be considered a mid-range power team for this test for a couple of reasons. Tests of the ultra-high-performance versions are readily available in the magazines which specialize in the subject, and we feel that the power team in our test car does a better job of meeting the objectives of a majority of buyers.

There are substantial differences in engine options. The 350 cu. in. L48 engine as installed in our test car uses a cast iron crank and hydraulic lifters with valve timing of 280° inlet, 288° exhaust, and 58° overlap. Intake lift is .39 in., exhaust .41 in. A 4V Rochester carburetor with 1.38 in. main throats and 2.25 in. secondary barrels operates

smoke the tires at the line at all.

The engine pulls strongly up to the automatic shift point which takes place at 4,500 rpm. There is no tire chirp when the shift from first to second gear is made at 48 mph and the shift from second to third takes place regularly just as you flash through the traps at the end of the strip with an indicated 85 mph on the speedometer. The tachometer has a yellow range from 4,800 to 5,200 rpm with a red band from 5,200 to 5,500 rpm. The power peak is at 4,800 though, so we also tried a few runs shifting manually at 5,200 rpm. At that speed we still weren't floating the valves, and we got the impression that the engine was willing to take at least another 500 rpm, but we didn't feel like twisting a new engine any faster. The extra 700 rpm before the shift from first to second gear didn't do anything for either the elapsed time or terminal speed, strangely, although it did mean

Power bulge is strictly cosmetic unless the extra-cost cowl induction system is ordered. In either case, it tends to hinder forward vision.

Fat eight-inch Goodyears were more than adequate to handle power served up by the 270-hp 4V 350. Single exhaust, however, was out of place at the Lion Dragway.

on an 8.5 to one compression ratio. Surprisingly, a single exhaust is fitted.

By comparison, the high-performance 454 cu. in. L56 engine uses a forged steel crank and 9.0:1 compression. Mechanical lifters actuate a wilder valve timing of 316° inlet, 302° exhaust, 80° duration, with .52 in. inlet and exhaust valve lift. Carburetion is by a 4V Holley with 1.69 in. main and secondary barrels, and a dual exhaust system with resonators is used. The large engines can also be ordered with cowl induction which allows the carburetor to gulp cold air from the high pressure area at the base of the windshield when maximum power is needed.

With the higher power set-ups the automatic transmission is usually replaced with a heavy-duty four-speed floor-shifted manual transmission coupled with a single dry plate clutch. With the L56 engine package the 3.31 rear-end ratio is standard with an optional 4.10 ratio available to those who place great emphasis on quarter-mile performance.

On that subject, we were quite inter-

ested in what the L48 engine would show us on the drag strip. After reviewing the specifications we were not expecting outstanding performance, so it was no surprise to find that the combination of 270 horsepower and the long gear ratio added up to some pretty nominal quarter-mile times. In fact, the big tires put so much rubber on the strip that it was only by winding the engine up to 2,500 rpm and holding solidly on the brake pedal until the Chrondek light turned green that we were able to

that we were going through the speed trap while still in second gear.

On the freeway, of course, it's a different story. At 65 mph the engine is loafing along at 2,500 rpm and you have to look at the tach to know whether or not the engine is even running. There is no engine or drive train noise at these speeds, and for that matter not much noise either. Naturally the 350 is not nearly as thirsty as the larger engines. Around town we averaged 11.8 mpg, on regular gas, which in-

Wheelspin required winding the 350 against the brake to 2,500 rpm, an academic exercise that does nothing to improve elapsed times.

creased to nearly 13 mpg out on the open highway.

Coil springs are used for suspension at all four corners, augmented by a .81 in. diameter front stabilizer bar. The front control arms are inclined, so that they will resist nose dive during heavy braking, and control arms are used with the linked Salisbury rear axle to resist acceleration squat. Weight distribution is 55%/45% front/rear. Although an SS350, our test car had the 15×7 Trans-Am styled wheels and the F60 raised letter tires normally fitted only with the SS454 package. We feel that these wheels and tires are worth their purchase price just on the basis of the considerable contribution they make to appearance, although the eight inches of rubber they put on the road also makes a major contribution in the areas of acceleration, handling and braking.

While we were at the dragstrip we also explored handling characteristics at the limit of adhesion. On very hard cornering the body rolls until the outside front springs are compressed solid — visually more apparent from the outside than the inside. The fat Goodyears hold mightily, resisting breakaway with a loud scream until the front-end finally breaks loose, and the car plows to a halt.

We got a more realistic appraisal of handling during a trip over some secondary roads winding through the local foothills. The SS350 gets through this sort of country in remarkably good or-

der. Its behavior is good enough to give you enough confidence so that you don't get on the brakes as soon or as hard going into a hairpin curve. Tire squeal gives adequate notice of impending difficulty, and after several miles of pressing quite hard there wasn't a single instance when we even thought we were going to get out of shape.

A major contribution to both ease and pleasure of driving is made by the combination of variable ratio power steering and the 14-inch diameter padded steering wheel. Power steering is a must with the wide tires and front-end weight bias, of course, and using it also allows a reduction in the overall steering ratio so that only 2.9 turns of the wheel are required to move from lock to lock. The small wheel allows maximum steering corrections with a minimum of arm flailing. It's mighty handy in the hills, but don't try to drive very far if the power steering unit ever fails (a very infrequent occurrence, we might add).

Usually a suspension set-up for any kind of decent handling means a very firm ride. In the case of the Chevelle SS, Chevrolet has compromised short of this effect. On a smooth highway the ride is, well, uneventful, and there's no awareness of being in a high-performance car. Small bumps are transmitted to the driver as much by noise as by feel — it seems as though the sound is picked up by the body structure. Over a rough cobblestone-type surface the wheels stay well put on the road and very little of the roughness is transmitted to the driver. Major bumps are quickly smoothed out, and the pitch control is excellent.

During the course of a year we test drive a wide variety of domestic cars,

and we often find them remiss in brake performance by comparison with their imported counterparts. Thus, we were pleasantly surprised to discover the brakes of the Chevelle SS to be nearly on a par with the best. Eleven-inch diameter vented cast iron rotors are used for the front brakes, with 9.5-in. drums at the rear, with the division of front to rear effort controlled by a modulating valve. A normal stop can be made from 60 mph in 175 feet with no need for steering correction. In a simulated panic situation we were able to reduce this distance to 141 feet by increasing the pedal pressure and making a few minor steering corrections. When we did lock the brakes, all four wheels locked together, and there was no swerve to the side which comes with rear wheel lock-up. After several such stops there was neither fade nor that unpleasant smell and smoke which frequently follows maximum service brake tests.

One of the more attractive styling features of the current crop of Chevrolets is the pronounced tumble home. However, this also means that the windows slope inward so far that they could interfere with one's head while entering or exiting from the car when they are up, especially in a parking lot where the doors cannot be opened fully. We know of no solution to this — handsome is as handsome does. Aside from this feature, access to the front seats is convenient, but a few contortions are required to enter or leave the rear seats.

Once inside on the standard bench seat (bucket seats are available for those who care) you look forward over what seems like an acre of hood. Visibility directly ahead and particulary toward the right front fender is obscured by the power bulge, which contributes a purely cosmetic effect except on those high-performance engines fitted with cowl induction. Visibility toward the rear quarters is moderatly obscured, but satisfactory in other directions.

Looking inside the Chevelle SS, you regard one of the better instrument packages we have encountered. A row of four circular gauges with white letters on a black background gives the impression of having been designed by automotive enthusiasts for automotive enthusiasts. The tach and speedometer flank the steering column. A clock is at the far right and supplementary temperature, fuel, and ammeter gauges complete the display. All controls are located within easy reach of the driver and arranged so that they may be operated without diverting attention from the road.

Seat belts are the usual mess en-

Unless a collapsible spare is installed, trunk room in the Chevelle is pretty marginal. Chevrolet should also furnish a cover for the spare to protect the luggage.

The Chevelle series got its last major body change in 1968, is due for another in '72. Sports coupe and the convertible are the two SS styles offered.

a Hurst shifter), drive train in general, and high operating costs. Nearly three-fourths of owners had experienced significant trouble, with the drive train being the major problem area.

Only a little more than half of the owners who returned questionnaires to us have their cars serviced regularly at dealers, with two-thirds of the owners expressing dissatisfaction with the cost and quality of dealer service. The most commonly expressed reason for not having service performed at a dealer was that it was the owner's preference to do his own mechanical work.

And what if we were to buy a Chevelle SS? How would we order it to be equipped? Well, first of all the car would be for family use — driving to and from work or on the occasional trip, but not for racing. We are attracted by the same features mentioned by our readers — road performance, ride and handling, and styling and in addition, the excellent brake performance. For appearance, we

countered in domestic cars. There are six loose belt ends flailing around in the front seat, not to mention the additional two shoulder harness ends at each side. A thoughtful encouragement not to use the center passenger belt or shoulder harness is provided by clips on the front of the front seat to which the loose ends may be attached. However they must be loosened and readjusted whenever the seat is moved forward such as when changing from a tall to a shorter driver — like every time the little woman decides to run up to the supermarket. We know this piece is about a Chevelle, but we still feel that every Detroit executive responsible for approval of seat belt installation designs should become familiar with the simple, effective, self-storing retracting arrangement on the Volvo 164.

Astro ventilation plus air-conditioning provide all weather comfort with windows up, and although some Chevelle owners have complained about the vent-

less side glass and expressed a desire for a return to wind wings, we applaud the contribution to style, cost reduction and all-around quieter driving made by the ventless windows.

In addition to our own behind-the-wheel impressions, we reviewed the comments of Chevelle SS owners who had returned questionnaires, mainly on '68 and '69 SS 396s, with a smattering of '67 and '70 models. The cars in our sample profile, mostly bought new, had an average of 23,000 miles put on them by their present owners, and were returning 10 mpg in town and nearly 14 on the open highway. Most liked features included road performance, ride and handling, and styling, as might be expected. Disliked features included the factory installed Muncie shifter (most of those really concerned had converted to

would order the SS equipment group plus the special instrumentation group and the sports steering wheel. Our power team would consist of the 350 cu. in. engine as installed in our test car, Turbo-Hydramatic transmission, 3.31 rear axle ratio and power steering. Naturally we would have a radio, probably AM. Air-conditioning needs are determined by geographic more than price considerations, but the extra cost is usually recovered at trade-in time.

But if we were buying an SS to go racing, well, pass the air conditioning, tinted glass and special light and appearance groups. In with the 454 cu. in. L56 engine, close ratio 4-speed box, 4.10 rear end, and 15×7 wheels with the F60 tires. And we think we would win our share.

Ron Hickman

1. Forced ventilation intake
2. Accessible wiper motor
3. Brake servo assist
4. Poor sparkplug accessibility
5. Oversized compressor
6. Cross-flow radiator
7. Side terminal battery
8. Hose merchant's delight

CHEVROLET CHEVELLE SS 2-DOOR SPORT COUPE

PERFORMANCE AND MAINTENANCE

Acceleration: Gears:
   0-30 mph . . . . 4.0 secs.— I
   0-45 mph . . . . 6.5 secs.— I
   0-60 mph . . . . .10.1 secs.—I, II
   0-75 mph . . . . .13.8 secs.—I, II
   0-1/4 mile . . . . 16.9 secs. @ 82 mph
Ideal cruise . . . . .70 mph
Top speed (est) . . . . .117 mph
Stop from 60 mph . . . . .141 ft.
Average economy (city) . . . . .11.8 mpg
Average economy (country) . . . . .12.6 mpg
Fuel required . . . . .Regular
Oil change (mos./miles) 4/6000
Lubrication (mos./miles) 4/6000
Warranty (mos./miles) 12/12,000
Type tools required . . . . .SAE
U.S. dealers . . . . .6280 total

*Power assisted as tested

SPECIFICATIONS AS TESTED

Engine . . . . .350 cu in., OHV 4V V-8
Bore & stroke . . . . .4.00 x 3.48 ins.
Compression ratio . . . . .8.5 to one
Horsepower . . . . . .270 (SAE gross) at 4800 rpms
Torque . . . . .400 lbs.-ft. @ 3200 rpms
Transmission . . . . .3-speed, automatic
Steering* . . . . .2.9 turns, lock to lock
                45.5 ft., curb to curb
Brakes* . . . . .disc front, drum rear
Suspension . . . . .coil front, coil rear
Tires . . . . .F60x15, belted 4PR Goodyear
Dimensions (ins.):
  Wheelbase . . . .112.0 Front track 60.0
  Length . . . . . . .197.5 Rear track 59.9
  Width . . . . .75.4 Ground clearance .4.6
  Height . . . . . . .52.7 Weight . . . .3650 lbs.
Capacities: Fuel . . .19.0 gals.   Oil . . .5.0 qts.
      Coolant . . . .17.0 qts.   Trunk . . . .12.8 cu. ft.

RATING

	Excellent (91-100)	Good (81-90)	Fair (71-80)	Poor (60-70)
Brakes	91			
Comfort		85		
Cornering		88		
Details		81		
Finish		88		
Instruments	94			
Luggage		84		
Performance			80	
Quietness		81		
Ride		85		
Room			80	
Steering	92			
Visibility		81		
Overall		85		

n/a — not available

BASE PRICE OF CAR

(Excludes state and local taxes, license, dealer preparation and domestic transportation: $2975 at Flint, Mich.

Plus desirable options:
$ 357 SS equipment
$ 74 270-hp L48 engine
$ 216 Turbo Hydramatic
$ 116 Variable ratio power steering
$ 100 Sports instrumentation & steering wheel
$ 408 Air-conditioning
$4246 TOTAL
$0.81 per lb. (base price).

ANTICIPATED DEPRECIATION

(Based on current Kelley Blue Book, previous equivalent model): $252 1st yr. + $611 2nd yr.

N/A — not applicable

The Long and The Short of it

As the crack in the intermediate dam widens, Ford
breaks out a long wheelbase sedan to capture those
who think big, while Chevrolet holds its ground in hopes
of luring the small car fan/By Jim Brokaw

Road Test

An economic hernia, followed closely by a body blow from the insurance industry, tolled the bell for the intermediate American automobile in 1970. Chronic symptoms of monetary malnutrition have lured car buyers away from the dubious value of the intermediate into either the compact and sub-compact areas, seeking a lower price tag for their means of conveyance, or up into the full-car ranks to search out more car for the buck. If this were the only problem to deal with, the manufacturers would simply milk the market till it was no longer financially sound to produce the intermediate, then let it slide gracefully into the mired limbo of cars that used to be, joining such tuskless mastodons as the Kaiser, Packard, Studebaker and the ultimate symbol of sheet metal birth defects, the Edsel.

Fortunately for our flagging national pride and morale, extenuating circumstances prevail which make it mandatory to dig in and fight to the bitter end for each and every piece of machinery built and sold in the U.S. In the old days, before the Bug, a failing model did not mean too much, as the lost buyers simply switched to another size or shape. The corporate coffers continued to wax healthy, and the annual statements exuded confident cheer and black ink. The buyers *are* switching to other models, but they belong to a different set of manufacturers and the truckloads of money which are being hauled out through New York and San Francisco are keeping the workers full of sake and strudel instead of beer and pizza. A lost sale may mean a lost job.

Some detailed scrutiny reveals that the bulk of the pre-1970 intermediate market consisted of two-door models whose prime appeal was to the ego and spirit of adventure possessed by the purchaser. Four-door models were badly butchered cousins of the star, whose dimensions were flogged, battered and stretched to accommodate the extra set of doors, with no regard to styling. Wheelbases and floor pans were commonly shared. One by one, led by GM, the car builders went over to a separate chassis for the four-door, more suited to the task of supporting four doors and two seats with leg and hip room for all. Chrysler joined the bandwagon in 1971 and Ford climbed aboard for 1972.

An unemotional and unprejudiced peep into the dyspepsia and hypertension of Detroit reveals that lurking behind that facade of indifference to the needs of the public and a pathological lust for longer-lower-wider, there resides a wealth of perception and raw in-

telligence. Chevrolet chose the premise that silicone and surgery can rejuvenate anything that is still possessed of sound basic construction, while Ford went the route of the transplant.

What we have is a pair of completely different automobiles being marketed as intermediates. The two-door Chevelle is as different from the four-door Chevelle as Raquel Welch is from your sister. The two-door is exemplary of the tried and true, with a few new tricks to keep you from being bored, not to men-

Top: Gran Torino Sport, modified to include a fastback roofline and a decorative hood scoop, gets you to thinking that Ford may be entering ideas of a return to racing. Not so, just one of the slickest of Ford's better ideas. Above: Chevelle has revised grille and headlights to distinguish '72 model.

tion the silicone. Still the basic, well-conceived, well-executed Chevelle, the '72 version offers a new grille, single-lamp "Power Beam" headlights, a wet look vinyl roof, new paint and a host of comfort and luxury options, at a slight extra charge. Some strategically located rubber plugs and strips reduce minor crunch damage, while the slow garroting of the smog monster results in a slightly more rapid strangulation of power and efficiency. Our Malibu had all of the options known to man, plus a few known only to the product planners. It comes off as a personal machine with compact dimensions, but not compact enough; very nimble and light-footed on the road, but sometimes a bit too light-footed, seating space is adequate, but leaves you feeling cramped. With the Chevelle sitting on a wheelbase only one inch longer than its little cousin, it comes off as a slightly oversized Nova. With the same power train, the only thing it can really do better than the Nova is carry three people in

the back seat.

The four-door Chevelle is a completely practical means of conveyance for five people, totally devoid of any detectable excitement. Visibility is good, ingress and egress are easily accomplished, the back seat is roomy and comfortable, with adequate leg and head room. The front seat is cramped, with a bad rake angle on the seatback.

Ford, being the last to jump into the dual wheelbase intermediate market, has had a chance to give the problem some heavy scrutiny. The Gran Torino Sport (modified to include a Sportsroof) is an execution of the realization that the only thing that is going to sell a two-door intermediate is styling. The graceful, flowing lines and the 60⁰ rake angle on the windshield are aerodynamically sound, with great possibilities for the big NASCAR ovals. The only flaw is the size. That beautiful, graceful beast is about a foot too long, and four inches too wide. Five inches chopped out of the vertical section from the front bumper back to the firewall would stir the juices of even a sporty car driver. But, Ford doesn't race anymore, and we need the extra foot out front to absorb the impact if and when we crash. Right?

Visibility is an inherent sacrifice in a fastback, but it isn't as severe as in years past, and an optional outside mirror on the right-hand door will help keep the traffic in sight. The integral headrest buckets are an improvement

))))

over last year's offering, but they are still contoured to put your gluteus maximus forward of the spinal column. That ain't how it's supposed to work.

The four-door Gran Torino is a whole different world. Sitting on a four-inch longer wheelbase, 118" to 114" for the racer, the Gran Torino (I hate to call it "GT," some insurance company will slap a surcharge on it) is Ford's look into the future. In spite of official estimates of a pending boom, it does appear that the money situation may get healthy, but it won't get into the Rockefeller range. With dollar demands cropping up all about us, sooner or later the Archie Bunkers of the U.S. are going to have to reduce the size of their cars, or increase the size of the monthly payments. Ford is betting that they'll go for smaller cars.

By producing a machine that has a wheelbase only one inch shorter than the 1964 Galaxie 500 XL, pride of the line, coupled with a Brougham interior which matches the LTD for quality, all that remains is to lure Archie into a test drive.

Like all machines locally built, there are several levels of Torino. The standard interior is satisfactory, but the Brougham is definitely uptown. The integrated headrest, nylon tricot upholstered, foam-lined seat has an additional pad for lumbar support. It works. Not only is it comfortable, but in a rad-

ical departure from industry SOP, the instrument panel is laid out in easy to read pods with functional gauges.

The power train in all four vehicles is nothing new, with the exception of the smog revisions. The Chevelles had the 350 ci 4V for the two door and 2V for the four-door. Oddly enough, the 2V was able to get through the slow starting 2.73:1 rear end and out-perform the 4V in spite of 10 more horsepower and a 3.31:1 rear axle ratio. The only place where the 4V came through was at the top end when the 2V began to run out of breath. Just to make the oddity complete, the 2V deferred to the 4V in fuel economy 11.68 mpg to 12.63 mpg. Part of this can be laid to the fact that the 4V spent more time at cruising speed than the 2V.

The Torinos were respectable down the Orange County drag strip, but slower than the Chevys. The 351-2V in the two-door should have pulled the 2V Chevy, as its torque curve peaks at 2000 rpm to the 350's 2400 rpm. The fact that the Torino is 540 lbs. heavier with 4 less horsepower, more than eats up the torque advantage.

The four-door, tipping the scales at 4,250 lbs. sported a 429-4V power plant. The 30 hp edge over the Chevys, backed up by a 42 lbs.-ft. advantage in torque was needed to remain in the ballpark. It's just basic physics that the heavier body needs more horses to overcome inertia. Surprise number two was the fact that it didn't pay an economy penalty, logging in at 11.52 mpg. This

is poor compared to some of the small engined imports, but in keeping with its domestic, desmogged, brethren.

Ride and handling was one of the areas that separated the two makes. The two-door Malibu had the trailering and heavy-duty suspension package. It got the job done, remaining stable and agile below 60 mph and exhibiting moderate harshness on road bumps. Suspension deflections were dampened rapidly, but tended toward twitchiness over 60 mph. The four-door was equipped with the standard suspension without the trailering package. Bump absorption was fine, but cornering induced some slop in roll control. Fortunately, the relative lightness and excellent weight distribution of the Chevelle, minimizes any suspension inadequacies.

Torino has a completely new perimeter frame chassis for '72, with coils all around and a four-link rear suspension with an anti-roll stabilizer bar. It works, but you have to have the right combination for the task at hand. The standard suspension is designed for those who ride in their cars in a relatively straight line and do not wish to be disturbed. The road isolation and vibration dampening is superb, the handling is not. There is an unpleasant amount of nose pitch in the standard setup which Ford will likely cure with a running change.

To get the same comfort with positive control over your machine, the cross country, or trailering, option is mandatory. It has good pitch control and favorable roll control, but does not penalize the passengers with harshness. A must for drivers.

The two-door fastback Torino is obviously a driver's car, requiring something more than cocoonlike isolation from the environment. The competition suspension is the ticket. Unlike the super heavy-duty set of springs in years past, the folks at Ford have managed to produce superior control without harshness. It takes a ride in one to truly appreciate it, but all the street handling you could expect from 4,000 lbs. of rubber and steel is there.

Quality control has always been good at GM, and it is getting better at Ford. The two are about on a par in the intermediate offerings. Luxury items are top quality going in, and are executed as well as can be expected in an assembly line environment. The lower quality items are nevertheless, properly installed and fit well. The only area where Chevy does not live up to their reputation is in the placement of the ignition system components. They are tucked away against the firewall behind the air cleaner. This won't bother the average motorist, but if your mechanic seems a bit testy after the semi-annual tune-up, you'll know why.

Top left & right: Chevelle dash panels are simple, functional. Bottom left and right: Torino base dash and optional full set of instruments.

LONG AND SHORT

One most welcome change on the Torino is the door latch which overrides the lock button. A second, equally welcome change, is the optional performance instrument cluster. Two large pods house the tach and speedometer, with five smaller pods enclosing the fuel quantity, water temp, ammeter, oil pressure and the eternal clock. There are back-up idiot lights for all functions including front seat belts.

Trailering options are available for both the Chevelles and the Torinos. Torino has a Class II option for 3,500-lb. trailers with a max tongue weight of 500 lbs. and a Class III package for 6,000-lb. trailers and 700-lb. tongue load. Chevy has trailering options, but they are specifically tailored to your needs. So, get the specs on your trailer and visit the local Chevy merchant.

Which is best? A very difficult question to answer, as each vehicle tends to overlap into a different category, but I choose the Fords. The four-door Gran Torino offers a new concept for intermediate sedans and is, at this testing, without peer. The Gran Torino Sport is a gallant effort to save a withering breed. The balance of handling and ride offered by the new four-link suspension, placing the roll center only eight inches off the road surface, affords a more stable high-speed ride than the Chevelle and less harshness with equal stability at low speeds. The four-door Chevelle has no salient faults, nor does it have any distinguishing features. That's the way we see it, so all you Chevophiles gather up your sack of rocks and please don't use rusty nails. /MT

SPECIFICATIONS

SPECIFICATIONS	Torino 2-Dr.	Chevelle 2-Dr.	Torino 4-Dr.	Chevelle 4-Dr.
Engine:	OHV V8	OHV V8	OHV V8	OHV V8
Bore & Stroke — ins.	4.00 x 3.50	4.00 x 3.48	4.00 x 3.50	4.00 x 3.48
Displacement—cu. in.	351	350	429	350
HP @ RPM (SAE Net)	161 @ 4000	175 @ 4000	205 @ 4400	165 @ 4000
Torque: lbs.-ft. @ rpm	276 @ 2000	280 @ 2400	322 @ 2600	280 @ 2400
Compression Ratio	8.6:1	8.5:1	8.5:1	8.5:1
Carburetion	2v	4v	4v	2v
Transmission	3-Speed auto	3-Speed auto	3-Speed auto	3-Speed auto
Final Drive Ratio	2.75:1	3.31:1	2.75:1	2.73:1
Steering Type	Power	Var. ratio power	Power	Var. ratio power
Steering Ratio	21.8:1	18.5-12.4:1	21.8:1	18.5-12.4:1
Turning Diameter (Curb-to-curb-ft.)	41.7	42.0	41.7	42.0
Wheel Turns (lock to lock)	3.7	5.5	3.7	5.5
Tire Size	G70-14	F78-14	H70-14	E78-14
Brakes	Manual disc/drum	Power disc/drum	Power disc/drum	Power disc/drum
Front Suspension	Coil/stabilizer	Coil/stabilizer	Coil/stabilizer	Coil/stabilizer
Rear Suspension	Coil/4-link	Coil/trailing arm	Coil/4-link	Coil/Trailing arm
Body/Frame Construction	Perimeter frame	Perimeter frame	Perimeter frame	Perimeter frame
Wheelbase — ins.	114	112.0	118	116.0
Overall Length — ins.	207.3	197.5	211.3	201.5
Width — ins.	79.3	75.4	79.3	75.4
Height — ins.	51.6	52.7	52.5	53.3
Front Track — ins.	62.8	60.0	62.8	60.0
Rear Track — ins.	62.9	59.9	62.9	59.9
Curb Weight — lbs.	4,040	3,650	4,250	3,510
Fuel Capacity — gals.	23	19	23	19
Oil Capacity — qts.	4 (1)	4 (1)	4 (1)	4 (1)

PERFORMANCE

PERFORMANCE	Torino 2-Dr.	Chevelle 2-Dr.	Torino 4-Dr.	Chevelle 4-Dr.
Acceleration				
0-30 mph	4.1	3.9	4.2	3.7
0-45 mph	6.7	6.4	6.7	6.2
0-60 mph	10.7	10.1	10.1	10.2
0-75	15.9	15.4	14.9	13.2
Standing Start				
¼-mile MPH	80	80	82	80
Elapsed time	17.9	17.3	17.3	17.8
Passing speeds				
40-60 mph	6.0	5.5	4.7	5.5
50-70 mph	6.6	6.4	6.2	5.9
Speeds in gears*				
1st ... mph @ rpm	49 @ 4400	43 @ 4000	47 @ 4000	39 @ 4000
2nd ... mph @ rpm	80 @ 4400	72 @ 4000	78 @ 4000	72 @ 4000
3rd ... mph @ rpm	95 @ 3500	93 @ 3500	98 @ 3500	94 @ 3500
MPH per 1000 rpm (in top gear)	27	26.5	28	26.8
Stopping distances				
From 30 mph	32 ft. 6 in.	34 ft. 11in.	34 ft. 7 in.	32 ft.
From 60 mph	138 ft.	147 ft. 3 in.	148 ft.	135 ft. 9 in.
Gas milage range—mpg	9.66-14.38/11.51 average	12.4-12.86/12.63 average	10.66-12.38/11.52 average	10.42-12.94/11.68
Speedometer error				
Car speed	28 43 49 59 70 80	29 44 49 60 71 81	29 44 49 59 69 79	29 44 49 62 72 82
True speed	30 45 50 60 70 80	30 45 50 60 70 80	30 45 50 60 70 80	30 45 50 60 70 80
Base Price	$3,166	$3,050	$2,950	$2,682
Options	$1,536	$1,710	$2,112	$ 688
Price as tested	$4,702	$4,760	$5,062	$3,350
Car of the Year Score	73.2	69.8	73.8	68.6

*Speeds in gears are at shift points (limited by the length of track) and do not represent maximum speeds.

By Gray Baskerville

Roger Baron, a 21-year-old machinist from Norwalk, California, doesn't fit into the stereotype gear-head mold. He's quiet, clean-cut, polite, and punctual—that's where it ends. He's a full-on hot rodder. Give him a Chevy with a big motor and he'll go for it. And if you think his '66 Chevelle, armed with something like 461 inches of big-inch bow tie, doesn't go for it, then try a steady barrage of 10.90s @ 128 mph on OCIR's clocks.

"What I originally intended to build was a nice little street/strip car, something with a complete interior and quick-connect mufflers so I could do a bit of serious cruising." That isn't *quite* how it began. You see, Roger works next door to Carl Smith. Smith happens to own a complete machine shop and fabrication facility, and, lo and behold, Smith's specialty centers around building all-out bracket

(continued overleaf)

Would you believe 0-60 in 1.26 seconds? Believe it . . . under the hood resides a fully blue'd 461 open-chamber Rat stuffed with TRW slugs, L88 rods, and Erson roller cam, topped by dual Holley 660s and a Weiand tunnel ram, and exhausted by Hooker. Rest of drivetrain consists of stout Turbo 400 trans (equipped with B&M full-manual valve body and 3500 stall converter), backed by 4.56-geared Dana rear narrowed 1 inch and fitted with Henry's axles. Koni coil-overs work with Lakewood traction bars to keep big slicks firmly planted. Stewart-Warner gauges and rollbar grace black and red leather factory-style interior.

Nice 'n' Nasty

Roger Baron's Rat-On Chevelle

Was Born

To Be Bad

Nice 'n' Nasty

bombers. You can guess the rest. Roger had this big-block '69 El Camino, and one of Smith's employees, Bruce Welsher, owned a similar '66 Chevelle. The upshot of the story is this: a trade was made, and Baron wound up with Bruce's beast. "I traded Bruce straight across for his unfinished Chevelle, and with the help of my brothers, Robert and Hal; Bruce Welsher; painters Steve Simbera and Steve Johnstone; and engine builder Carl Smith of Carl's Custom in Paramount, California, I've now got a quiet sleeper."

I really can't say how quiet Roger's sleeper is because we did our rod test at Orange County International Raceway drag strip, and I was on the phone when he uncorked the '66 in the pits. It may not have sounded like the cackle of a top fueler, but I don't have to remind you that the cacophony produced by 461 inches of rat isn't exactly what you would call a gentle murmur in the valley of love. And doing 0-60 clockings isn't all that easy either, especially when you're trying to watch the '66's speedo, run a stopwatch, and fight the effects of some instant acceleration.

First, I had to crawl over a diagonal support tube, which is part of the full roll cage made from 1¼-inch by .125-inch wall chrome-moly tubing, into a near-perfect interior. Then, Roger reached for the floor-mounted B&M shifter, rattled it around for a while, and it was bleach box time. After a quivering burnout, mixed with a series of chirpies, we were off to the races.

Up front is simply a .030-inch over 454 Chevy V8. I say simply because there is nothing trick about the bored, balanced, and blueprinted '77 rat attack. True, the Carl Smith-prepared

fat-block features an align bored, stress relieved, power honed, decked, and detailed cylinder block. The engine also is fitted with a fully radiused, straightened, polished, and index-ground stock steel crank, while the balance of the reciprocating assembly consists of TRW open-chamber pistons and polished, peened, and re-sized L88 steel rods. Meanwhile, the fat rat remains well lubricated thanks to a TRW high-volume oil pump and an 8-quart "dooner" pan.

Camshafting is in the form of a Sig Erson-style, dual-pattern roller (.650-inch on the intakes, .660-inch on the exhausts) tied into a valvetrain package made up of Erson roller tappets, Crane 1.7:1 rocker arms, Crane pushrods, Erson retainers, Manley valves (2.19-inch intakes, 1.88-inch exhausts with ⅜-inch stems), and Erson triple-wound valve springs. A pair of '78 open-chamber heads (ported, matched, and cc'd by Carl's Customs) plus a Weiand tunnel ram intake and two Holley 660-cfm carburetors complete the rest of the induction system.

Now when you've got a torque peak of 525 ft.-lbs. at 4200 rpm, you have to hook it up or you'll find yourself shot down. Gettin' a grip on the starting line is left up to a combination of Koni coil-over shocks, a set of Mura-massaged 32-inch traction bars, a Dana "pumpkin" fitted with 4.56s feeding into a pair of Henry's axles, and two big-by-large Goodyear slicks.

The Chevelle's stance, achieved by a front suspension that has been dropped 2 inches, and a wheel/tire combination made up of 15x3½-inch and 15x10-inch Center Lines sporting both 28x14-15 and 30x14-15 Goodyear

tires, ensures the car looks mean, not obscene. Save for the hood scoop, race-style rolling stock, and ear-shattering exhaust note, Baron's barn burner remains a successful conclusion to what a British rod magazine would call, "the Empire Strikes Black." **HR**

HOT ROD MAGAZINE'S ROD SPECIFICATIONS

1966 Chevelle Two-Door Sedan
Roger Baron, Norwalk, California

ENGINE:
Engine Type .... 1977 Chevrolet V8
Displacement .... 461 cubic inches

DRIVELINE:
Transmission .... 1969 Turbo 400 fitted with a B&M valve body and 3500-rpm stall converter
Rearend .... Dana 12-bolt narrowed 1 inch and fitted with 4.56 ring and pinion

CHASSIS:
Frame .... 1966 Chevelle augmented with a six-point roll cage made from 1¼-inch by .125-inch wall chrome-moly tubing
Front Suspension .... 1966 Chevelle
Rear Suspension ...... 1966 Chevelle fitted with Lakewood traction bars, Koni coil-over shocks
Spindles .... 1966 Chevelle
Springs .... Front: 1966 Chevelle; Rear: Koni
Shocks .... Front: Gabriel; Rear: Koni
Brakes .... 1966 Chevelle augmented with a Mr. Gasket "line lock"
Wheels .. Center Line; Front: 15x3½-inch; Rear: 15x10-inch
Tires .... Goodyear, Front: 28.0 x 14.0-15; Rear: 30.0 x 14.0-15

MEASUREMENTS:
Wheelbase .... 9 feet, 10 inches
Weight .... 3400 pounds
Overall Height .... 4 feet, 9 inches
Overall Width .... 6 feet, 2 inches
Overall Length .... 16 feet, 5 inches
Track ...... Front: 6 feet; Rear: 6 feet, 1 inch
Stopping .... 40 feet @ 30 mph
Turn Radius .... 36 feet, 10 inches
Color .... Black Centari acrylic enamel by Steve Johnstone
Instruments .... Stewart-Warner
Performance .... 10.96 @ 128.98 and 0-60 mph in 1.26 seconds
Cost $9000

Mystery Machine

The Z-16 Chevelle Legend: A Combo Of Myth And Fact

The legends surrounding the Z-16 Chevelle, rooted in fact but by now enhanced by fiction, portray the car as one of the most intriguing musclecars of the horsepower era.

Consider, for example, the statement that the Z-16 didn't need a posi. Due to the car's no-twist, heavy-duty convertible frame (even with the grand goddess of torque 375hp, 420-ft./lb. 396, which was similar to the L-37 in the '65 Corvette lineup), the rearend would lay down a dual strip of black, equal on both sides with its stock 3.31:1 open axle. It wasn't one light strip and one dark one—both were the same shade. And, of course, the car was so quick that it couldn't be beaten on the street. It ruled the streets. How many cars have been parked on *that* throne?

Mystery surrounds even the name, because Z-16 doesn't appear anywhere on the vehicle. Its markings showed it to be a Chevelle Malibu sport coupe, model 13837, with the SS 396 option. Z-16 was the RPO (regular production option) number, although enthusiasts claim that Chevrolet called the car the Z-16. Magazine articles of the time recommended that Chevrolet call it Z-16 after the option number; it was the first pre-Z28 Chevy to use this code as a name. (Interestingly, Chevrolet interoffice memos list Maverick as a possible name for this car.)

Of course, there was nothing regular about this regular production option, and its cost was a heart failure-inducing $1501. This was big bucks in 1965, especially considering that the base price on a standard Malibu SS was $2431.

For the extra $1501, the RPO Z-16 included the special 396 engine and various comfort and convenience op-

tions. The 375hp 396 big-block was Chevrolet's new high-performance replacement for the then-outdated 409, which was finally dropped from the Impala SS lineup in December 1964. At GM's proving grounds in Mesa, Arizona, this 396 was known as a revived and revised version of the infamous '63 Mark II Daytona mystery engine. In January 1965, when the 396 was ready for passenger cars, it was introduced in the brand-new Chevrolet Caprice and was offered in a higher-performance form in the Corvette. (The Vette engine was a high-winding, mechanically cammed torquer, whose exact configuration is well-known.)

However, when the 375hp 396s were dropped into a special run of 396-powered Chevelle SSs in Kansas City, Missouri, it was obvious that the Z-16 would be next-to-impossible to acquire. Just 200 were scheduled to see the light of day, but when the assembly lines quit, exactly 201 had been produced. And to this day it still isn't clear whether all of these 396s were hydraulic tunes; some may have been solid-lifter-cammed. But even with hydraulics, the rev potential was up there with the big boys in the 6000 rpm range. It was factory-rated at 375 horsepower at 5600 rpm, and its torque equaled 420 ft./lbs. at 3600 revs, via 11:1 compression and a four-barrel Holley carb.

What were the other extras? First, on the outside, the car looked like any other '65 Chevelle SS, but there were several subtle differences. The most obvious one was the black-painted and chromed grille bars extending across the rear deck lid and taillight board. These bars were die-cast (rather than pressed-out metal), then chromed. Also, the rear panel was dressed with a rectangular Malibu SS 396 emblem

high on the passenger side above the special grille bars. This emblem coded the cubes to the curious, and a 396 in a mid-sized Chevelle was news in 1965!

The Malibu SS emblem was moved from the rear quarters to the front fenders just behind the wheelwell opening, another minor difference. On the front fenders were more 396 Turbo-Jet emblems with crossed checkered and Chevy flags.

On the inside, Z-16s came with a special 160mph speedometer, an in-dash 6000rpm tachometer, bucket seats, console, a clock mounted on top of the dash and a Multiplex AM/FM stereo mounted below the dash panel. The car was luxurious, too; speed wasn't Chevrolet's primary concern. The horsepower theme went hand-in-hand in those days with comfort and convenience options.

Rumor had it that the Z-16 was to go to VIPs, which may have been true in light of its limited production run and the fact that demand easily exceeded supply, despite the $4500 price tag and the lack of sales brochures and advertising. Dan Blocker ("Hoss," on the then-popular television series "Bonanza") supposedly owned one—whether as a gift or a purchase is not known. (Perhaps his big image fit in with the car's big-cube image!) Executive types got Z-16s, too, according to legend, as did certain Chevy dealers and other celebrities.

An interesting rumor circulated at Green Valley Race City in Texas, where we recently photographed this car. In hushed tones, people related the story of how the then-president of GM (or of Chevrolet—take your pick) got the last Z-16 off the line—number 201. This extra one over the projected

Mystery Machine

This '65 Z-16 could be the lowest-mileage original in existence—the odometer read an ultra-low 17,461 when we recently photographed the car. Most Z-16s came with a vinyl top, but Tom's has a rare uncovered roof.

The '65 Chevelle body was in its last model year before a major design change, which is another reason the Z-16 is so desirable today. The 375hp 396 was offered on a wide scale in 1966, but the '65 body style and the car's special engineering make the Z-16 a curiosity and a legend today. Restored and excellent originals easily fetch more than $20,000.

The factory dual exhausts exit to the side immediately behind the rear wheels, although many of these cars were modified (for sound and exhaust flow purposes) with pipes exiting straight out the back under the rear bumper.

This large emblem on the front fenders was unique to Z-16s in 1965; the only 396 offered was the special 375hp big-block.

The '65 Z-16 is most easily distinguished from the rear, where special die-cast and chromed grille bars run across the deck lid and extend into the taillight board. The rectangular Malibu SS 396 emblem, unique to the '65 Z-16, is on the passenger side above the grille bars.

The front grille was '65 Chevelle pure and simple...no Z-16 hints here that we detect.

run was supposedly cranked out especially for this president. Well, the car was so distinctive that this individual immediately put it in storage, where it remains today. Imagine a brand-new Z-16 out there somewhere just waiting for a collector to run into Chevy gold—a "Z-16-in-a-barn" story!

In addition to the convertible frame that was part of the package, the rest of the suspension was beefed up. Power-assisted front drum brakes used 11-inch station wagon brake shoes housed in cast-steel wheel hubs with shotpeened ball studs. This car also had rollbars front and rear, plus a 15:1 overall power steering gear that was slightly quicker than the 17.5:1 ratio on other '65 Chevelles. Perhaps even more special than the heavy-duty frame was the extra set of control arms (four instead of two) to prevent axle wind-up on hard acceleration. The 396 was backed by a four-speed Muncie featuring a 2.56:1 first gear and splined to the torquey engine with Chevy's 11-inch heavy-duty clutch.

Tom Wright, owner of this Chevelle Z-16, is more than a casual admirer of this muscle Chevy. In 1967-'68 his col-

Notice the factory wheel covers, stock to the Z-16, on these factory tires and wheels; they were made to look like mags. Fourteen-inch wheels mount 7.75x14 Firestone gold-striped tires.

Chevrolet built 201 Z-16s in 1965 but could have sold hundreds, maybe thousands, more despite the hefty $1501 premium for this historic option.

Every Z-16 came with an assortment of comfort and convenience extras, in addition to the mandatory four-speed Muncie. Notice the wood-grain steering wheel, console, buckets, in-dash tach, Multiplex AM/FM stereo and the clock on top of the dash.

The six-grand tach is between the speedometer/odometer and the round gauge that includes amps, water temperature, oil pressure and fuel indicators.

A dual-snorkel air cleaner tops the 375hp 396. Notice the stock chromed valve covers, plus the metal 396 emblem on the air cleaner lid.

Mystery Machine

The 396 is topped by a Holley four-barrel. A Holley dealer told Tom that his Z-16 mounted a 3310.

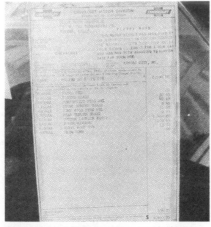

This original Z-16 invoice, or window sticker, isn't from Tom's car, but it is typical and lists a number of options, culminating in that final huge price tag that was in Cadillac country in 1965!

lege roommate owned a Z-16, and the pair power-shifted this Chevy around campus, where it was unbeaten in the classic street stoplight peel-outs so common in the Sixties. Tom claims his big-block GTO was no match for the king 396 Chevelle. "I couldn't touch it!" he says.

So in 1984, when Tom ran across a Z-16 at a swap meet in Fort Worth, he decided he just had to have one. He succeeded in tracking down his roommate's old SS, a yellow car with a black top; however, the owner refused to sell. But Tom kept looking, and in Alabama he finally found this regal red 17,000-mile original, which he proceeded to buy and trailer home to Garland, Texas.

According to Tom's research of the car's background, this Chevelle was once a race car. Its engine had been pulled for quarter-mile racing; but once the owner was through racing, he reinstalled the engine to factory specs, and put the car into storage.

As far as we know, Tom Wright's is the lowest-mileage original Z-16 in existence—until that sneaky "president" pulls his '65 Chevelle SS 396 into the light of a car show. ●

Special:
SUPER SPORT REPORT

REVIEWING AMA SPECS FOR 1970 L78 AND LS6 CHEVELLES

By Wayne Scraba

Purchasing and/or restoring a vintage supercar can involve far more than dealing with sheetmetal, upholstery trim and running gear. It is very important to track down pertinent paperwork that either accompanied the vehicle when new or was made available for it later on. This paperwork may include dealer showroom albums, fingertip fact books, parts manuals, owner's manuals, paint samples and era road tests. There are many reasons to collect this information, but perhaps the most important is the verification of equipment and options on a particular vehicle.

While searching for a personal muscle machine, the author "stumbled" across an interesting assemblage of factory paperwork on the 1970 SS Chevelle. It's contained in a thorough specification catalog of all solid lifter (396/375 and 454/450) Chevelles from the 1970 model year. This spec list was prepared by Chevrolet for the American Automobile Manufacturer's Association in 1969. This information is so important and rare that we've decided to share some of it with you. Follow along as we examine "AMA form 40-A".

BODY—TYPES AND STYLE NAMES

	Malibu
2-Door Sport Coupe, 5-Passenger	13637
2-Door Convertible, 5-Passenger	13667

CAR AND BODY DIMENSIONS

Model	Sport Coupe	Convertible
WIDTH		
Track-front	60.0	
Track-rear	59.8	
Maximum overall car width	75.4	
LENGTH		
Wheelbase	112.0	
Overall car length	197.2	
Overhang-front	37.5	
Overhang-rear	47.7	
HEIGHT		
Passenger distribution, front and rear	2-3	
Trunk cargo load (lbs.)	200	
Overall height	52.6	52.9

Model	Sport Coupe	Convertible
COWL HEIGHT	38.1	
Rocker panel to ground (front)	8.5	
Rocker panel to ground (rear)	2.2	

	Sport Coupe		Convertible
Windshield slope angle		53.0	
GROUND CLEARANCE			
Bumper to ground-front		14.3	
Bumper to ground-rear		15.1	
Angle of approach		25.5	
Angle of departure		21.0	
Minimum running clearance		4.6	
FRONT COMPARTMENT			
Effective head room	37.5		38.3
Effective leg room-accelerator		42.8	
Shoulder room		58.2	
Hip room		59.7	
Upper body opening to ground	48.5		48.6
REAR COMPARTMENT			
Effective head room	36.3		36.9
Minimum effective leg room		32.3	
Minimum knee room		0.7	
Shoulder room	56.9		47.9
Hip room	52.9		50.4

Model	Sport Coupe	Convertible
Usable luggage capacity	14.6	8.5
Liftover height	25.9	
Position of spare tire storage	Horizontal; right side of trunk	
Method of holding lid open	Boxed hinges with torsion rod	

POWER TEAMS

Displacement	Carburetor	Compression	BHP	Torque	Transmission	Axle, Std.	Axle, Opt.
Turbo Jet 396 V8 Z25/L78	One 4 bbl	11.0.1	375 @ 5600	415 @ 3600	4-speed man. (2.52 low) 4-speed man. (2.20 low) HD 4 spd. man. 3-spd. Auto.	3.55:1	4.10:1
Turbo Jet 454 V8 Z15/LS6	One 4 bbl		450 @ 5600	500 @ 3600	HD 4-speed man. (2.20 low) 3-spd. Auto.	3.31:1	4.10:1

Model	Turbo Jet 396-375	Turbo Jet 454-450
ENGINE—GENERAL		
Type, number of cylinders	90° V8 overhead valves	
Bore and stroke, nominal	4.126 x 3.76	4.251 x 4.00
Piston displacement (CID)	402	454
Numbering system, left bank	1-3-5-7	
right bank	2-4-6-8	
Firing order	1-8-4-3-6-5-7-2	

Model	Turbo Jet 396-375	Turbo Jet 454-450
Compression ratio, nominal	11.0:1	11.25:1
Cylinder head material	Cast iron	
Cylinder block material	Cast iron	
Number of mount points, front	1	
Number of mount points, rear	1	
Engine installation angle	4°-46'	
Taxable horsepower	54.5	57.8
Published HP @ engine rpm	375 @ 5600	450 @ 5600
Published torque @ engine rpm	415 @ 3600	500 @ 3600
Recommended fuel	Premium	
ENGINE—PISTONS		
Material	Aluminum impact extruded	
Description	Domed head, slipper skirt	
Weight (ounces)	23.12	26.80
ENGINE-RINGS		
Function: # 1 ring	Compression	
# 2 ring	Compression	
# 3 ring	Oil	
Top ring material	Cast alloy iron, barrel face, molybdenum inlay	
Second ring material	Cast alloy iron, inside bevel, taper face, chromeplated	
Compression ring width	.0770-.0780	.0770-.0775
Compression ring gap	.010-.020	

Model	Turbo Jet 396-375	Turbo Jet 454-450
Oil ring material	Multi-piece (2 rails and 1 spacer expander) Rails-steel, chromed OD; Expander-stainless steel	
Oil ring width	.1870-.1890 assembled	
Oil ring gap	.015-.055	
Expanders	in oil ring assembly	
ENGINE—PISTON PINS		
Material	Chromium steel	
Length	2.90-2.950	
Diameter	.9895-.9898	

Type	Locked in rod (pressed)	
Clearance in piston	.0025-.00035	.00030-.00040
Direction and amount of offset	On center	
ENGINE—CONNECTING RODS		
Material	Drop forged steel	
Weight (ounces)	27.84	29.44
Length, center to center	6.130-6.140	
Bearing material	Premium aluminum	
Overall length	.847	
Clearance (limits)	.0009-.0025	
End play	.015-.023	
ENGINE CRANKSHAFT		
Material	Forged steel	

Model	Turbo Jet 396-375	Turbo Jet 454-450
Vibration damper type	Rubber mounted inertia	
End thrust taken by:	Bearing number five	
Crankshaft end play	.006-.010	
Main bearing material	Steel-backed insert; copper alloy or premium aluminum lining selected for application	
Clearance, # 1	.008-.0020	
#2, #3, #4	.0011-.0023	
#5	.0017-.0033	
Journal diameter, # 1	2.7509	2.7503
#2	2.7510	2.7505
#3	2.7505	2.7505
#4	2.7505	2.7505
#5	2.7510	2.7510
Crankpin journal diameter	2.199-2.200	
ENGINE—CAMSHAFT		
Material	cast alloy iron	
Bearing material	Steel-backed babbit	
Number of bearings	5	
Type of drive	Chain	
Crankshaft gear material	Steel sprocket	
Crankshaft gear material	Nylon teeth w/aluminum hub	
Number of timing chain links	50	
Timing chain width	.740	
Timing chain pitch	.500	

Model	Turbo 396-375	Turbo Jet 454-450
ENGINE—VALVE SYSTEM		
Lifter type	Mechanical	
Valve rotator (s)	None	

123

Special:

Rocker ratio	1.70:1
Operating clearance, intake	.024
Operating clearance, exhaust	.028
Intake valve opens (°BTC)	44°
Intake valve closes (°ABC)	92°
Exhaust valve opens (°BBC)	86°
Exhaust valve closes (°ATC)	36°
Intake valve duration	316°
Exhaust valve duration	302°
Valve opening overlap	80°
Intake valve material	Alloy steel, aluminized face and head
Intake valve material	5.204-.5.224
Intake valve head diameter	2.185-2.195
Angle of seat, intake	46° seat; 45° face
Stem diameter, intake	.3712-.3717
Stem to guide clearance, intake	.0010-.0027
Intake valve lift	.5197
Exhaust valve material	High-alloy steel, aluminized face and head
Exhaust valve head diameter	1.875-1.885
Angle of seat, exhaust	46° seat; 45° face
Stem diameter, exhaust	.3705-.3710

Model	Turbo Jet 396-375	Turbo Jet 454-450
Stem to guide clearance, exhaust	.0010-.0027	
Exhaust valve lift	.5197	

ENGINE-VALVE SPRINGS

Outer spring pressure: closed,	69-81 lbs. @ 1.88''
open	228-252 lbs. @ 1.38''
Inner spring pressure: closed,	26-34 lbs. @ 1.78''
open	81-99 lbs. @ 1.28''

ENGINE—LUBRICATION SYSTEM

Type of lubrication: Main bearings	Pressure
Connecting rods	Pressure
Piston pins	Splash
Camshaft bearings	Pressure
Tappets	Pressure
Timing chain	Centrifugally oiled from cam bearing
Cylinder walls	Pressure jet cross spray
Oil pump type	Gear
Oil pressure @ 200 RPM	40 psi
Oil pressure sending cnit	electric
Oil intake, type	Stationary
Oil filter system	Full flow
Capacity less filte	4 qts.
Engine service ·equirement	MS

Model	Turbo Jet 396-375	Turbo Jet 454-450

ENGINE—EXHAUST SYSTEM

Type	Dual with resonators
Number of Mufflers	2 mufflers and 2 resonators
Exhaust pipe diameter, main	2.50 x .082-inch wall thickness
Exhaust pipe diameter, branch	2.00 x .069'' wall thickness (muffler to tailpipe)

CRANKCASE VENT SYSTEM

Type	Ventilates to induction system
Location	Left front rocker cover

ENGINE—FUEL SYSTEM

Carburetor type	Holley 4150 series
Fuel tank capacity	Approximately 20 U.S. gallons
Filler location	Behind hinged rear license plate
Fuel pump type	Mechanical
Location	Lower right front of engine
Pressure range	7.50 to 9.00 psi
Fuel filter type and location	Fine-mesh plastic strainer in gasoline tank and paper filter in carburetor fuel inlet
Choke type	Automatic
Intake manifold heat source	Exhaust crossover
Air cleaner type	Oil-wetted paper element
Idle speed, manual trans.	750 rpm @ neutral
automatic trans.	700 rpm @ drive

Model	Turbo Jet 396-375	Turbo Jet 454-450

ENGINE—COOLING SYSTEM

Type	Pressure	
Radiator cap relief psi	15 ± 1	
Thermostat type	Choke	
Thermostat opening point	177°-183°	
Water pump type	Centrifugal	
Gallons per minute @ 2000 rpm 24 gpm		27 gpm
Drive type	V-belt	
By-pass type	External	
Radiator core type	Tube and center	
Cooling system w/heater	23 qts.	22 qts.
w/o heater	22 qts.	21 qts.
Optional	24 qts.	23 qts.
Lower rad hose type	Molded, single	
Lower rad hose diameter	1.88-in.	
Upper rad hose type	Molded, single	
Upper rad hose diameter	1.50-in.	

Model	Turbo Jet 396-375	Turbo Jet 454-450
By-pass hose type	Molded, single	
By-pass hose diameter	.745	
Fan blade type	7-blade, staggered	
Fan diameter	18-in.	
Fan cut-out type	Thermo-modulated, viscous coupling	

ELECTRICAL—SUPPLY SYSTEM

Battery make and model	Delco Remy 1980030	Delco-Remy 1980080
Voltage rating	12 volts	12 volts
Number of plates	66	78
Amp. hour rating	61 amp. hr. @ 20 hr.	62 amp. hr. @ 20 hr.
Battery location	Right-side engine compartment	
Terminal grounded	Negative	
Generator type	Delco-Remy	
Model	1100837	
Ouput @ engine idle	13 amps	
Regulator type	Delco-Remy	
Model	1119515	
Type	Vibrator	
Regulated voltage	13.8-14.8 amps @ 85°F	

ELECTRICAL-STARTING SYSTEM

Starter motor type	Delco-Remy	
Model	1108418 w/std.; 1108430 w/auto.	
Model	Turbo Jet 396-375	Turbo Jet 454-450
Starter rotation	Clockwise	
Starter switch type	Solenoid	
Starter engagement type	Positive-shift solenoid	
Starter pinion location	Rear	
Pinion tooth count	9	
Flywheel tooth count, std. and auto.	168	
Flywheel tooth face width	.4100-.4220	

ELECTRICAL—IGNITION SYSTEM

Distributor type	Conventional breaker point	
Optional system	None	
Coil make and model	Delco-Remy # 1115293	
Amps, engine stopped	4.0	
Amps, engine running	1.8	
Distributor make	Delco-Remy	
Distributor model	1112000	1111437
Centrifugal advance begins @	1000 rpm	
Intermediate advance	15 @ 1800	17 @ 2000
Max advance	36 @ 5000	26 @ 3800
Vacuum advance begins @	6.00 in. hg	7.00 in. hg
Vac. adv. max degrees	15° @ 12 in. hg	12° @ 16 in. hg
Vacuum source	Carburetor	
Timing, initial	4° BTDC @ 750 rpm-manual; @ 700 rpm-auto.	
Breaker pint gap	.019-inch	
Cam angle	28°-30°	

Model	Turbo Jet 396-375	Turbo Jet 454-450
Timing mark location	Torsional damper	
Spark plug make and model	AC No. R43T	

SUPPLEMENTARY CARBURETOR INFORMATION

Engine	Transmission	Carburetor	Carb. model	Number used	Barrel size
396 V8 &	Manual	Holley	3967477	one	1.69'' primary
454 V8	Automatic	Holley	3969898	one	& secondary

Thread	14mm
Tightening torque	25 lbs.-ft.
Spark plug gap	.033-.038-in.
Ignition cable conductor type	Linen core impregnated w/electrical conducting material
Ignition cable insulation type	Rubber with neoprene jacket
Spark plug protector	Neoprene
Electrical suppression	@ ignition cable

CLUTCH DRIVE UNIT (manual transmission)

Make and type	Chevrolet single dry disc, centrifugal
Pressure plate type	Diaphragm, bent-finger design
Total spring load	2450-2750 lbs. 2600-2800 lbs.
Number of driven discs	1
Clutch facing O.D. and I.D	11.00 x 6.50-in.
Total effective area	123.70 sq. ins.
Clutch thickness	140-in.
Release bearing type	Single row ball
Clutch torsional damping	Coil springs

DRIVE UNITS (manual transmission)

Number of forward speeds	4
Std. transmission ratio, 1st. 2.52:1	2.20:1

Model	Turbo Jet 396-375	Turbo Jet 454-450
Std. transmission ratio	2nd 1.88:1	1.64:1
	3rd 1.46:1	1.27:1
	4th 1.00:1	1.00:1
	Rev. 2.59:1	2.26:1

Shift lever location	Floor
Transmission lube capacity	3 pts.
Lube type	MIL-L-2105B
SAE viscosity	SAE 80

DRIVE UNITS—AUTOMATIC TRANSMISSION

Make and model	Turbo Hydra-Matic 400
Type	Torque convertor with planetary gears
Selector location	Lever, steering column; floor-mounted when used with optional console and bucket seats
Gear ratio and selector pattern	P-Park
	R-2.08:1
	N-Neutral
	D-2.48:1, 1.48:1, 1.00:1
	L2-2.48:1, 1.48:1
	L1-2.48:1
Number of torque convertor elements	3
Max. ratio at stall	2.10:1
Type of transmission cooling	Water
Nominal torque convertor diameter	12.20-in.

Model	Turbo Jet 396-375	Turbo Jet 454-450

DRIVE UNIT—PROPELLER SHAFT

Number used	1
Type	Straight tube
Dimensions, O.D., length, wall	3.250-in O.D. x 56.34-in. long x .065-in. wall thickness
Slip yoke type	Yoke
Number of teeth	27
Spline O.D.	1.1750-1.1752-in.
Universal joint type	Chevrolet cross
Number of universal joints	2
Rear attachment method	U-bolt
Bearing type	Anti-friction
Lubrication	Pre-packed

DRIVE UNIT—AXLE

Type	Semi-floating, overhung hypoid pinion and ring gear
Limited slip type	Cone clutches or dual-disc clutches
Pinion offset	1.50-in.
Number of differential pinions	2
Ring gear diameter	8.875-in.
Pinion adjustment method	Shim
Pinion bearing adjustment	Collapsible sleeve
Rear axle capacity	4.25 pts.
Rear axle lube type	MIL-L-2105B
SAE viscosity	80

Model	Turbo Jet 396-375	Turbo Jet 454-450	
AXLE RATIO—TOOTH COMBINATIONS			
Axle ratio	3.31:1	3.55:1	.410:1
Number of pinion teeth	13	11	10
Number of ring gear teeth	43	39	41

DRIVE UNIT—WHEELS

Wheel type and material	Short-spoke steel disc
Rim size	14 x 7-in. JJ
Attachment type	Stud
Wheel stud circle diameter	4.75-in.
Number and size of nuts	Five hex 7/16-in. UNF-2B

DRIVE UNIT—TIRES

Tire size	F-70 x 14
Tire type	Fiberglass bias belted
Full rated inflation pressure, front	24 psi cold; 30 psi hot
rear	28 psi cold; 34 psi hot

Special:

BRAKES—PARKING

Type of control	Foot pedal apply, handle release
Control location	@ instrument panel, left of service brake
Park brake operation method	@ rear service brakes

Model	Turbo Jet 396-375	Turbo Jet 454-450

BRAKES—SERVICE

Brake type	Disc front and drum rear
Adjusting mechanism	Self-adjusting
Special valving	Metering and proportioning valve
Standard brake booster type	Delco-Morraine integral power unit
Effective brake area	106.1 sq. ins.
Gross lining area	118.1 sq. ins.
Total brake swept area	332.4 sq. ins.
Front rotor diameter	11 ins.
Inner rotor working diameter	7.180 ins.
Rotor working width	1 in.
Rotor type & material	Vented, cast iron design
Rear drum nominal diameter	9 ins.
Wheel cylinder bore, front	2.938 ins.
Wheel cylinder bore, rear	.8750 in.
Master cylinder bore size	1.125 ins.
Master cylinder displacement distribution	73% front; 27% rear
Brake pedal arc ratio	3.53:1 @ 100-lb. pedal load
Front brake lining type and material	Riveted, molded asbestos
Front primary lining size	5.96 x 2.21 x .41 ins.
Front secondary lining size	5.96 x 2.21 x .41 ins.
Rear brake lining type & material	Bonded, molded asbestos
Rear primary lining size	9.01 x 2.00 x .17 ins.
Rear secondary lining size	9.01 x 2.00 x .17 ins.

Model	Turbo Jet 396-375	Turbo Jet 454-450

STEERING

Standard steering type	Manual with energy-absorbing column
Optional steering type	Variable ratio, power-assist
Optional steering adjustment	Tilt with five inches of vertical travel
Steering wheel diameter	16.25 x 15.50 ins. (oval)
Turning diameter, wall to wall	45.5 ft.
Turning diameter, curb to curb	42.0 ft.
Manual steering gear type	Semi-reversible, recirculating ball nut
Manual steering gear ratio	24:1
Manual overall steering ratio	28.7:1
Number of turns, lock to lock	5.5
Power steering gear type	Integral gear with vane-type pump
Power steering manufacturer	Saginaw
Power steering gear type	Semi-reversible, recirculating ball nut
Power steering gear ratio	16.1:1 to 12.4:1
Power overall steering ratio	18.7:1 to 12.4:1
Number of turns, lock to lock	2.9
Power steering pump drive	Crankshaft
Steering linkage type	parallelogram
Linkage location	Front of wheels
Tie rod number	2
Steering axis, inclination @ camber	7¾° to 8¾°
Upper bearing type	Ball stud with non-metallic surfaces

Model	Turbo Jet 396-375	Turbo Jet 454-450

Lower bearing type	Ball stud with non-metallic surfaces
Wheel alignment (@ curb wt.); Caster	N 1½ to $ degrees
Camber	0 to P 1 degree
Toe-in	⅛ to ¼ in. (outside of track)
Steering spindle type	Forging with pad for brake mounting
Inner wheel bearing diameter	1.2493 to 1.2498 ins.
Outer wheel bearing diameter	.7493-.7498 ins.
Thread size	¾-20 NEF (modified)
Wheel bearing type	Taper roller

SUSPENSION—FRONT

Type	Independent, SLA type w/coil spring, concentric shock absorber and spherically jointed knuckle at each wheel
Spring type	Coil
Spring material	Alloy steel
Spring size	11.7-in overall height, 3.63-in I.D., .659-in. bar dia.
Spring rate	435 lbs. per in.
Spring rate at wheel	150 lbs. per in.
Stabilizer type	Link
Stabilizer material and size	H.R. steel w/ .812-in. O.D.

SUSPENSION—REAR

Type	Linked, salisbury axle fixed by control arms
Drive and torque taken by	Control arms
Spring type	Coil

Model	Turbo Jet 396-375	Turbo Jet 454-450
Spring material	Alloy steel	
Spring size	9.00-in. overall height, 5.50-in. I.D., 553 bar dia.	
Spring rate	160 lbs. per in.	
Spring rate at wheel	155 lbs. per in.	
Spring mounting insulation type	Rubber	

CONVENIENCE EQUIPMENT

Power windows	Optional
Power seats	Not available
Radio type (s)	Optional AM pushbutton, AM-FM pushbutton, AM-FM stereo
Rear seat speaker	Optional
Power antenna	Not available
Clock	Optional
Tachometer and gauges	Optional
Air conditioning	Not available
Speed control	Not available
Dome lamp	Standard
Glove compartment lamp	Standard
Luggage compartment lamp	Optional
Underhood lamp	Optional
Courtesy lamp	Optioanl
Map lamp	Optional
Fingertip washer control	Optional

CURB WEIGHT

Model	Curb Wt. Frt.	Curb Wt. Rr.	Curb Wt. Total	Fuel Wt.	Coolant Wt.
SS 396 (L78) 2-Door Sport Coupe	2111 lbs.	1615 lbs.	3726 lbs.	122.4 lbs	32.9 lbs.
2-Door Convertible	2103 lbs.	1668 lbs.	3771 lbs.	122.4 lbs	32.9 lbs.
SS 454 (LS6) 2-Door Sport Coupe	2091 lbs.	1615 lbs.	.3706 lbs.	122.4 lbs	32 lbs.
2-Door Convertible	2098 lbs.	1633 lbs.	3731 lbs.	122.4 lbs	32 lbs.

ACKNOWLEDGEMENT

The author would like to thank Brian Wilson of Chevrolet Motor Division Public Relations for his assistance in compiling the information included in this article. The research performed by Wilson and the other unsung "heros" at Chevrolet is impressive and certainly above and beyond the call of duty.

EQUIPMENT DIFFERENTIAL WEIGHT

Equipment	Curb Wt. Frt.	Curb Wt. Rr.	Curb Wt. Total	Comments
Turbohydramatic	54 lbs.	11 lbs.	65 lbs.	With L78 396
Turbohydramatic	45 lbs.	9 lbs.	54 lbs.	With LS6 454
Bucket seats	11 lbs.	9 lbs.	20 lbs.	
Floor console	6 lbs.	3 lbs.	9 lbs.	With 4-speed trans.
Floor console	11 lbs.	4 lbs.	15 lbs.	With Turbo Hydramatic
Power steering	29 lbs.	2 lbs.	31 lbs.	
Cowl induction	7 lbs.	7 lbs.	14 lbs.	
Evap. emission	4 lbs.	1 lb.	5 lbs.	
AM radio	6 lbs.	2 lbs.	8 lbs.	
Stereo radio	12 lbs.	4 lbs.	16 lbs.	

FRONT SUSPENSION REBUILD

REJUVENATING YOUR CHEVELLE'S FRONT END FOR THAT BRAND-NEW FEELING

Text and Photography by Eric Pierce

1. The balljoints are the heart of the front suspension, with the lower joints doing most of the work of supporting the car and absorbing much road shock. It's best to replace both uppers and lowers at the same time.

L et's face it, every car has a suspension, but few of us pay much attention to it unless we're changing it in some way—raising it, lowering it, or making it more heavy-duty. Adding traction bars or chrome is news; rebuilding it, unfortunately, is not. Besides, renewing a worn suspension system sounds like a lot of work that nobody will ever see or even appreciate.

In 1964 General Motors introduced its A-body line, an all-new—if thoroughly conventional—design. The Chevy version was the Chevelle. So successful was this chassis setup that it was carried through virtually unchanged into the early Seventies. While many A-bodied

2. A balljoint separating tool and the smaller-but-identical tie rod end separator (shown) are used to safely separate the front suspension components.

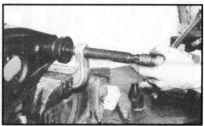

5. Superior Frame's Dan Conner uses this special tool to press the new lower balljoints into place. Clamped in a vise as shown, the tool supports the control arm from the bottom while squarely pressing the new part in from the top.

6. A sharp chisel is used to clip the heads off the original rivets. This job is most easily done with the upper control arm still in the car, although it can be accomplished with the arm held in a vise. Rivet bodies are then driven out with a hammer and short drift.

3. A floor jack or heavy-duty bottle jack is used to compress the coil spring while the balljoint is loosened. The anti-sway bar is removed, the safety chain wrapped through the spring, and then the jack is slowly lowered to release the spring's tension. Go slowly and stand well back and to the side!

4. Here we see the "hammer method" of balljoint and bushing removal demonstrated. A heavy, sharp rap on the edge as shown should pop the balljoint loose and free of the arm. Repeat, if needed.

Bow Tie cars have rolled up one, two, or even 300,000 miles, many could be considered worn out in the suspension department. Thanks to the conventional nature, simplicity, and durability of the A-body suspension, however, a restoration job can be done almost completely at home. If your Chevelle has lost the light, tight, and lively feel for which it has become famous, here's the low-buck lowdown on how to get the feeling back.

Once the decision has been made, a call to Just Suspension should be your first order of business. Just Suspension, owned and operated by Bill Kanouse, specializes in complete front suspension parts for all American cars from 1936-'87. In addition to being able to supply *any* suspension part or parts you might need or desire, Just Suspension is also a storehouse of knowledge that can help you select the *right* parts for the use you plan for your car.

As Bill pointed out to us, it's easy to undo the work done by factory engineers by mismatching components. Too much of any component (too heavy springs, too stiff shocks, too thick anti-sway bars, etc.) can be as bad—or worse—than too little, and one must strive for balance. For our '64 Malibu SS (283, automatic transmission, no air condition-

ing) Bill suggested a *complete* suspension rebuild—along with new KYB Gas-a-Just shocks and a mild set of anti-sway bars, front and rear. It sounded good to us.

Next we contacted Manny Martinez of Superior Frame & Alignment and asked if he'd show us a few home-style methods of disassembling and assembling the Malibu's front suspension system. As Manny's chief suspension technician, Dan Conner, demonstrated, the only stumbling blocks for the do-it-yourselfer are safely separating the spindle/balljoint assembly and pressing the lower balljoints into the lower control arms. Of course, the alignment is best left to the experts, but the rest can be done in a home shop with a minimum of special tools.

Dan began the disassembly by removing the front springs. This can be a very dangerous operation, so take proper precautions before starting. The shock is removed and a length of heavy chain is wrapped in, around, and through the spring. This will do much to control it if it

REBUILD

7. Just Suspension's upper balljoints bolt into place utilizing the new bolts, lock washers, and nuts provided. Clean up the mounting area of the arm to ensure bolts seat and tighten properly.

9. Frame and alignment shops use special "cups" to drive the new bushings into place—after removing the old ones with the same hammer method used with the lower balljoints. You can make your own tools from various-size pipe nipples with pipe caps on the ends. Use a large, solid vise and watch your fingers.

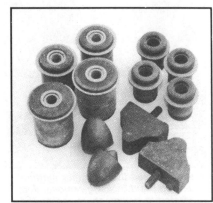

8. The replacement rubber bushings are exact duplicates of the factory parts. Larger ones are for the lower control arms, while the small ones are for the uppers. Bump stops should be replaced, too, especially if the car is to be lowered.

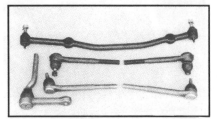

10. A complete rejuvenation should include new steering arms, tie rod ends, and an idler arm assembly to eliminate any steering play for optimum control. These items simply bolt on. Don't forget to pre-lube the tie rod ends and bushings.

should launch itself in your direction. (A suddenly released coil spring contains enough stored energy to seriously injure a person.) With the car elevated on jackstands, a heavy-duty floor jack is then positioned below the lower control arm and used to lift it, compressing the spring to its normal ride height. The lower balljoint-to-spindle nut is then backed off several turns, *but not removed*! A balljoint separating tool (known as a pickle fork) is then used to loosen the tapered shaft from its tight fit with the spindle. When this has been accomplished, the nut that was left in place for safety reasons can be removed. The jack is then *slowly and carefully* lowered, releasing the tension from the coil spring. Should the jack slip during this operation, the safety chain will contain the spring, but stand well back and to the side just in case! The jack is then removed from beneath the control arm, and the spring itself is removed. The operation is then repeated on the opposite side.

The upper and lower control arms are then unbolted and removed, the spindle having been released from the upper balljoint in the same manner as the lower one. The rubber bushing removal technique is easily mastered. The idea is to place the arm above a large vice, the jaws opened just enough to permit the bushing to pass

through. A good-size hammer is then used to smack the bushing sharply and squarely, dislodging it from the arm with a single (or perhaps a second) blow. It'll only come out one way and, by doing the job in one blow, you minimize the chance of tweaking the arm itself.

While the lower balljoints are removed with the hammer-and-vice method, the upper balljoints are riveted in place and require a different removal technique. A sharp steel chisel—is used to cut the heads off the old rivets. A drift is then used to knock the remainder of the rivet out of the holes, thus

freeing the balljoint without damage to the control arm. The new upper balljoints go into place using the special bolts included with the replacements.

While the old ones are easily removed as mentioned previously, the new ones must be pressed into place. Dan used a special tool designed specifically for this purpose, but recommended that an enthusiast take his lower control arms and new balljoints to either a chassis shop or automotive machine shop and pay a small fee for having this job done. It's possible to drive the new joints into place with a homemade tool, but it's too easy to crook or damage them to justify the

REBUILD

11. *Optional, but highly recommended, is an anti-sway bar. Just Suspension can assist you with the choice of the best bar for your car. Polyurethane sway bar bushings are recommended.*

12. *The rear-suspension upper and lower control arms can be treated exactly as the front control arms were: Hammer the old bushings out and drive the new ones in. If one arm is done at a time, you won't have to remove the axle. The eccentric goes back in the same position.*

small savings.

The rubber bushings, however, can be done at home with no problem. Tools to drive the bushings into their arms can be made from short pipe nipples and caps obtained from a plumbing supply store. The tools must fit squarely on the bushing shoulder (as close as possible to the rubber without actually contacting it). This gives a firm surface that won't deflect as the bushing is driven into place. A bit of white grease will also help them slide into place. Should the arm distort during the installation so that the bushing is fully in position but the arm is crooked where it surrounds the bushing, don't worry. Simply lay the arm on the floor with the bent side down and whack the arm into shape around the bushing. A large drift punch is sometimes helpful.

From here on, the job is a simple matter of removing and replacing bolt-on components. All the steering arms, the idler arm, and links were unbolted and the new ones simply bolted on in their place. Dan recommended that all greased joints be pre-lubed before they're bolted into place. The upper and lower control arms are bolted back into place, and the old alignment shims are reinstalled. The four rear-suspension links are simple, each being removed and rebushed in turn to save the trouble of removing the axle completely.

We elected to replace the front coil springs on this car as they had become somewhat saggy with age. Just Suspension supplied a pair of new ones, that were longer so they could be "cut to taste." We wanted to lower the front about an inch—for aesthetic reasons.

Because the spring pockets on A-body cars are designed with shapes that accommodate the coil spring's "tail," the springs must be cut only in full coils to fit within the pockets.

Because heat will alter the spring rate and sometimes even destroy its temper, a carbide blade was used to snip two coils. The final measurement was only ¼-inch lower than our intended 1-inch overall drop, and we had yet to install the new KYB Gas-a-Just shocks, which would have the effect of raising the car slightly as well. While this method gave us the ride height we wanted, there are too many variables to recommend it for all applications. A safer, though slower, method would be to install the new springs uncut first, then cut *one coil only* and check the height. Note the amount of drop caused by cutting one coil and use that distance to figure the effects of additional cuts. As noted, rubber spring pocket cushion spacers can be used to fine-tune the

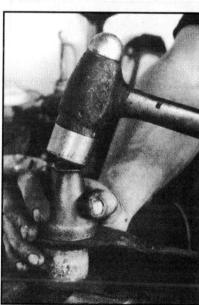

13. *If rear arms distort as the new bushings are being driven in, they're easily straightened using your hammer and the vise. Again, make your own bushing driver.*

overall height.

While we were freshening up the suspension, we decided to add a little frosting to an already fine cake. At Bill Kanouse's suggestion, we elected to bring our early A-body suspension up to later-model specifications by adding a few se-

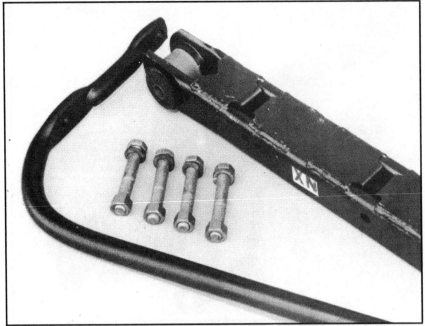

mounts and end links allow us to get all we can out of the mild bar, but without any detriment to ride quality. After Dan gave the car the careful alignment that's the trademark of Superior Frame & Alignment, we hit the streets for a test drive.

The thrill is back! Even though our '64 had shown little evidence of wear other than lower balljoints, the new components proved how wrong we could be. Lulled by time, we hadn't noticed how badly the ride and handling had deteriorated even though the car showed only 70,000 miles on the clock. From back roads to boulevards, *this* is how Chevelles should handle—firm and solid; light, tight, and lively. ●

14. *Another option is the new boxed rear lower control arms and rear anti-sway bar. This bar works with the thicker front one to reduce body roll in corners and gives the car a much flatter feel when pushed hard.*

15. *One bit of technology developed in later years that greatly complements the suspension system is the gas-filled shock absorber. Just Suspension suggests KYB Gas-a-Just units for excellent control and good ride.*

16. *A good check-out and wheel alignment is an absolute must once you've got your car back together.*

lect components developed over the years. At the rear, a set of boxed lower control arms was substituted for the original open-channel set. This gave us slightly denser rubber bushings, greater arm strength, and the internal reinforcement necessary for use with a rear anti-sway bar. Of course, a fairly mild rear anti-sway bar was included to improve overall balance and handling without affecting the car's ride. A pair of KYB Gas-a-Just shocks helped firm things up in the rear. At the front, a semi-stout

Just Suspension front anti-sway bar that matched this car's light weight and our desire for a good ride. Polyurethane bushings at the frame

OUR SOURCES

Just Suspension
Dept. CHP
P.O. Box 167
Towaco, NJ 07082
(201) 335-0547

Superior Frame & Alignment
Dept. CHP
888 Chambers Ln.
Simi Valley, CA 93065
(805) 581-0954

OTHER SOURCES

If you're looking for additional suspension information for your A-body Chevelle, contact these sources:

Energy Suspension
Dept. CHP
960 Calle Amanecer
San Clemente, CA 92672
(714) 361-3935

H-O Racing
Dept. CHP
4708 D8 Marine Ave.
Lawndale, CA 90260
(213) 973-7078

Kanter Auto Products
Dept. CHP
76 Monroe St.
Boonton, NJ 07005
(201) 334-9575

Mr. Suspension
Dept. CHP
P.O. Box 396
Montville, NJ 07045
(201) 299-8019

TRW Automotive Aftermarket Div.
Dept. CHP
8001 E. Pleasant Valley Rd.
Cleveland, OH 44131
(216) 447-1879

STREET MACHINE BUILDUP

A Tired '67 Chevelle Turns Into A Show-Winning Street Machine
By Bruce Caldwell

Building a street machine means different things to different people. A set of custom wheels and high-performance tires is enough for some, while others aren't satisfied until every part on the vehicle has been modified. Bob and Debby Gustafson of Eatonville, Washington, are of the latter school, so we figured their '67 Chevelle Super Sport 396 street machine would be a perfect buildup experiment.

The Gustafsons' original idea was to build a daily driver, but their finished product is so nice that they entered it in some car shows before returning it to street duty. This Chevelle represents what it takes to transform a beater into a super street machine. All the work was done by professionals, but individuals on a tighter budget can do it on their own, one area at a time.

The most obvious change is the paint. The wild Bob Cody paint job combines with Cragar Pro Tech wheels and B.F. Goodrich Radial T/As to create a standout—and that's even without the trick engine, suspension, inte-

rior and detailing changes. The body has been restored to stock, which means lots of dings and dents have been removed. The fenders and one of the doors were replaced rather than salvaged, and the rear quarter panels had to be straightened since the car at some point had been rear-ended. Even the roof had to be repaired because someone had walked on it! Bob Cody removed the roof dents with a shrinking hammer; the headliner had already been removed since the entire interior was slated for a makeover.

Kondar Acrylic primer surfacer (DZ-7) covers the bodywork, and the brilliant yellow topcoat is '76 Corvette Yellow Deltron acrylic urethane. The Hugger Orange, Ditzler fleet color No. 70837 red and Ditzler fleet color No. 60972 pumpkin graphic stripes are separated by ⅛-inch gold leaf stripes done by Steve Creach. The paint job is topped with five coats of Ditzler Delglo acrylic urethane (DAU-82). After the paint had been buffed out with rubbing compound, Roy Dunn of Dunn Hi-Tech

Signs pinstriped the Chevelle.

To complement the stunning exterior, the Gustafsons wanted more performance than the tired 396 was capable of providing. Jay Norton of Norton's Precision Engines provided a balanced and blueprinted 427-cubic-inch big-block with 10.25:1 pistons, a Crane cam and kit, an Edelbrock Performer intake manifold, a Holley 600cfm double-pumper carburetor and a Mallory ignition. The engine is backed up by a Muncie four-speed with a Hurst shifter, McLeod clutch, flywheel and scattershield.

Bob and Debby are especially enthusiastic about the suspension: A nine-inch Ford rearend with disc brakes replaces the Chevy 12-bolt unit. Mike Conte of Conte Enterprises in Graham has a kit for both this rearend swap and for rear disc brake conversions.

The Ford rearend has been narrowed to 57 inches to make it easier to run big tires without installing wheel tubs. The nodular center section is equipped with 3.90:1 gears. Since the

BUILDUP

1. The starting point of our street machine buildup is this well-worn '67 Chevelle SS 396. A cheap red paint job hid the car's real flaws.

2. We completely stripped the Chevelle in preparation for a custom paint job. Here, Bob Cody removes the bumper, which was sent out for new chrome.

3. If you don't have a tool specially designed for removing windshield wipers, place a shop rag under the screwdriver blade so you don't gouge the cowl vent panel.

4. As each piece is removed, it's labeled to facilitate replacing the look-alike pieces.

5. Even though the interior had been gutted, taping the area made cleanup easier. Both sides of the door glass should be taped.

6. Repaired areas like this fender are fogged with a guide coat of Ditzler's black primer. (The car was primered in red oxide.)

7. The guide coat is then sanded with 320-grit on a long board to reveal any low spots or other imperfections. The black paint stays in the low spots.

8. After each round of sanding and guide coating, more Kondar primer surfacer is applied. Getting a car straight takes lots of time and materials.

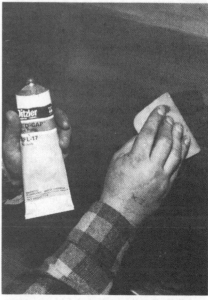

9. Ditzler's Red-Cap spot putty is spread thin over minor flaws and sanding scratches.

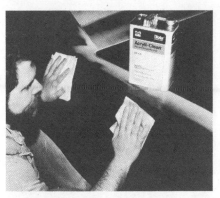

10. While wet-sanding with 400-grit paper on a rubber sanding sponge, Bob keeps a moist rag nearby; you can also use a big sponge.

11. Wax and grease remover is often used to clean off sanding debris; one rag is for applying and another for wiping off.

12. We chose Ditzler's Deltron acrylic urethane because of its high gloss and durability. Deltron is catalyzed paint; be sure you have ample ventilation and a top-quality respirator when using it.

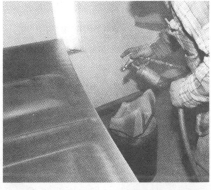

13. The doorjambs are painted first. A small touch-up gun controls overspray.

14. To make sure the back edges of the hood receive ample paint, Bob removes the hood. Only the edges are painted with the touch-up gun.

15. The hood is placed back on the car without hinges. Tops from spray cans block the hood up to the proper height.

16. Just before applying the color coats, the car should be wiped down with fresh tack rags.

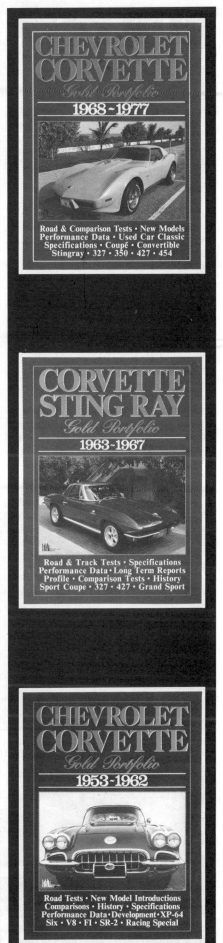

BUILDUP

rearend comes equipped with mounting tabs, the installation of Conte Enterprises' triangulated four-bar kit was a snap. Aldan coil-over shocks replace the stock coil springs and shocks. The Conte rear disc brake kit uses JFZ four-piston aluminum calipers with new rotors that can be taken from a '68-'72 Mustang or Cougar. JFZ front disc brakes are also used.

Mike Conte is also responsible for the car's trick tinwork. The entire engine compartment is detailed with sheets of .040-inch bead-rolled aluminum. The panels are fitted with Dzus fasteners for quick and easy removal.

After Conte Enterprises finished with the Chevelle, Mike Sader fabricated an exhaust system at Walt's Muffler and Radiator in Puyallup. The whole spotless undercarriage is painted black.

The car didn't have much of an interior when Bob and Debby bought it. Debby wanted it to be luxurious, so rather than use a reproduction upholstery kit, Bob Jasper of Jasper's Custom Auto in Tacoma built an interior befitting the Chevelle's new status, using camel-colored mohair in a combination of pleats and diamond tucks. The door panels and trunk match the seats, and a custom dashboard and center console were fabricated.

The finished car is a showpiece, but it's also capable of daily use. Its looks, performance, handling and comfort all spell out "first-class." And that's all anyone could want in a super street machine! ●

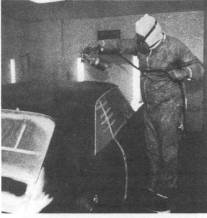

17. Notice that Bob holds the air hose away from the car as he paints the roof.

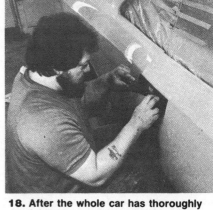

18. After the whole car has thoroughly dried, it's block-sanded with wet, ultra-fine sandpaper, which is the equivalent of 1200-grit.

19. Use 3M Fine Line masking tape to lay out the graphic stripes. Careful measuring ensures that both sides of the car are symmetrical.

20. Taping off graphics is a long, involved job. The stripes on the Chevelle even go through the doorjambs.

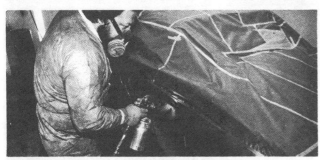

21. Each stripe must be painted separately and allowed to dry overnight before the next color is taped off and painted.

22. Steve Creach gently applies the gold leaf to the sizing (adhesive for the gold leaf), using a cotton ball to wipe off the excess material.

23. New rubber weatherstripping is installed throughout the car. A wooden paint mixing stick is handy for pushing the rubber into place without scratching the fresh paint.

24. Scab wheels and tires were used during the painting process; the new B.F. Goodrich Radial T/A tires and Cragar Protech wheels vastly improve the Chevelle's looks.

25. Our car was painted with the engine out. The fresh blueprinted 427 from Norton's Precision Engines was painted Chevy orange and then installed in the detailed engine compartment.

26. This trick nine-inch Ford from Conte Enterprises replaces the stock 12-bolt rearend. The unit has polished disc brakes, a four-bar system, coil-over shocks and a heavy-duty sway bar.

27. Conte's rear disc brake kit uses JFZ calipers and Ford rotors. Everything has been polished and fitted with stainless steel brake lines.

28. The Ford rearend as it's installed under the Chevelle. These rearends have a well-deserved reputation for strength and durability.

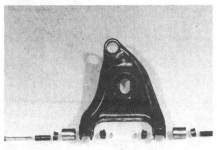

29. Conte Enterprises' lower A-arm urethane bushing kit is designed for Chevelles and similar cars.

30. Mike Conte welds steel inserts into the A-arms so the urethane bushings can be used.

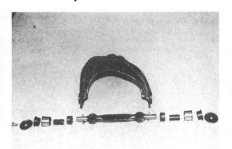

31. The upper A-arm kit. Mike calls the bushings "zero deflection" urethane bushings since they give more road feel.

32. The Conte Enterprises front disc brake kit as it's installed on the Chevelle. Polished JFZ calipers with new Chevelle rotors and gas shocks have been installed.

33. The Ford rearend, one-inch-diameter sway bar, four-bar setup and coil-over shocks as seen from below the Chevelle's rear suspension.

34. Mike was responsible for crafting the bead-rolled aluminum panels in the engine compartment, after first making cardboard templates for each piece.

35. A power shears cuts out the aluminum panels, and rough edges are smoothed with a file.

BUILDUP

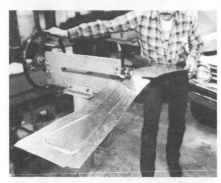

36. Mike bead-rolls the panels for additional strength and good looks. This step requires care to get nice, straight lines.

37. Mike with the panel that goes over the radiator after it was notched to clear the radiator cap and bead-rolled.

38. The interior of the Chevelle was a mess. We completely gutted the car during the renovation.

39. You need a commercial sewing machine with a power foot to work the heavy fabrics. Bob sews welting to a section of mohair.

40. The camel-colored mohair is stitched in a pleated pattern with diamond tucks at the top of the seat cushions.

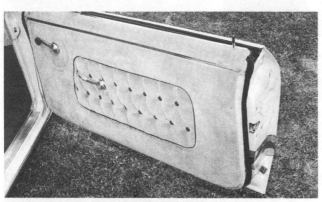

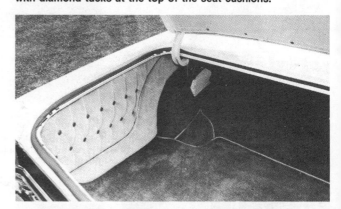

41. The diamond tucks also look great in the center of the door panels.

42. The trunk is as plush as the interior with its diamond tucks and carpeting.

43. A long, narrow piece of ¼-inch plywood is used to mount the custom gauges. Owner Bob Gustafson marks hole centers for the various components.

44. The metal face of the dashboard is chromed; reassembly is a difficult and tedious job.

45. The finished custom dashboard uses Stewart-Warner gauges.

46. Bob Jasper's custom interior is beautiful. The stock Chevelle bucket seats have been re-covered with camel mohair.

47. The powerful 427 big-block engine is detailed with chromed accessories and pinstriping. The Mallory coil mounts on the aluminum firewall panel. Even the hood hinges are chromed.

48. The Muncie four-speed transmission is equipped with heavy-duty McLeod clutch parts and a scattershield.

49. Reversed Cragar Protech 14x7-inch rear wheels run with 245/60R14 B.F. Goodrich Radial T/As.

50. Beautiful paint and wild graphics (above) make the Chevelle a standout both on the street and at car shows. The graphics work well with the stock SS 396 hood scoops (left). Roy Dunn gets the pinstriping credit.

51. The Super Sport is impressive from any angle. All the chromed parts and trim pieces have been either replated or replaced with new pieces.

'67 CHEVELLE BUILDUP SOURCES

BIG O TIRES
11321 Meridian Ave. South
Puyallup, WA 98373
206/841-2300

CODY CUSTOMS
(by appointment only)
206/847-2325

CONTE ENTERPRISES
28002 110th Ave. East
Graham, WA 98338
206/847-4666

DITZLER AUTOMOTIVE FINISHES
P.O. Box 3510
2155 W. Big Beaver Rd.
Troy, MI 48048
313/564-5500

DUNN HI-TECH SIGNS
5426 35th Ave. S.W.
Seattle, WA 98126
206/938-5994

JASPER'S CUSTOM AUTO
13908 50th Ave. East
Tacoma, WA 98445
206/537-7866

NORTON'S PRECISION ENGINES
(by appointment only)
206/474-4759

WALT'S RADIATOR & MUFFLER
318 Meridian Ave. North
Puyallup, WA 98373
206/848-2532

Bold graphic stripes give Bob Gustafson's '67 Chevelle a feeling of motion, even when it's standing still. Bob Cody deserves a hand for the trick paint job.

Job Jasper re-covered the interior with beautiful camel mohair by combining pleats and diamond tucks. The dash, which is filled with Stewart-Warner gauges, and the console are both custom items.

There's plenty of horsepower to back up the engine's strong looks: It sports 427 cubic inches of big-block punch. The trick aluminum panels are Mike Conte's handiwork.